THE PRICE THEY PAID

A TRUE STORY

THE PRICE THEY PAID

ENDURING WOUNDS OF WAR

MICHAEL PUTZEL

To Jeff,
from the angel on the plane

Washington
Dec 17, 2019

TRYSAIL PUBLISHING

The Price They Paid: Enduring Wounds Of War

Trysail Publishing
Washington, DC
www.trysailpublishing.com

ISBN: 978-0-9861321-0-0

FIRST EDITION

Cover and book design by Gwyn Kennedy Snider
of GKS Creative

This is a true story. Every effort has been made to verify
the accuracy of the events, names, and places described
in this book. Memories of individuals differ, and as time
passes, personal accounts may vary or change. No attempt
was made to alter or augment any of the accounts or
information herein.

For more information, visit www.michaelputzel.com.

To Ann

TABLE OF CONTENTS

PRINCIPAL CHARACTERS

Major James T. Newman, commanding officer, C Troop, 2/17 Air Cavalry

Captain Chuck Vehlow, West Pointer, Newman's most trusted Cobra gunship pilot

Lieutenant Ed Kersey, West Pointer, platoon leader of "the Blues," C Troop's aero rifle platoon

Major Bill Zierdt, the first Condor

Specialist 5 Richard Frazee, Huey crew chief

Specialist 5 Gary Schuler, Frazee's door gunner

Specialist 5 Ricky Miller, crew chief of a Huey known as "Gunky"

Flora Newman, Major Newman's first wife

Roger and Ronald Newman, Major Newman's two sons born before the war and disowned

Jay Newman, Major Newman's favorite son, born after the war

Robert L. Howard II, son of a C Troop sergeant killed in the A Shau Valley

Condor pilots:
Captains Malcolm Jones, Jim Kane, Gary Swift, Rick Daly

Warrant Officers James Casher, Mike Sherrer, Steve Karschner, Ed "Pappy" Papin

INTRODUCTION

This is not the story I set out to tell. That was the story of a flawed hero, a remarkable military leader who rose from obscurity to become a legendary air cavalry commander whose men would follow him into hell—and did. They went, in part, because they knew if they got in trouble, he would come to get them. And he did. His name was James T. Newman, and he was an Army major when I met him as a war correspondent during the deadliest, most intensive helicopter campaign of the Vietnam War, or ever, for that matter. Years later, when covering political candidates, presidents, world leaders of many stripes, I often reflected on Newman and puzzled at what seemed to be his innate understanding of what was demanded of him as a commander. He was certainly not the only leader with what people call "command presence," but physically and on paper he seemed an unlikely candidate for the role. Short in stature and uneducated, he walked with a limp he couldn't hide and spoke with diction and profanity that instantly exposed his humble upbringing in the rural South. He was neither profound, nor particularly curious, yet his superiors listened to him as a wise man, and his officers and men idolized him. He was eerily calm in a crisis and brave to the point of foolhardiness.

The men liked him in part because he "led from the front," a tenet of famed cavalry commanders like the North's Philip Sheridan and the South's J. E. B. Stuart. They also liked that he scoffed at Army regulations that didn't help accomplish the mission and protected them when they disobeyed rules he regarded as unnecessary. Newman expected and received unquestioning loyalty from his troops, and he made them fierce and skillful warriors.

What I did not know was that he returned from Vietnam a different person. The day he was buried at Arlington National Cemetery nearly four decades after his Vietnam service, I learned that he came home from the war, walked out on his wife, left two sons behind, and never spoke to the boys again. On the verge of being groomed for high military office, he committed a series of inexplicable transgressions that doomed his career.

His first family never found an adequate explanation.

"Vietnam changed him," they said. It was all they knew, and it became their mantra. He married again, miserably, and acquired and walked out on women the rest of his life. He doted on a third son, born after the war, and spoiled him whenever he could. That son cherishes his memory.

What I came to understand as I spoke with those who had followed—even worshipped—Jim Newman was that the war changed them all. Some self-destructed as soon as they got home; others enjoyed successful careers, marriages, children, then crashed many years later. I found only a couple who soldiered on and never looked back. There was not one pattern or one course they followed. Nor did they necessarily fail at what they tried to do. Few talked about the war after they got home, at least not with family, neighbors, or coworkers. But they all grappled with their experience one way or another. Many still do.

The Americans who actually fought enemy troops in Vietnam, perhaps a third of those who served in the war zone, are forever changed by the experience in ways they can't explain to others or, often, even to themselves. No one told them they would keep paying for their service, perhaps for the rest of their lives. Although some contend Vietnam was different in the American experience, that the soldiers were unappreciated because the war grew unpopular at home and was lost in the end, evidence indicates the long-term effects on those who directly engage the enemy in other wars are not so different. What has changed is that we now look for those who suffer afterward and try to care for them.

The search for war's less visible victims has yielded new layers of innocents who also paid a price, especially the wives and children of veterans, who struggle to understand what happened to their heroes.

This story, then, is about those men, the helicopter pilots and crewmen who flew for Condor Six, the call sign of the commander of C Troop, 2nd Squadron, 17th Air Cavalry, 101st Airborne Division, and about those who waited for them to come home.

FAREWELL AT ARLINGTON

WET SNOW FELL ON THE FIELDS OF WHITE GRAVESTONES as his family and a band of aging Condors from his old unit watched the honor guard lift Major Jim Newman's flag-draped casket onto a caisson. A plastic cover kept the flag dry but muffled its colors. One of the horses in the team of six whites and grays shook its bridle as it flicked flakes from its ears. White-gloved soldiers moved like animated stick figures, reaching ever so slowly for the old commander's coffin, raising it with absolute precision in endlessly rehearsed motions, following no audible command. They slid the box onto the wagon bed as the mourners closed on the scene, converging toward each other as they neared the troops and stopped. Hardly anyone looked around to see who else was there. All eyes were on the soldiers in dark blue dress coats and gold-striped pants. The horses stepped off, easing the shoulder-high wheels of the caisson into motion on the shiny-wet street.

The band of mourners—a little girl with red hooded cape and umbrella, ex-cavalry soldiers in black Stetsons, an aging first sergeant with jump boots and a cane—fell in behind the caisson as the little troop made its way to Section 64, Arlington National Cemetery. Past the bleak gray walls of the Pentagon, the snow now sticking on the ground and grass, the cortege trooped through the maze of closely spaced white gravestones, identical but for their engravings.

Family and friends gathered around the grave site as the Army band played "America, the Beautiful." By prior agreement with military officials, the major's youngest son, who goes by Jay, took the seat of honor reserved for next of kin. Two older sons unhappily stood their distance with their mother. His kid sister Elaine, the one he liked, sat next to Jay's wife and young daughters. On her left, in a scarlet-lined black hood, sat Pat, the black-sheep sister who shot and killed her husband in a trailer down in Georgia. Jay's mother, Kim, the second wife, wasn't there, but on Pat's left, in the last chair, staring straight ahead at the casket, was Cheryl, the last wife, another casualty on home soil. Standing in the open, their

Cav hats protecting their faces, stood clutches of Condors, the men who served him nearly four decades earlier, who never forgot, and came to say good-bye.

Many of the Condors weren't there, of course. Some had been killed in air crashes after the war. Others died young. Many were far away. One, a promising pilot who planned to go to medical school after Vietnam, was living in a filthy, falling-down shack in the woods of Washington State. One way or another, war changed them all.

Chaplain Stanford Trotter, wearing gold braid, his hat bill embellished with the "scrambled eggs" of a senior officer and the golden oak leaves of an Army major on his shoulder straps, began with a familiar reading from the Gospel of John: "Jesus said to her, 'I am the resurrection and the life. Those who believe in me, even though they die, will live, and everyone who lives and believes in me will never die.'" The Protestant service never varies. Time is tight. The nation's military buries a couple dozen veterans a day at Arlington. "'Do not let your hearts be troubled. Believe in God, believe also in me. In my Father's house there are many dwelling-places. . . .'"

In a brief eulogy that Jay asked me to deliver at the grave site, I mentioned that Jim was severely wounded during his first tour in Vietnam and, many years later, found and thanked the crew chief of his aircraft for saving his life by using his belt as a tourniquet to stanch the blood pouring from Jim's boot.

Jim Kane, one of those in the small crowd gathered around the grave, stared at the casket, somber and attentive, his eyes unblinking in the falling snow. He knew he would not be standing there were it not for the personal courage and flying skill of Major Newman. He was not alone. Quite a few others credited Newman with saving their lives. At least a dozen of the men who served under Condor Six in Vietnam were there to say farewell. They came from all over the country and from foreign lands as well.

Major Newman's wartime colleagues come to say farewell at Arlington National Cemetery.

It was February 18, 2009, thirty-eight years to the day since Major Newman had flown his command ship through a storm of fire to retrieve four crewmen of a U.S. Army medevac helicopter that had been shot down at a besieged firebase in Laos. His decision to go in and get those men when a crew from their own unit determined it was too dangerous earned Condor Six the first of two nominations Newman received for the Medal of Honor. Only six days earlier, he had driven his Huey helicopter into a grove of trees and deliberately cut off the treetops with his main rotor blade to haul Jim Kane and Jim Casher to safety after their Cobra gunship was shot down and surrounded in enemy territory.

Richard Frazee, Jim's sometime crew chief in those days, put it best: "It always amazed me how so many people with so many different backgrounds and personalities could all find common agreement on the value of this one man. Jim Newman was a man of immeasurable courage who made us all feel invincible and hard-pressed to keep up."

He couldn't save them all. Thirteen of his Condors were killed while he commanded the troop. He never forgot them.

Former infantry officer Ed Kersey, looking out at the cold, miserable, gray weather at Arlington, had a flashback to Vietnam. He remembered riding in Major Newman's Huey in the western mountains, bumping their heads on the cloud ceiling and dipping ever lower to keep the ground in sight. At the grave, the temperature crept above freezing, and the snowflakes started to melt as they landed on the cavalrymen's hats. Kersey looked over at Jim Kane and saw a big drop about to slip from the brim of Kane's Stetson. It was blood red! He saw another on Chuck Vehlow's hat. The microfine red-clay dust from their base at Khe Sanh, the color they had scrubbed for weeks to get out of the pores of their skin after the Laos operation, was still embedded in the felt of their beloved black Cav hats. As they stood paying respects to the man who had led them through those dangerous days, the dust that had permeated their skin and clothes and hair was now being drawn from the felt to the surface of their hats by the melting snow. It was dripping onto the ground at Newman's grave.

"In sure and certain hope of the resurrection to eternal life through our Lord Jesus Christ," the chaplain intoned, "we commend to Almighty God our brother, James Newman, and we commit his body to the ground; earth to earth, ashes to ashes, dust to dust."

The pallbearers stretched the flag above the casket, folded it crisply, and as the officer in charge knelt to hand the bundled blue star-spangled triangle to Jay, a flock of Canada geese swept over the heads of the mourners in V-formation, hooked a turn in the air a hundred yards off, and made a second flyover before the mourners. A Cobra gunship platoon couldn't have executed the maneuver more gracefully or with better timing.

A squad of riflemen, standing off among the grave markers in the snow-blanketed field, fired three volleys over the grave, and a lone bugler played the haunting strains of "Taps."

Jim Newman was at rest. The mourners split up into three groups, those who had known him before the war, those who followed him into combat, and Jay's family and friends who were born afterward and knew an altogether different Jim Newman.

ED KERSEY'S LESSON

Ed Kersey remembered how he met Jim Newman. The young West Pointer had just finished jungle warfare school in Panama, and he arrived in Vietnam itching for a fight. Kersey's only brother, a helicopter gunship pilot nearing the end of his second yearlong tour in Vietnam, was killed in a freak accident on a mission with the 1st Air Cavalry Division. That was on Labor Day, 1970, the night before he was scheduled to fly to Hong Kong for R & R. Ed was on leave himself, getting ready to go to Vietnam, when word came he'd lost his brother. Suddenly, he was the sole surviving son, a status that automatically excused him from combat duty, but he wouldn't think of it. He wanted revenge. Kersey buried his brother and, despite his parents' agony, resolved to pursue his dream of commanding troops in battle. "I felt that I needed to go, I wanted to go, and I have the utmost admiration for my parents for not asking me to get my orders canceled," he wrote after the war. The day after he arrived "in-country" a few weeks later, he came down with typhus that he had picked up from a bug in Panama and spent his first week at war in a U.S. Army hospital at Bien Hoa, outside of Saigon.

Lieutenant Kersey, a slim, blond soldier whose father and grandfather were veterans of wars, was determined to avoid a staff job. He had orders to report to the storied 101st Airborne Division up north and was waiting for a military flight to take him there when he met a warrant-officer pilot heading back to C Troop, 2/17, an air cavalry unit of the 101st. The pilot, who had been sent to Tokyo for treatment of an accidental gunshot wound, was returning to duty with "Charlie Troop." He told Kersey the troop had the best commanding officer around and might have an opening for an infantry lieutenant to command its aero rifle platoon (ARP). The platoon, known as "the Blues" or by its acronym, pronounced "Arp," was a small ground unit normally led by a junior infantry officer like Kersey.

Charlie Troop was mostly helicopters. Like its horse cavalry predecessors, the troop rode out ahead of the division's main ground forces to scout the enemy, fix his position, and engage him in a skirmish to test his strength. Instead of horses, the Vietnam-era troop used quick little bubble-faced OH-6 observation helicopters and protected them with AH-1 Cobra gunships, slender, mean-looking fighters that carried assorted rockets, fast-firing miniguns, and grenade launchers. To support the scout and gun platoons and transport the aero riflemen, the troop had a lift platoon, consisting of UH-1 Hueys, the familiar workhorses of Army aviation. The Blues platoon was kept ready at all times to fly into combat zones to conduct ground reconnaissance, secure downed helicopters, or skirmish with enemy troops spotted from the air. The soldiers intentionally provoked enemy contact but got in and out fast, leaving protracted fights to larger units. It was just the sort of thing Kersey was looking for.

Like all newbies headed to the 101st, Kersey had orders to report to the replacement detachment at the division's headquarters, Camp Eagle, where he would be assigned to a slot in one of the various units that made up the 18,000-man division. Instead, he jumped in a jeep with the C Troop pilot he had met and went straight to Phu Bai, a subsidiary base where C Troop was headquartered a few miles down the road near the historic capital of Hue. When he walked into Newman's office in a dirty shack where all such buildings were referred to as hooches, the major asked him what he was doing there.

"I wanna kill bad guys," he said, "and I understand you do a lot of that."

Newman must have liked the look of him or perhaps his brash, no-nonsense attitude like Newman's own. He told the green lieutenant that to join the unit he would need permission from the executive officer of the squadron, one level up from the troop. The CO picked up the phone and called squadron headquarters at Camp Eagle, then loaned Kersey his jeep and driver to take him there for a personal meeting. After a brief chat, the executive officer called division headquarters and arranged the assignment. Kersey still had to report to the replacement detachment as a formality to pick up his paperwork, and when he got there, a major chewed him out for going around the regs.

It was typical Newman. He was a stickler for military discipline under some circumstances, but he had no patience for bureaucracy and little respect for careerists up the chain of command who kissed ass and pulled rank. He supposed he brought his attitude with him from the enlisted ranks.

The officer at Division "threatened me with death or something," Kersey recalled. He thought it absurd, as if the staff officer were threatening to send him to Vietnam.

As required of all new troops assigned to the 101st, Kersey was sent off for a week of specialized combat training to learn some of the tactics the division had developed for fighting regular North Vietnamese Army (NVA) troops, who were better equipped and trained than the Viet Cong guerrillas down south. When he got back to C Troop, it was late in the afternoon. He reported to the orderly room and learned Newman was down on the flight line. The troop executive officer said the Blues, whom Kersey was supposed to command, had been in the mountains all day and were pinned down by North Vietnamese troops. It was too late in the day to get helicopters into the area to extract them, and Newman was planning to lead the lift platoon to get them out in the morning. Kersey was told he could ride along to see how things were done and would meet the men in his platoon when they all got back to Phu Bai.

Kersey had no idea the situation on the ground was more dire than a mere firefight. Bravo Troop from the same squadron had dropped a team of a half-dozen L Company Rangers into Three Rivers, a fog-shrouded junction where steep, jungle-green mountains towered over three narrow river valleys. The Rangers, who were there to conduct stealthy reconnaissance, not to look for a fight, stumbled onto a much larger North Vietnamese unit that quickly attacked. Two Rangers were killed and another was wounded before the survivors could call for help. Charlie Troop put the Blues on the ground, but they quickly got into trouble themselves, and grunts from Delta Troop, the squadron's full-size infantry unit, were flown in as further reinforcement. Leaders on the ground and back at headquarters quickly realized the Americans had encountered a superior force of North Vietnamese regulars, but before the helicopters could go back to extract the beleaguered troops, the weather closed in and the soldiers on the ground were trapped.

Lonnie Turner, a nineteen-year-old sergeant and assistant squad leader for one of the Blues platoon's six-man squads, was with his men in a low spot near a creek bed where the Rangers had been hit. They caught glimpses of North Vietnamese troops in the distance moving toward them. A medevac chopper had tried to get in to evacuate the wounded Rangers, but it ran into intense enemy fire and abandoned the mission. A Bravo Troop Huey made the next attempt, slowing to a hover just above the ground to give the Blues a few seconds to get a rope around one of the wounded Rangers and tie his dead companion's body to one of the aircraft's landing skids. The Huey tried to lift them out to a safer place where the aircrew could haul the dead and wounded men on board, but the hillside erupted with ground fire from the enemy troops, and the Americans on the ground heard the snap of bullets as they hit the ship. The door gunner made a motion to cut the rope, and one of the soldiers slashed the line holding the wounded Ranger just as the Huey took off. The body of the dead man still tied to the skid dragged through the brush until the aircraft could gain altitude and get away. Turner's squad was resting at the bottom of a knoll when one of the surviving Rangers came down and bummed a cigarette from him. The Ranger nodded his gratitude and turned and walked about twenty feet back up the rise. A rocket-propelled grenade fired from the shoulder of a North Vietnamese gunner hidden in the trees hit the Ranger and exploded, cutting him in half at the torso. Shrapnel from the explosion blew in all directions, and Turner heard it swoosh just over his head as shards of hot metal cut down the acting platoon leader, a staff sergeant only a notch above Turner, and took out Turner's squad leader as well. Both were severely wounded. Turner, suddenly the senior man around, told the four men left in the squad to wrap the dead and wounded in ponchos and carry them about two hundred yards to the top of a mound, where Delta Troop was dug in on higher ground. The rain and mud made it slippery work, and the light was fading in the mountains just before sunset. Turner told the men to park the dead Ranger by the side of the trail and they would go back to get him the next day.[1]

"I can still see those dark, cold mountains, and it sends shivers up my spine," Malcolm "Mac" Jones, the commander of the lift birds, said years later, recalling his image of the region. People think of Vietnam as tropical, but winter brought cold air to the mountains. Cold and damp, often rainy, and made more miserable by the ominous fog. To Jones it was bleak, foreboding, and evil just to look at. That was Three Rivers.

Jones, Newman, and other officers in the squadron sat up that night brainstorming how they could get the troops out of there. They discussed zooming into the gorge, slipping into the landing zone, and doing instrument takeoffs to climb out without hitting the mountains on either side. They considered using ground-controlled approach radars from faraway fields. They knew it was conceivable in other circumstances, but none of them had flown under instrument flight rules since flight school, certainly not into and out of a blind gorge.

Instruments in Army helicopters were primitive, and Hueys rarely flew where their pilots couldn't see. There weren't even manuals on board for the tactics they were discussing. Newman and Jones went to a briefing at squadron headquarters, where they and other officers confessed they were stymied by the weather conditions and the difficult, mountainous terrain. Lieutenant Colonel Robert Molinelli, tough-minded commander of the 2nd Squadron, dictated a direct but dangerous course. He wanted Newman to lead the way into the gorge, followed by Jones and his flight of five Hueys, known as "slicks." While Newman monitored from above, the Hueys would dash up the gorge following a fork in the river, pick up seven soldiers each, scoot back down, and drop them on a sandbar at the mouth of the river. They would have to make three trips in and three out along the same route, an inherently dangerous tactic that gave the enemy ample opportunity to anticipate and ambush them along the way. Somebody pointed out they wouldn't have enough fuel to make that many trips in and out. Molinelli said he'd have some five-gallon jerry cans unloaded on the sandbar and that the crews could refuel there. Newman and Jones looked at each other, realizing what they were being ordered to do. It was suicide.

Lieutenant Kersey didn't know any of that. Back at Charlie Troop, he went to find the supply sergeant to get outfitted for his new command. The sergeant handed him the rucksack that had belonged to the previous platoon leader, who completed his tour and went home. It was still packed with canned rations and dry socks and had hand grenades and claymore mines hanging from it. The sergeant also gave him his predecessor's M-16 rifle and some ammunition and told him to be on the flight line at 0600 hours, 6:00 a.m., to meet Major Newman. That night, in the hooch that was to be his new home, Kersey tore down the M-16 as he'd been taught, taking it apart piece by piece to make sure all the parts were clean and working. He fretted that he hadn't fired it or zeroed its sight before carrying the weapon into action, but there wasn't time for that now. When he arrived on the flight line before dawn, the supply sergeant showed up with three cases of C rations—canned beans, chopped meat, snacks—twelve individual meals packed in each case. In military nomenclature, each plain cardboard box was labeled were "Meal, Combat, Individual," but soldiers universally called them C-rats. They were the staple diet of troops in the field. "Take 'em," the sergeant said. Kersey resisted, saying the choppers were just going out to pick up the troops and they would eat when they got back, but the sergeant insisted. "You never know what's gonna happen," he said.

On the way out, Kersey rode on a bench of canvas stretched over a tubular aluminum frame in the cargo compartment of Newman's command-and-control chopper, the rations and his personal gear on the metal floor in front of him. He didn't have a headset, so he had to rely on the crew chief shouting over the engine noise to relay instructions. He was told there would be a flight of twelve lift birds forming up behind Newman's Huey to follow the command ship in one at a time and pick up the troops on the ground. As they headed west toward Three Rivers near the Laos border, Mac Jones followed Newman at the head of his lift platoon. Jones was so scared he had no spit. As they flew over pale green rice paddies on their way to the mountains, a guerrilla on the ground fired up at Jones's helicopter. Normally, the pilot would have reported that instantly to alert the gunship escorts to answer the rifle fire with a hail of rockets and blazing miniguns. But there were no gunships on the mission. The cloud ceiling was too low, and there was no room for Cobras to maneuver in the narrow, twisting gorge. Jones's five slicks were going to have to run the cloud-shrouded gauntlet six times, flying "low and slow" with no gunships to pursue enemy machine gun crews. Jones was afraid if he opened his mouth his voice would break over the radio and his platoon would know how terrified he was. So he said nothing.

As often happened in autumn in the northern part of South Vietnam, thick, gray clouds dipped into the valleys, making them all but impenetrable to helicopters, whose pilots couldn't fly where they couldn't see. Lieutenant Kersey didn't know where they were and had never seen such terrain, but he could watch the clouds closing in as the helicopter followed a river up a valley to the junction of three rivers. Pretty soon, the clouds obscured the ridgelines on both sides as Newman slipped lower and lower to keep sight of the ground. Then they were down on the deck, flying level perhaps fifty feet above a streambed to reach the site where Newman knew the ground troops were waiting anxiously in a landing zone they had cleared in the dense forest to await their ride out.

Suddenly, a hail of automatic-rifle fire from the trees on both banks of the river shot toward the helicopter. "Taking fire! Taking fire!" the door gunner screamed as he and the crew chief grabbed the handles on their floor-mounted M-60 machine guns, swung the barrels toward the muzzle flashes they had seen, and returned bursts of fire from both sides of the Huey. The rat-tat-tat noise exploded in the cargo bay around Kersey. Newman flew on, as if nothing were happening. Kersey was stunned. It was the first time he had been in a fight with people who were trying to kill him.

Wind whipped through the open doors of the chopper, spraying rain about and soaking Lieutenant Kersey, who wondered why he didn't know it got so cold in Vietnam. He was shivering, chilled through, and couldn't stop his hands from shaking. He told himself it couldn't be fear.

Newman found the landing zone where his troops and two platoons from Delta Troop were waiting. He punched a hole in the sky to drop to the valley floor and wait for the train of slicks to catch up, but it was too late. No one else could get in through the clouds. The helicopter circled for a few minutes, and Kersey watched the backs of the pilots' helmets. He could see them talking by radio, but he couldn't hear what was being said.

"I willed my body to relax and, for a moment, stopped shivering," he wrote later. His wet jungle fatigues clung to his skin. "I can never remember feeling more alone."

Kersey pulled a topo map from the side pocket of his trousers but couldn't figure out where they were. There was hardly any terrain visible through the fog, and he had never tried to read a map from the air. Watching the crew, calm now after the brief firefight, he saw them looking at each other and speaking by intercom; without a flight helmet, he guessed they were talking about him.

The door gunner leaned down and shouted into his ear: "Hey, Lieutenant, get ready to get out. The Old Man's going to put you on the ground. You need to take your platoon. The lift birds are weathered out. They're on their way back to Phu Bai, and we'll be back to get you when we can."

"Excuse me?" the lieutenant shouted back. The gunner repeated Newman's instructions as the helicopter swung in a tight right turn and swooped toward the opening in the trees, shuddering as it slowed and slipped over the treetops into a clearing and the skids touched down.

Kersey kicked the cases of C-rats out the door and jumped to the ground with his pack and rifle. His boots sank in the mud.

Four men came running toward the helicopter, each holding one corner of a poncho stretched between them. Kersey looked in and saw a man blown in half. The men swung the poncho and its bloody contents on board. Newman looked over his shoulder at his sad cargo and turned back to lift off and get away. A couple of wounded were boosted aboard.

As the bird roared off overhead, scattering rain and leaves, grass and twigs in its wake, the lieutenant squinted through the debris and saw a cluster of soldiers standing nearby. He walked over and told them he was Lieutenant Kersey and was looking for the aero rifle platoon.

"That's us," they said. "Where are the lift birds?"

It was left to the new platoon leader to tell them their ride wasn't coming. His officer training, with its countless challenges to analyze his situation on the spot and decide what to do, kicked in. Kersey called for the platoon sergeant and was told he had been wounded the day before and medevaced out. He asked who was the next senior man in the leaderless band that made up his unit and determined there were three buck sergeants, one of whom had been promoted a couple months before the others.

"Okay, you're the new platoon sergeant," he told Lonnie Turner, the nineteen-year-old E-5, the pay grade of a sergeant with three chevrons on his sleeve. Overnight, Turner had gone from assistant squad leader to senior enlisted man in the platoon. "How are we fixed for ammunition, rations, claymores (remote-controlled mines), and trip flares?" They had half the ammo they'd come with but no rations, claymores, or trip flares. Nobody had expected them to be stuck in the mountains overnight. With four men wounded the day before, Kersey's platoon had nineteen Blues left, including himself. The others were wet, cold, and hungry. At least, the lieutenant had eaten—and had brought them food.

He told Turner to move his men back to the perimeter, distribute the C-rats, and wait until the weather cleared and the lift birds could get back in.

With his platoon and two other platoons from Delta Troop, there were about ninety people on the ground, surrounded by at least two enemy battalions. There was no air cover; no relief birds were on the way. Even under-strength, as North Vietnamese battalions frequently were, the Americans were outnumbered probably five to one and outgunned as well. Kersey sought out the captain in command of Delta Troop, who told him to tell his men to get in their holes and stay there. Kersey soon discovered that the aero rifle platoon soldiers traveled so light they didn't have entrenching tools to dig foxholes. The weather didn't clear before dusk, and they were stuck for another night.

About 2:00 in the morning, a runner from Delta Troop came down to tell Kersey the captain wanted to see him. The lieutenant made his way in the dark to the captain's command post, a poncho propped up with a stick at each corner and a flashlight underneath with a red filter to preserve night vision and reduce the chance they'd be seen by the enemy. A radio relay team back in Phu Bai had picked up an enemy transmission and decoded it, concluding that two North Vietnamese Army battalions were going to launch a coordinated attack at 8:00 a.m. to overrun their position. They had figured out where the American force was holed up and concluded it was vulnerable. Kersey's orders were to break camp at first light, about 6:00 a.m., and start out on foot to the northwest with his platoon climbing through jungled forest over the next ridgeline, down into a valley and up along another ridgeline to a point where they could be rescued when the clouds opened up.

The weather was miserable: raining, cloud cover down to about three hundred feet, and cold, relentlessly cold. Before dawn, the men were rousted out, grumbling, and told to pack up as quietly as they could, collect all their weapons and gear, fire their last mortars into the woods to get rid of them, and spike the mortar tube with a high-temperature thermite grenade so they wouldn't have to hump the heavy weapon. For some reason, maybe because they didn't have a grenade that would melt the metal, the men buried the mortar tube. That was not the last they'd hear of it.[2]

The men in the three platoons ran as much and as fast as they could in the thick forest, slipping and sliding in the mud and underbrush blanketing the steep hillsides. Two long guns, firing from the closest U.S. artillery battery at Fire Base Bastogne, lobbed giant explosive projectiles along the route, trying to hold off attacking forces. At near-maximum range of more than twenty miles, the guns were dangerously inaccurate, posing almost as much threat to the Americans they were trying to protect as they did to the enemy.

"We ran that whole day," Kersey remembered. They clawed their way up a high ridge, heavy packs on their backs and rifles in hand.

It was sliding in wet clay more than running, but they managed to stay ahead of their pursuers. They reached the top of the ridgeline as the light faded late in the afternoon, and they set up a night defensive position in case the North Vietnamese caught up with them in the dark.

Years later, Kersey learned from an intelligence officer who had served in the radio relay unit back at base that the North Vietnamese, frustrated by the Americans' early-morning escape, put a small contingent on their tail to chase them but sent the bulk of their forces on a shortcut through the woods to set up a classic L-shaped ambush on the route they expected the Americans to take. In fact, the NVA guessed right, and the GIs would have walked into the deadly trap, but the Americans misread their map and inadvertently turned into another valley before reaching their assigned checkpoint. They avoided the ambush without realizing it. The weather broke enough that afternoon for a scout helicopter, a bubble-faced mosquito called a "loach" or "little bird," to fly over the area and locate the retreating platoons.

The pilot spotted the men on the ground, but the weather was closing in again, and he told them he was breaking station until it cleared enough to bring in the relief birds. Not thirty seconds later, the troops heard an explosion echo through the gorge. The little bird had flown into a "granite cloud" and burst into flames on the murky mountainside across from them while trying to climb to safety. The platoons struggled down another two hundred yards to a place where they could girdle enough trees with plastic explosive to blast a clearing for a single helicopter to land. As the Hueys slipped in one at a time, the nineteen men of C Troop's aero rifle platoon were the first ones out.

C Troop Huey settles into hastily cut landing zone to extract Blues Platoon from the A Shau Valley after the soldiers escaped from an enemy ambush.

Kersey sprawled on the floor with the last of his men, lying against his pack, dead tired. He had been on the ground for three days, most of that time on the run. He was cold, wet, hungry, and still terrified. But they were on their way home. About halfway back to their base at Phu Bai, Kersey saw the pilot, Mac Jones, turn around and look at him. He read on the captain's face an unforgettable expression of sympathy, empathy, sadness, shock—all those and more. The next thing he knew, the four helicopters carrying the

Blues were swinging in a wide, 180-degree turn and heading back to the area they had just escaped.

Kersey tugged at the crew chief's sleeve. "What's up?"

The crew chief triggered his microphone and got on the intercom with Jones, who told him to take off his helmet and give it to Kersey so he could tell the lieutenant himself. Jones turned around in his seat to look at the green lieutenant as he told him the loach they had lost was from Charlie Troop. The two-man crew, pilot Franklin Alvin Hamm, and the observer/crew chief, Sergeant Bruce Charles Halbach, were presumed dead, but Major Newman wanted Kersey's platoon to go back to recover the bodies. Jones saw the new guy's jaw drop. Kersey was just beginning to breathe again for the first time in two days, and Jones watched as shock and amazement spread across his face.

The helicopters dropped the Blues back into the forest in late afternoon with instructions to set up a defensive position for the night because they were a thousand yards below the crash site and would never find it in the dark. Just before nightfall, a supply bird swooped overhead and dropped them some gear, including two body bags for their mission the next day. That night Kersey and his new acting platoon sergeant zipped themselves into the waterproof body bags, a privilege of rank. It was warm and dry inside, and no bad guys showed up to harass them. At first light, they and the rest of the Blues scrambled up the ridge to the crash site and found the remains of the two crewmen still in their seats in the burned-out loach. They loaded the scorched bodies into the body bags and called in the choppers to get them out. "I can still see the walls of that gorge shrouded in mist and feel the coldness that went through you when you knew you had to fly into that place," Warrant Officer Bruce Emerson wrote to his colleagues years later.

On his first combat mission, Ed Kersey had learned a critical lesson about Major Newman: Condor Six never left anyone behind.

GEORGIA

SHE WAS HATLESS IN THE COLD, WET SNOW, her close-cropped, graying sandy hair not quite long enough to cover her ears, with no heavy winter coat to protect her from the unaccustomed chill. Her white blouse was buttoned at the collar, the wide lapels of her black jacket suggesting dignity, if not high style. Her lips were firmly sealed, her eyes not quite hidden by slightly shaded glasses.

On an otherwise empty street through Arlington National Cemetery, Flora Rogers Newman stood with the other outcasts from Jimmy's life as she waited for the soldiers to transfer his casket from the hearse onto the caisson. On her left, wearing a patriotic tie with red-and-white stripes down one side and white stars on a blue field on the other, stood her elder son Roger, his bare hands folded over his suit jacket, the pale skin of his high forehead exposed to the bitter weather. On her right, a black hood with scarlet lining hiding her eyes, stood Jimmy's sister Pat, ostracized by her older brother even before she shot and killed her husband in the trailer they called home. Pat often carried a gun, and some who knew that wondered if she was packing even there, in the shadow of the terror-struck Pentagon. To Roger's left was the stooped figure of Jimmy's last father-in-law, an aging Korean War vet now reduced to a hobble when not slumped in his wheelchair. His daughter Cheryl, dressed in black from head to toe, was in line to collect Jimmy's pension if their marriage, at least his third, wasn't challenged in court. Flora and Jimmy's second son, Ronald, lingered off to one side, shooting the scene with a camcorder. Having decided to go to the funeral only at the eleventh hour, he wore a wool sport jacket and tie, his left hand tucked into a jacket pocket for warmth. Bareheaded, his distinctively high forehead resembled those of his father and older brother.

Flora met Jimmy on a school bus in Georgia coming home from a basketball game in 1951. He was only fifteen, known to some as a ballplayer but not much of a student, and he seemed to switch at will from the high school in his hometown to the rural high school ten miles down the road in the village of Welcome, where Flora lived. She was already seventeen, the youngest of nine children, and was aiming to become the first in her family to finish high school. She knew who he was—it was a small school where everybody knew everybody—but she had never paid much attention until that night she was sitting in the next to last row on the bus when he crawled over the seat-back and slid down to sit next to her. She was a cheerleader but had hardly ever had a date when they started seeing each other. She had no idea he was thinking of quitting school to join the Army.

Jimmy Newman grew up in Newnan, Georgia, a dusty farm town about forty miles southwest of Atlanta and the same distance due east of Alabama. In the 1940s, when Jimmy was a boy, Newnan was a strictly segregated county seat closer in mindset to rural Alabama than to the big, cosmopolitan city Atlanta is today. Its history is entwined with that of the American South. The town narrowly escaped destruction during Sherman's Civil War march through Georgia, but it was hardly unaffected. Newnan was the site of seven field hospitals to treat the wounded in the last year of the war, earning it the moniker "hospital city of the Confederacy."

The town's heritage also is entwined with King Cotton and the slaves who made farming it profitable. And racism did not end with the war. If anyone outside the South ever heard of Newnan, Georgia, it was probably because the town was the site of one of the most notorious lynchings in American history. A local black laborer known as Sam Holt to some and Sam Hose to others was blamed for the murder of a young white man from a prominent Newnan family and the rape of the man's wife in April 1899. He was tracked down by bounty hunters and a train-car load of vigilantes. They bound him and returned him to Newnan, where a mob of white people, hundreds strong from nearby and as far away as Atlanta, beat and mutilated the prisoner before they set him afire and burned him at the stake. Holt's supposed implication of an accomplice as he was being tortured triggered a second lynching in a nearby town two weeks later, even as the second victim's white employer, a Confederate war hero, stood before the mob to insist on the man's innocence and demand he be turned over to authorities for trial.[3]

For decades afterward and to some extent even today, white people in Newnan practiced a casual sort of racism that simply assumed separation of blacks from whites. The word "niggah," pronounced with the soft Southern "r," was used in everyday speech in the Newmans' household and by many whites in town to refer to people of color. While it certainly implied a connotation of inferiority, the word was not necessarily used in hatred, although it could be. When farmhands gathered to help each other during harvesting, baling, or other operations that required many workers, everyone labored together, but at the Newmans' farm, as elsewhere, it was understood that whites ate at a table indoors or on the porch; blacks ate outside.[4]

By the beginning of the twentieth century, Newnan's cotton mills were in decline, but peaches were becoming a cash crop.[5] On Jimmy's paternal grandparents' farm, they raised both. His grandparents lived in the main house, surrounded by orchards, and Jimmy's family occupied a smaller home on the same land but with fewer amenities. His grandfather, Xenophen Orlando Newman, known to all as X. O., was a prosperous planter with perhaps a thousand acres. X. O.'s house was said to be the first in Coweta County to have running water. He also owned the general store, where Jimmy learned to run the register and where he was permitted to spend the nickel he got from his grandfather for going to church on Sunday.

Jimmy Newman's grandparents, Xenophen Orlando Newman and his wife, Suzie Mae Foster Newman, who was part Cherokee Indian. Jimmy was said to be X. O.'s favorite grandchild.

As a little boy, Jimmy was a towhead, but his hair darkened as he grew up and began thinning when he was still a young man. At his first home, the water was drawn from a well with a bucket on the porch out back, and everybody used the outhouse. By the time his father inherited the big house—without the farmland—it had electricity and a gas stove. Jimmy's much younger brother Jack, born the year Jimmy joined the Army, remembered that the children took baths in a washtub with water heated on the stove. It was warm, but never hot.[6] Their parents and grandparents were not educated people and lived a modest life, but they weren't poor. Jimmy's grandfather took a special shine to his first grandchild and would do anything for him. When Jimmy was four years old, X. O. gave him a goat that the boy hitched to a cart and rode around the yard. He also got to stand in front of his grandfather's seat on the tractor and steer with the wheel. Granddaddy dug a fishing pond across the road from the house where the children learned to row a boat. Jimmy liked to sink the boat and make everyone swim for shore. There were water moccasins in the pond, but he told people they wouldn't bite if people just threw rocks at them. Apparently, no one got bitten. Elaine was two years younger than Jimmy and worshipped her big brother. He told her once that if she'd build a dam in a stream to make a pond where he could float his toy boat, he would give her a cigarette. The kid sister dutifully built a dam, and he was good to his word. They both smoked—and both got dreadfully sick. She never touched another cigarette. Jimmy did, and the habit may have caused his lung cancer many years later.

From Elaine's point of view, Jimmy was always a leader. He seems to have been one for other children as well. When they played "Cowboys and Indians," he decided who would be the cowboys and who would be the Indians. The other children in the neighborhood looked up to him for guidance, too, asking, "Jimmy, what we gonna do?"

Jimmy was brave about most things. But when he was a little boy the family got some chickens for Easter, and one of them chased him around the yard and wouldn't let him get through the door into the house. Years later, when he was a young man, one of the neighborhood girls put a baby chick up to his ear to show how it peeped and Jimmy almost jumped out of his skin. He was scared to death of live chickens.[7]

The boy could be headstrong, like many of the Newmans, and sometimes downright reckless. He and Elaine were playing with their cousins Stanley and Sammy in the barn loft one day, when he tied a rope around Elaine's leg and told her he was going to push her out the loft door but would catch her up short with the rope before she hit the ground. To everyone's surprise, he did it. It almost pulled Elaine's leg off.

"It was the only time I ever knew my grandmother to switch him," Elaine said.[8]

Jimmy's father, Sam Newman, did not hesitate to use corporal punishment, a common practice even at school in those days. Jack said there was nobody who could strip his belt off faster to deliver a whipping than their father. It was a trait Jimmy carried with him into adulthood, taking a belt to his own boys—until he came home from the war.

Jimmy's relationship with his father was colored more, however, by something else. All the children remembered growing up with his drinking.

"When I say an alcoholic, lemme explain, just so you know," Jack said, speaking in his soft, west Georgia accent. "It's not like me and you sittin' down and havin' a drink and we get drunk. You never saw my father take a drink. Ever. Of anything. He had a bottle stuck between towels in a boot in the closet, in a raincoat pocket, on the walkway with a bucket turned upside down over it. All you saw was him gettin' drunker and drunker. He'd leave the living space, go wherever the bottle was, turn it up. I'm sure bubbles must have been flying to the bottom, because many times I didn't see him but I heard him say, 'Ach-hhhh' when it finished burning on the way down. That's the kind of drinking I'm talkin' about, binge drinking . . . He might go six months without drinking, but when he drank, he would drink for days, and he'd cease to consume food. Luckily, we grew up in a small town where we knew personally many of the doctors, so we had friends that would put him in the hospital, straighten him up intravenously, and he'd come home, and he'd look ten years younger than when he left."

When Elaine was a little girl, her father called her "Bunk," and she remembered that he used her to stoke his awful habit. Her mother tried to hide the liquor from him, but he'd call his daughter into the room and say, "Bunk, you know where my jug is," and she would go and fetch it.

Jimmy wasn't old enough to drive a car legally when he began dating Flora, but that didn't stop him. His father had a friend who used to come over to the house on Saturdays to get drunk. When the men were well into the bottle, Jimmy took the man's big, boxy green Dodge to go pick up Flo and take her to the movies. They'd go to a drive-in sandwich shop in Arnco Mills, where everybody in her family worked at the blanket mill. She and Jimmy always ordered the same dinner: grilled cheese sandwiches and chocolate milk. Then they'd go to the late movie at the theater in Newnan's main square or to the drive-in movie outside town. They often double-dated with a boy in Flora's class, who was going with a girl who had a reputation as what they called cheap. Flora and Jimmy called her a little whore. Jimmy took her out once, and the other boy, perhaps to get even, took Flora. When Jimmy found out later what had happened, he pulled a knife and told the kid never to try that again. It was the first sign of Jimmy's jealousy, a trait that eventually rose to the point of paranoia.

"I guess you'd call it love," Flora said years later of her first and only steady relationship. "Now I'd call it stupid."

Elaine grew to despise her drunken father as her older brother did and, as a teenager, was embarrassed if she had a date and the boy would come to the door when her father was slobbering drunk. She and Jimmy each decided in their midteens to escape. Jimmy joined the Army. A year later, at fifteen, Elaine chose marriage.

In January 1952, one year after he met Flora on the school bus, Jimmy climbed on another bus and went off to Fort McPherson in Atlanta to enlist. Flora said she never had a clue.[9]

He was only sixteen, not old enough for military service, but his granddaddy played checkers at the courthouse every Saturday and knew a thing or two about how to get things done. X. O. had the Coweta County ordinary, the equivalent of a probate judge, file a "Delayed Certificate of Birth" saying that James Taylor Newman, son of John Sam Newman and Judith Camp Newman, was born April 25, 1934. That would have made him seventeen when the delayed certificate was signed on January 10, 1952—old enough to enlist with his parents' permission, which he may have faked as well. An affidavit filed years earlier by his mother's attending physician attests to his true birth date exactly one year later, April 25, 1935.[10]

The United States was at war in Korea when Jimmy Newman volunteered in the winter of 1952. The Korean Peninsula jutting south from the Chinese mainland had been held by Japan when the Japanese surrendered at the end of World War II, and Korea was divided by the Allies at the 38th Parallel, the North to be controlled by the Soviet Union and the South by the United States. On June 25, 1950, the North invaded the South, and Korea exploded into the first hot battleground of the Cold War. The surprise attack nearly drove the overwhelmed South Korean and American forces into the sea before the defenders clawed their way back to the old boundary. Months of bitter stalemate and inconclusive peace talks followed.

The Army sent Private Newman to Fort Benning outside Columbus, Georgia, for basic training. The base was only about seventy-five miles from Newnan, but it was a new world for a boy who had rarely left home. Jimmy took to it and shined. After the compulsory eight weeks of basic training, he got into Jump School, a notoriously tough three-week course that turns out hardened physical specimens unafraid to leap out of airplanes and famed for their *esprit de corps.*

Private First Class James T. Newman was two months past his seventeenth birthday when he graduated from jump school and became a paratrooper. The Army thought he was eighteen.

Jimmy and Flora, whom he and everyone in both their families called by her childhood nickname "Coot," wrote each other practically every day that he was away. When he came home on leave after parachute training, he gave her his first silver wings, the ones with the open parachute in the center worn on a uniform over the heart. As was the custom among paratroopers, he broke the pin off the back to ensure that no pretender could wear the wings.

Front and back of Newman's first jump wings with the pin deliberately broken off the back.

Jimmy took to jumping so well that he eventually qualified as a senior, then master parachutist.

Sam Newman may have been a hopeless binge drinker, but he had his own auto repair shop at one point and held down a job for years commuting to Marietta to work for Lockheed, the aircraft manufacturer. He was on a team of a half-dozen men, all the others engineers, who strung miles and miles of wiring for the C-130 Hercules cargo plane and later the C-5A jumbo jet. Jimmy bragged about that years later while engaging in a bit of résumé polishing that would have had his father a graduate of Georgia Tech and himself a college kid. Neither was any such thing, but Sam wired those airplanes, and Jimmy acquired the skills to keep any car on the road, tank in the field, or, as it turned out, helicopter in the air.

SOLDIER BOY

IT WAS THE 1950S, HEYDAY OF THE AMERICAN AUTOMOBILE, and Jimmy grew up loving cars, the one affair that lasted his whole life. The Army recognized his talent for fixing them and took him out of the infantry to make him a wheeled vehicle mechanic. The old horse cavalry had migrated to jeeps, tanks, and armored personnel carriers, and it wasn't long before Jimmy got a job driving or fixing the rolling stock. He was a good soldier, so outstanding that he was picked as crew for one of the tanks from Fort Bragg that drove up Pennsylvania Avenue in the first inaugural parade for the former General of the Army, President Dwight D. Eisenhower, on January 20, 1953.[11]

Private Newman received orders to go to Korea that fall to join the 187th Airborne Regimental Combat Team. But an armistice ended the fighting on July 27, and so Newman was sent instead to meet his new unit in Japan, where the United States still maintained substantial forces nearly two years after the Allied occupation ended in 1951.

Before shipping out, he got a thirty-day home leave and returned to Newnan, where he and Flora Rogers were married on December 28, 1953. A week later, he went overseas. His young bride stayed with her mother to await his return, and on September 11, 1954, Jimmy and Flora's first son was born. They named him Roger.

A few months later, in July 1955, Jimmy was reassigned to Fort Bragg in Fayetteville, North Carolina, home of the 82nd Airborne Division. Flo and the baby joined him there, and they set up house in one of the tawdry, one-bedroom shacks that ringed the base. They'd stay in one place till they got tired of it or Jimmy got promoted, then move into something a little bit better. By the time Roger, a classic Army brat, went away to law school, he counted thirty-three addresses.

The Army was Jimmy's life, and he was determined to be a good soldier. He kept his uniforms creased and clean, polished his brass, and spit-shined his boots. The discipline suited him, and he applied one-man rule and uncompromising expectations to his family as well.

Roger's little brother, Ronald, was born in August 1956, when the family was living at Fort Campbell, Kentucky. Jimmy, still a wheeled vehicle mechanic by military specialty, was rising through the enlisted ranks and beginning to demonstrate the leadership talents that would flower years later in Vietnam. The family bounced around from Fort Campbell to Fort Jackson in South Carolina, then back to Bragg before Jimmy was shipped abroad again, this time to West Germany. He took his wife and children with him to live in a military-provided apartment in Budingen, a walled medieval city where U.S. armored cavalry units trained for decades after World War II.

Home movies from the Newmans' three years in Europe show Platoon Sergeant James T. Newman in buff physical condition and starched fatigues loading heavy equipment on trains, participating in firing exercises in the field, and riding in armed convoys along narrow German roads and through picturesque Old World villages.

At one point, he's got his head under the hood of a broken-down convoy vehicle.

More telling in the silent movies are the images of his two little boys, wearing identical plaid shirts, their hair trimmed short, learning to toss baseballs in the air in the parking lot of their Army compound. Surrounded by 1950s American cars, they caught the balls in their new, still-stiff leather baseball mitts. In between movements of military convoys and parachute demonstrations, there are images of Roger and Ronald climbing on the swing sets and a jungle gym in the yard, watching their father tuning the family car, hunting for Easter eggs around their apartment. Their mother kept the camera on as the boys pulled presents from under the Christmas tree and passed them around the room in an annual ritual shown in three successive winters in Germany. Even Saint Nick made an appearance in full regalia. Superman outfits, an electric train, and big-boy bicycles were huge that first year. So were toy guns with holsters. Snowball fights, skiing in the street, and wrestling with Daddy after a fresh snowfall were all captured on film.

The family drove a black Volvo PV fastback, one of the few foreign cars the Newmans ever owned.

Roger remembered his soldier father as a strict disciplinarian with a flaring temper. As part of his uniform, Platoon Sergeant Newman wore a khaki web belt with a brass tip at one end and a carefully hand-polished brass buckle at the other. It had to be fastened just so. More than fifty years after those days in Germany, when Roger was in kindergarten, he still recalled the snapping sound that belt tip made as it zipped through the belt loops when his father jerked the band from his trousers to deliver a whipping. Belt in hand, Sergeant Newman folded it in half and snapped the two parts together, making a frightening crack that let his boys know what was coming. It was Roger's introduction to what he thought of as military discipline. He didn't regard it as cruel, just tough and, of course, painful. There were rules, and breaking one meant getting whipped. He and his little brother weren't bad boys, but they occasionally ran afoul of their father's unbending expectations. One firm rule was that Roger and his little brother had to eat everything on their plates at dinner. Ever since he has been old enough to make his own rules, Roger has refused to eat beets, onions, broccoli, or asparagus, the vegetables his father ordered him to finish because they were supposed to be good for him. But he still craves Wiener schnitzel, the breaded and fried veal cutlets he adored when the family ate out in a local restaurant. Budingen, near Frankfurt, served as a garrison for U.S. armored cavalry troops from the end of World War II until 2007. For generations, the American military presence was a fact of life in the region, and Army families could move with ease around towns and cities where Germans came to accept them as neighbors and a valuable addition to the local economy.

One of the rituals Roger remembered fondly was helping unpack his father's duffel when he returned from field exercises. The sense of smell is said to be the best remembered of human senses, and decades later, if Roger picked up the scent of heavy cotton canvas, he instantly thought of his father's bag and the uniforms packed inside.

An exemplary soldier, Newman rose through the enlisted ranks without a hitch. Near the end of his tour of duty in Germany, he was up for promotion from E-7, platoon sergeant, to E-8, master sergeant, the rank signified by three chevrons with a rocker under each one. He had spent ten years in the Army but was only twenty-six or twenty-seven years old when he went before the promotion board. A master sergeant is supposed to be a tough, grizzled noncom, hardened by experience, a father figure to the green recruits. Newman didn't fit the image. The head of the promotion panel, Colonel James W. Sutherland Jr., whom Newman would encounter again many years later in Vietnam, told him, "You're entirely too young to be an E-8. What I want you to do is go back and fill out the paperwork for a direct commission" as an officer.[12] The most junior officers, second lieutenants, were mostly just kids in their early twenties, straight out of the academy, an ROTC program, or Officer Candidate School, OCS. They were bound for command, slated to lead, but they rarely garnered much respect from the enlisted ranks until they had proven their mettle. Newman told the colonel he'd apply, but he didn't much like officers and had no ambition to be one. He went back to work as an acting platoon leader of his reconnaissance platoon that didn't have a commanding officer at the moment and thought no more of the recommendation until his company commander called him on the carpet a couple weeks later and told him they were both in big trouble. The colonel had ordered a special inspection of the company, and the whole unit would be up days and nights preparing every square inch of buildings and every piece of assigned equipment for tough, unforgiving eyes.

"What'd you do?" Newman asked the CO.

"No, it was you," the CO shot back. "Colonel Sutherland told you to fill out the paperwork for a direct commission, and you didn't do it."

That was the Army way. The failure of a subordinate was the responsibility of his commander. Now, everyone in the company would pay for Newman's ignoring the colonel's recommendation—unless he did as he was told.

Newman's commander told him he had already made the appointment for the sergeant's physical and that the clerk had the paperwork ready for Newman to fill out, "so until you get that done, you're not doing anything else." Newman did as ordered, the papers went off to the Department of the Army in Washington, and his commission was approved shortly after his return to the States. He went to work at Fort Bragg one day as an E-7 platoon sergeant with three chevrons and two rockers sewn on his shoulder and came home with the single gold bar of a second lieutenant on his collar.

In one sense, he was starting over. At twenty-seven, Lieutenant Newman was ranked with freshly baked college graduates five and six years younger who got their commissions through part-time, university-based ROTC programs or as graduates of the Army's Officer Candidate School at Fort Benning, which churned out classes of new lieutenants known as "90-day Wonders." The promotion, of course, raised his pay. But it also put him in line for command of a unit, a job he didn't know he'd been born to do. It was 1962, and Vietnam was barely a blip on anyone's radar screen. There were no U.S. combat forces there yet, only advisors, trainers, and some Special Forces volunteers. Newman was given a reconnaissance platoon in a ground cavalry squadron at Fort Bragg, but the appointment didn't last long. A superior officer saw something he liked and brought the new officer into battalion headquarters as the operations officer. Newman moved up from there to a staff job at the division level, which looked good on paper but meant he was a junior cog in the Army's notoriously bureaucratic and rank-conscious organizational structure. He kept jumping out of airplanes for fun and won his Century Wings in 1963, signifying he had made one hundred parachute jumps, but he was restless in his job and looking for adventure.

A fellow officer invited him to go flying in an OV-1C Mohawk, an odd-looking new armed reconnaissance airplane with twin propellers, two seats side by side and a triple tail. Newman was hooked at takeoff. Another friend told him helicopters were more fun—"The sonofabitch will fly itself if you can get it off the ground"—and the Army had more of them than fixed-wing aircraft. So Newman applied to rotary-wing flight school, which in those days began at Fort Wolters in Mineral Wells, Texas. Commissioned officers such as Newman were regarded as temporary aviators who would return to their assigned branch—usually infantry, armor, or artillery—after their tour with a flight crew or in the command structure of a helicopter unit. Unlike the Air Force, which required all pilots and copilots to have commissions, the Army selected promising volunteers from the enlisted ranks to train them to fly. If they succeeded, they were promoted to warrant officers, and many of them spent their careers flying or training others but were not eligible to command regular units. Unlike commissioned officers, who are addressed as "Sir" by subordinates, warrant officers are universally called "Mister."

Candidates who made it through the first three months of primary training were sent on to Fort Rucker in the rolling wiregrass country of southeastern Alabama. Newman planned to leave his family behind at Fort Bragg to let the boys finish the school year while he started training at Wolters, then reunite when he got to Fort Rucker. But he was gone less than a week before he drove home to North Carolina on a Wednesday, rented the house in Fayetteville, packed up, and took Flo and the boys with him to Mineral Wells on Saturday. Flo said he couldn't stand to be alone. She hated the old base—Mineral Hell, the soldiers called it. Snow was falling in Texas when they arrived with their two little boys in tow.

The principal training aircraft at Fort Wolters was the Korean War–era H-23, a helicopter familiar to anyone who has watched the opening scene of the long-running television comedy *M*A*S*H.* It could be used for reconnaissance, as an ambulance with open-air litters mounted on the skids, or for limited supply or troop transport. It had only two, three, or four seats, depending on which configuration was being used. Classes began with the fundamental principles of flight, but students looked forward to their most critical test: the first solo. No one got past Fort Wolters without one, and most would-be pilots discovered it wasn't that easy. Newman's friend who told him a helicopter would fly itself probably had never tried it.

A helicopter, or rotary-wing aircraft, has five main controls, only one of which, the throttle, is familiar to a driver who has learned to handle a car or motorcycle in the two-dimensional world. The cyclic, a bent stick that rises from the floor between the pilot's legs, steers the aircraft to the right, left, forward, or back. To the left of the pilot seat is the collective, a lever that controls the pitch of the rotor blades and thus the rate of climb or descent. At the end of the collective is the throttle, a grip that is twisted to control the speed of the rotor blades, similar to the throttle on a motorcycle. And finally, the pilot's feet rest on two pedals that control the tail rotor, a vertical blade that counters the tendency to twirl downward like a maple-seed pod. Without the tail rotor or a counter-rotating blade, the craft's fuselage would simply spin inevitably downward until it hit the ground. The challenge is that all the controls are interrelated, that is, changing one requires nearly simultaneous adjustment of the others to keep the craft flying properly. For instance, raising the collective to increase the pitch of the rotor blade slows down the engine, requiring the pilot to open the throttle just enough to maintain position. The increase in power raises torque, which tends to make the helicopter body spin to the right. That can be corrected by pressing harder on the left pedal. It's a lot of things to do at once—not counting the buttons at the end of the cyclic for intercom and radios and, sometimes, a cargo release button or gun trigger.

The novice pilot learns quickly that raising the helicopter off the landing pad and bringing it to a hover takes concentration and intricate coordination. Newman, then a first lieutenant, learned how, but it took some getting used to. The first time he got his hands on the controls, he liked to say, he couldn't keep the machine inside a five-mile area, but he improved to the point he could play tic-tac-toe with his helicopter, hopping from square to square in the exercise area. His biggest challenge was the required class on weather and its effects on flying. He studied the material but had trouble grasping it. He made it through, however, and said years later the meteorology he learned came in handy flying in the awful conditions he encountered in the A Shau and mountains west of Khe Sanh. Newman did his solo at Wolters, got thrown into the pool at the Holiday Inn—a ritual for student pilots after making their first flight alone—then picked up his family to move to Fort Rucker to learn instruments, fly the earth's contours at treetop level, and get into and out of tight landing zones.

One of the most important skills they all had to learn was autorotation, the saving grace of a helicopter that enables a pilot to make a forced landing without power. It is possible to control a rotary-wing craft in a powerless glide—but the crew gets only one chance to find a place to land and guide the ship in, pulling pitch at the last moment to slow the forward motion without falling out of the sky or tumbling backward. Autorotation saved lots of crews and aircraft in combat, including several that flew for Newman.

When he got to Fort Rucker for instrument training and aviation tactics, he had to learn to fly the H-19, a huge, ungainly aircraft that pilots hated. Newman claimed it took three men just to hold the collective to keep the helicopter flying.[13] Without the hydraulic controls of the more modern Huey, the H-19 demanded strong pressure on the left pedal to keep the craft "in trim," flying steadily forward. Newman would come to dread that strong left pedal.

WAR

WHILE JIM NEWMAN WAS LEARNING TO FLY HELICOPTERS, the war in Vietnam struck home.

At 2:00 a.m. on Saturday, February 7, 1965, Vietnam time, half a world away and a dozen time zones ahead of the eastern United States, North Vietnamese troops of the 409th sapper battalion attacked the U.S. military headquarters of about a thousand Americans advising South Vietnamese troops in the Central Highlands. The headquarters and nearby Camp Holloway Army Airfield were strategically located in Pleiku, a small provincial capital on a high plateau in the center of the country's rugged highlands region.[14][15][16] Although unacknowledged at the time, the North Vietnamese had begun "a new era in our revolutionary war, the era of combining guerrilla warfare with conventional warfare," coordinating operations by Viet Cong guerrillas from the South with well-disciplined regular-army troops from the Communist-led northern half of the country. The two Vietnams were separated at that time by a demilitarized zone (DMZ) along the Ben Hai River. The 1954 Geneva Accords that ended French colonial rule in Indochina established the temporary buffer, supposedly until a popular election would reunite the two halves under a single government.

The North Vietnamese sappers opened fire on the U.S. headquarters with rocket-propelled grenades in a fifteen-minute barrage that killed one American and wounded seven. As the headquarters troops, unaccustomed to combat, dove for cover, more sappers from the same unit launched a mortar attack on Camp Holloway, the nearby airfield where most of the U.S. helicopters and small reconnaissance planes in the highlands were based. The mortars rained into the camp's living quarters, where ill-prepared and poorly protected soldiers of the 52nd Aviation Battalion, most of them helicopter maintenance people, scrambled for cover. The sappers dashed onto the airstrip on foot, firing rifles to keep guards at bay, hurling hand grenades at parked planes and helicopters as they ran. Some paused long enough to set demolition charges to blow up as many aircraft as they could. Nine Americans were killed, 125 were wounded, and ten helicopters and planes were destroyed in the coordinated attacks. It was the worst direct assault the Americans had experienced against one of their own bases in Vietnam. The number of U.S. military personnel advising and training South Vietnamese troops, flying air missions, and running counterinsurgency operations against Viet Cong guerrillas had swelled to twenty-three thousand by that time, but few of them were directly engaged in combat. Elite Special Forces teams, distinguished by their green berets, recruited and led indigenous hill-tribe fighters to support the South against the Communist North, but the bulk of U.S. Forces worked in support roles.

The United States had been trying to buck up the South Vietnamese ever since the French were defeated in 1954, but the plan wasn't working. The Pentagon Papers revealed later that by early 1965 U.S. officials thought the South Vietnamese government was nearing collapse. "The most optimistic estimate was that the VC would take over within a year," according to the secret government analysis leaked by Daniel Ellsberg when he was working for a government contractor in 1971.[17]

When the enemy escalated its campaign by attacking Americans directly, President Lyndon Johnson told his National Security Council, "I've had enough of this." Activating a contingency plan he had previously directed the Pentagon to prepare, the president ordered reprisal air raids against targets in North Vietnam. Forty-eight hours later, the enemy struck again, blowing up a new four-story hotel built to billet American soldiers in Qui Nhon on the coast, seventy-five miles east of Pleiku, where the first strikes had hit. Twenty-two Americans were killed in the follow-up attack, many of them crushed in the rubble of the building. Twenty were wounded.

President Johnson responded that time with Operation Rolling Thunder, taking the war to the North with a sustained bombing campaign. He also ordered units of the 3rd Marine Division to go ashore and guard the sprawling air base at Danang, a staging area for the air raids against the North. Bigger things were planned. Much bigger.

Only three years earlier, the Army had been paying scant attention to the potential uses of helicopters in combat, concentrating instead on the traditional armor, infantry, and artillery that it expected to use if the Soviet Union and its Eastern European allies swept into Western Europe. A handful of senior officers advocating air mobility had been ignored for years. The focus changed in an instant when Defense Secretary Robert S. McNamara, a systems analyst, not a hidebound military officer, ordered the generals to conduct a quick and comprehensive study of military mobility and specifically told them to "give unorthodox ideas a hearing."[18]

McNamara demanded they report back to him in four months—lightning fast for the Army bureaucracy. Near the end of the study, the Army staged a mock air and ground assault on an entrenched enemy position to show McNamara and the Pentagon brass what it could do. Using twin-propeller Mohawk armed reconnaissance planes as low-level bombers, big helicopters as machine-gun and rocket platforms, and a fleet of thirty Hueys to land the infantry and seize the supposed enemy position, the "airmobile" force rose over a hill behind McNamara and the assemblage of dignitaries and landed troops on the high ground beyond them, taking the objective within two minutes. The secretary was so impressed that the only question he asked was how much it cost. An experimental division was quickly assembled at Fort Benning, Georgia, to develop the airmobile concept, a giant step toward making helicopters an integral part of military operations.

After the Viet Cong struck the compounds in Pleiku and Qui Nhon, the Army moved quickly to stand up that experimental unit, renamed it the 1st Air Cavalry Division, assigned it the old yellow shoulder patch with black diagonal stripe and horse's head symbolizing the unit's roots, and ordered men and equipment loaded aboard ships to fight a new kind of war in Vietnam. The first contingent landed that September in Qui Nhon, the coastal town where the Viet Cong had blown up the Americans' hotel. The United States believed it had the most powerful Army in the world and that it could fly troops into combat faster than anyone had imagined. Within months those troops would be tested in the Battle of the Ia Drang Valley, one of the bloodiest engagements of what was to be nearly ten more years of war. The Army needed lots of helicopters—fast—and pilots to fly them.

Newman got to Fort Wolters to begin primary rotary-wing flight training about three weeks after the Pleiku attacks. He was among the first helicopter pilots to go through the advanced course at Fort Rucker after the buildup began and graduated on October 25, 1965.

Fifteen of the forty-nine graduates in his class got orders for Vietnam. Most of the others, including Newman, would follow in the coming months. Newman was assigned to the 1st Air Cav at Fort Benning. It was on its way to war, but he got picked to stay behind and ferry brand-new UH-1 Hueys from the Bell Helicopter plant in Fort Worth, Texas, across the Southwest to Oakland, California, for shipment to the war zone. His flight records indicate that ten days after graduation from flight school he qualified in the B-model Huey then bound for the war zone and soon after was certified to fly the latest D-model.

A group of a dozen pilots went hopscotching across the desert, each with his own aircraft, searching for civilian airports where they could buy fuel because their choppers didn't have the range to make it to a military base. The pilots had fun flying and logged lots of solo hours. It was one of the few times since joining the Army that Newman was largely on his own, finding his way, making his own decisions, and he loved it. He went on to Fort Benning, where, having missed the deployment of the 1st Air Cav to Vietnam, he was assigned to the 173rd Aviation Company. It was soon to be renamed the 173rd Assault Helicopter Company to describe its newly defined combat role. Roger, then eleven, was impressed when his daddy started flying because Newman brought his flight helmet home every night in a green helmet bag and wore a cool, bomber-style flight jacket that cut off at the waist. The jacket was made of sage green satin and a blaze orange lining with the thought it could be turned inside out by a downed pilot to signal his position to rescuers. Newman had quit wearing regular fatigues to work and put on a one-piece, flame-resistant flight suit instead.

At the end of the year, he was promoted to captain and ordered to the war zone with the 173rd. The slick crews called themselves the Robin Hoods, and they painted a yellow Robin Hood–style cap adorned with a red feather on the nose of their aircraft. The slicks were the workhorses of the Army throughout the Vietnam War and for years afterward. They were called Hueys because the original Army designation of the aircraft when it was accepted from Bell Helicopter in 1960 was HU-1A, more or less pronounceable as "huie." The Army later reversed its nomenclature from "Helicopter, Utility" to "Utility Helicopter," but the nickname stuck. The passenger models that were used to ferry troops and supplies to the field were called "slicks" by soldiers because they were easily distinguished from early gunship models that had heavy rocket pods hanging off each side of the fuselage. The slicks were armed, but only with M-60 machine guns that the crew chief and a door gunner manned from either side of the rear cargo compartment. Slicks ferried troops in and out of landing zones, carried supplies and ammunition, and served as command-and-control or chase ships for airmobile operations. The Robin Hoods were protected by the Crossbows, a fleet of "B-model" gunships that were Hueys with a cluster of nineteen rocket pods behind the doors on either side. The Robin Hoods went over together on the Navy troop ship *General Walker* among nearly five thousand men headed to Vietnam as part of the buildup. Newman started a letter to Flo the first day at sea and added to it every day for three weeks. When he got to Vietnam, he dropped it in the mail in one thick envelope and continued to write her most days.

When the Robin Hoods arrived at Lai Khe, a village about thirty-five miles north of Saigon, they found that a work detail from a U.S. infantry brigade in the area had pitched a dozen big canvas tents for them in an old French rubber plantation near the airfield. The tall, symmetrically planted trees with their broad, green leaves afforded welcome shade from the tropical heat. Two big ice chests filled with beer were left for the arriving pilots as a welcoming gift from the grunts who would soon be riding to war in the Robin Hoods' helicopters.

Major Ernie Bruce, who shared a tent with Newman and a dozen other pilots when they arrived at Lai Khe, remembered he had been asleep on a cot in the darkened tent for about an hour when everyone was shaken awake by the boom and screaming of artillery shells flying a few hundred feet above them as an American battery south of the runway fired a salvo off into the night toward an area known as the Iron Triangle, a free-fire zone where anyone alive was presumed to be an enemy. The Army called it harassment-and-interdiction fire just to keep anyone out there on his toes or, preferably, hiding in a hole. When the howitzers paused, a machine gun on the perimeter opened up to rattle off a few hundred rounds in hopes of driving off anyone trying to attack the base. Every night was noisy like that.

About four o'clock in the morning, the pilots were awakened again, this time startled by a strange squawking noise outside the tent. Bruce heard the click of several pistols as his fellow pilots cocked their .45-caliber service weapons. He slipped his own out from under his pillow and coaxed a round into the chamber. The men imagined their tent surrounded by Viet Cong guerrillas who were signaling each other with strange sounds. At the first sign of light, a brave young captain slipped out of the tent, pistol in hand, to confront the noisemaker.

"Shit!" the others heard him say. "A goddamn rooster is perched on top of the tent." They had survived their first night at war.

The American base, with a runway long enough to accommodate four-engine C-130 cargo planes, soon engulfed the village, and the local Vietnamese quickly learned to supply everything from laundry service to bar girls and marijuana to their new neighbors.

The Americans built bunkers out of sandbags for protection from mortar attacks, and soon the tents were replaced by modest wooden cabins that GIs throughout Vietnam dubbed hooches.[19] The pilots got the best quarters, often only two to a cabin, with their names painted on signs that hung outside their doors. The Robin Hoods dubbed their new home, of course, Sherwood Forest.

Captain Newman, right, relaxing with fellow officer outside operations shack in Sherwood Forest base camp.

The Army was in such a rush to get its helicopters flying in Vietnam that it quickly exhausted the supply of junior pilots and began plucking senior officers with previous flight experience from their cushy staff jobs while it raced to put enlisted men through flight school and promote them to warrant officer rank, the lowest rank permitted to fly helicopters. The 173rd Assault Helicopter Company was authorized one major, a few captains, a dozen lieutenants, and about thirty warrant officers. All were expected to be qualified pilots. But when they arrived in Vietnam, the Robin Hoods had thirty-three majors, leaving junior captains like Newman lucky to be assigned to fly "right seat," the copilot's position in a Huey. Fortunately for the junior officers, as well as the aging majors, the military bureaucracy was exploding as the U.S. combat role escalated. Long Binh, the secure headquarters of the U.S. Army in Vietnam just outside the capital of Saigon, was desperate for staff officers, and many careerists left frontline units for air-conditioned offices and most of the comforts of stateside military bases. That opened flying spots in chopper units. Captain Newman soon got his own helicopter and crew and was appointed a section commander, giving him nominal authority over four Hueys.

The title didn't really mean much. Everybody flew what were known as "ash and trash" missions, hauling supplies and ammunition from base to base and out to troops in the field. The section commander could set the order of takeoffs and landings and such, but most mission-critical decisions were made at a higher level. They were all learning the tactics of airlifting the infantry—grunts—into cleared landing zones in the thick jungle of the Iron Triangle. The Viet Cong stronghold was laced with underground tunnels dug, maintained, and expanded into vast complexes with sleeping quarters, meeting rooms, even hospitals. The most notorious tunnel network surrounding the nearby village of Cu Chi became a popular tourist attraction after the war, when the victors enlarged the tunnels to enable comparatively tall Westerners to hunch over and explore how their determined enemy survived the carpet bombing and superior armament of the Americans.

When the Robin Hoods arrived at Lai Khe, they had only one pilot with any combat experience, and he was soon transferred to fly a general above the fighting. The rest of them learned what little was known about combat assaults and resupply under fire by flying with the Tomahawks, another helicopter unit stationed nearby. Much of what they knew, they made up flying troops and supplies in and out of makeshift landing zones carved out of jungle forest between Saigon and the Cambodian border.

They also learned that adventurous soldiers in a war zone could add creature comforts not provided on official equipment lists. The company commander discovered that one of his enlisted men was a skilled con artist. The enterprising soldier was designated the "company scrounger" and assigned one of the unit's two small trucks to barter or steal anything he thought the unit could use. At one point, he located an unassembled Quonset hut that he decided would be just the right size for an officers' lounge. He traded it for a surplus pistol, and the pilots obligingly ferried the parts from another base to Sherwood Forest, where it was assembled, outfitted with tables, chairs, and a beer bar, and named the Blue Boar Inn for the tavern in Howard Pyle's classic *The Merry Adventures of Robin Hood.*

Newman kept that in mind years later and had his own skilled scroungers for even bigger prizes.

The captain had been in-country for more than six months and was regarded as a proficient combat pilot when he was picked to resupply a beleaguered company of grunts from the 1st Infantry Division that was locked in a firefight with enemy troops. The company reported by radio that it was running out of ammunition and urgently needed resupply. Newman was flying Huey 091, a slick identified by the last three digits of its tail number: 65-10091. That UH-1 would one day find a place in American history, but on September 18, 1966, it just happened to be available for a mission.

Private First Class Ed Walsh had been made crew chief of 091 about ten days before, and Newman became its regular aircraft commander. It was the first time either had been given his own helicopter—they usually filled in for others—and they immediately liked working together. The four-man crew consisted of two officers and two enlisted men. The person designated to be in charge was the aircraft commander, who in civilian parlance would be regarded as the pilot. A second flight-trained officer, whom the Army called "pilot" but who actually was the copilot, was universally referred to in Vietnam as the "peter pilot."[20] The crew chief, an enlisted man, sat in a pocket behind the peter pilot and was responsible for maintaining the craft on the ground and supervising any passengers or cargo. He also manned one of two machine guns mounted in the open doorways on either side of the aircraft. The door gunner, frequently a fill-in from an infantry unit in the field, manned the M-60 machine gun on the left side, behind the aircraft commander's seat. Walsh remembered the door gunner on that resupply mission was named Battista. No one could remember the peter pilot's name. He was a warrant officer, brand new in-country, and none of them had flown with him before.

The stranded company they were assigned to resupply was in the Iron Triangle, not far from Sherwood Forest, but there was a heavy fog that Sunday and practically no visibility. Newman "couldn't see jack," as he put it, but after they took off, the weather lifted just enough for him to pick out a creek bed leading to the embattled encampment. He dropped down to about thirty feet above the water and followed the twists and turns of the creek at 100 knots, so fast that the slightest miscalculation would put them in the water or trees. They slipped into the beleaguered landing zone twice, dropping their loads to the soldiers waiting directly below. "Ole dumb-ass me," as Newman called himself long afterward, made the mistake of going out the same way once more. Helicopter combat tactics weren't as advanced as they became later in the war, but it was pretty basic knowledge in any military unit that it was dangerous to follow the same course again and again. Walsh said there just wasn't any other choice with the ceiling so low and no other way to navigate into the camp. Coming out the last time, still flying as fast as he could at low level, Newman saw three or four guerrillas with AK-47 assault rifles pop out of the jungle on the creek bank and fire up at his Huey as it swept overhead. The VC (Viet Cong) were on the left side of the aircraft, close enough for eye contact, and the gunner Battista opened fire with his M-60, knocking at least two of them to the ground. It was too late. The first round to find its target crashed through the clear plastic "chin bubble" at Newman's feet and bounced off the steel "chicken plate" that flight crews wore on their chests as body armor. He watched the bullet fall harmlessly into the open ashtray on the instrument panel. The next bullet splintered his left ankle, knocking his foot off the pedal. The sudden pressure on the other pedal pushed the rudder to one side and spun the rear of the aircraft, nearly throwing the chopper into a tailspin. Blood squirted from Newman's boot as the peter pilot, who was trained to keep his hands and feet lightly on the controls just in case, grabbed hold and pushed his cyclic stick forward hard trying to regain control of the aircraft. His commander's blood spattered them both and sprayed the console. But Newman's leg was jammed between the pedal and the cyclic on his side. The peter pilot screamed for his commander to get his feet out of the way. It was no use. Newman's leg was stuck.

Walsh, the crew chief, was watching out the right side of the aircraft and hadn't seen the enemy troops on the ground, but he realized his ship was in trouble because it was suddenly lurching sideways with its tail swinging wildly back and forth. He heard the shouting and realized what was happening. Crew chiefs were supposed to be familiar with all the parts of their aircraft, and Walsh knew a maneuver even pilots often didn't. He dove across the cargo compartment and yanked an emergency release that dropped the back of Newman's armored seat onto the floor. Newman, strapped into his safety harness, fell backward away from the cockpit. Walsh jumped over the wounded officer, grabbed his leg, and pulled it free. The anonymous peter pilot regained control at about thirty feet off the water and headed back toward the home airstrip at Lai Khe.

Walsh unbuckled Newman from the seat and, with a hand from his gunner, pulled the helpless Newman backward onto the floor. He could see blood pouring from the captain's boot and thought the man might bleed to death before they could get him to the hospital. Walsh whipped off his own belt, wrapped it around Newman's thigh, and twisted it hard to cut off the circulation to his leg. Newman always said that makeshift tourniquet saved his life. There's no question the peter pilot, whoever he was, saved them all. When 091 landed at Lai

Khe, waiting medics hurriedly shifted Newman onto a stretcher and transferred him to a waiting medevac chopper for a fast flight to the military hospital at Vung Tau. There, he was loaded aboard a U.S.-bound ambulance plane with other severely wounded troops. Ed Walsh didn't hear of him again for nearly forty years. Despite separate attempts over the years, neither man ever identified the peter pilot.

Huey 091, however, brought Newman and Walsh back together. Walsh figured his former aircraft commander had probably lost his foot and left the Army, but he hoped one day to be reunited with him. Walsh himself was wounded slightly in a later incident but finished his tour and got out of the Army after his three-year hitch was up in 1968. He found a job doing sheet-metal work for a subcontractor on the giant C5A military transport jet. He was laid off in a cutback and took a civil service test that landed him a position as a school custodian in his native Springfield, Massachusetts, where he has lived all his life.

Newman's official performance reviews for his combat service were laudatory, but the review period of his last evaluation officially ended the day before he was shot, and so it didn't mention the incident. However, tacked to the back of the official record is an addendum written by Major Ernest E. Bruce Jr., the unit's executive officer. "There is one important event" that was left off Newman's OER, the Officer Evaluation Report, Bruce wrote. "I feel it must be mentioned.

"Captain Newman was transferred from the First Platoon to the Second Platoon in order to become the Section Commander of the Second Airlift Section. Approximately one week after taking over the section, his section was given the mission of resupplying the 3rd Brigade, 1st Infantry Division, which was on a combat operation on the northern edge of the Iron Triangle. The resupply was initiated under a cloud ceiling of one hundred to two hundred feet. This placed the helicopters in a very vulnerable position with respect to enemy ground fire. He elected to continue this important mission of resupply to the combat unit in spite of the poor weather. Captain Newman [led] his section in an outstanding manner. He took different routes on each sortie to keep from establishing a pattern. On the last lift, he overflew a small clearing, and . . . a squad of Viet Cong [was] waiting with automatic weapons. They had heard the helicopters approaching and fired point blank at Captain Newman's helicopter. One bullet smashed through Captain Newman's foot causing major bone damage and profuse bleeding. Captain Newman was the Aircraft Commander and his pilot was a fresh graduate from flight school who had been in Vietnam only several days and had only a few dozen flight hours after graduating. Captain Newman immediately radioed his section which was following him and directed fire from their door guns on the Viet Cong. The infantry passengers saw three Viet Cong drop from the fire. Captain Newman led his flight back to the home station and only when out of danger did he release control of the aircraft to the inexperienced pilot. At this time he was approaching a state of shock from massive blood loss. After three days in the intensive care of the hospital ward to offset the blood loss, Captain Newman was evacuated to CONUS (Continental United States).

"He has been recommended for the Distinguished Flying Cross for his heroism and outstanding devotion to duty."

The major's undated note,[21] corroborating Newman's and Walsh's accounts, was found in Newman's personnel file two years after his death.

As the Internet sprang into use and Vietnam veterans started looking for each other over the network, a friend of Walsh's came across an e-mail address for a Major James T. Newman and passed it along to Walsh, who messaged his long-ago aircraft commander that their old chopper was going to fly again. Huey 091, having been repaired, hit again, repaired, and shot down in Vietnam, all within a few months, was hoisted out of the jungle in January 1967 and shipped back to the States for rebuilding. It was used for training at Fort Rucker and missions for the Navy, National Guard, and the National Aeronautics and Space Administration before being declared surplus in 1995 and turned over to an airplane museum in Texas. The museum later donated it to the Smithsonian Institution in Washington to be the iconic Vietnam centerpiece of an exhibition called "The Price of Freedom," an exploration of more than two centuries of Americans at war. In 2002, a band of veterans was organized to fly the freshly overhauled old bird across the country on a ten-thousand-mile farewell tour, ending on the National Mall in Washington with delivery to the Smithsonian's National Museum of American History.

Newman, right, and Ed Walsh, the crew chief he credited with saving his life, at the opening of an exhibit featuring their helicopter, Huey 091, at the Smithsonian Institution's National Museum of American History in Washington. The helicopter in which Newman was wounded on his first combat tour anchors the Vietnam section of an exhibition called "The Price of Freedom: Americans at War."

Walsh, one of the Huey's first crew chiefs, was tapped to escort his old charge across the country, and he contacted Newman to ask for a reunion when they passed through North Carolina. Walsh wasn't sure Newman was coming, and as the afternoon dragged on, he almost gave up hope they would see each other again. Then, near the end of the day, the major showed up, sought out Walsh, and hugged him in gratitude—an awkward show of emotion for the usually standoffish retired officer who tried never to get too close to his men. They talked about their brief comradeship early in the war, when 091 was new and they were young.

Newman thanked Walsh for saving his life and told him he had fought the Army to stay in and get recertified to fly. He never mentioned the lives he saved on his second tour or the medals he collected for heroism.

Walsh almost broke down when Newman thanked him all those years later. "After a guy tells you to your face he wouldn't be alive except for you—and then you find out he went on to save all those other people—well, I realized it was the most important thing I ever did."[22]

COMEBACK

FLORA NEWMAN DIDN'T KNOW HER HUSBAND HAD BEEN WOUNDED until several days later when she picked up a letter from the Red Cross at lunchtime. She had the afternoon off from work in a local doctor's office and stopped to check for mail. Newman had told the Army not to notify her until he got back to the States. The same day that she received his letter saying he'd been hit, mailed from a military hospital in Vietnam, he called her from Alaska. The ambulance plane bringing wounded back from the war had landed in Anchorage to refuel. Newman had been pouring sweat when they loaded him aboard the plane in tropical Vung Tau, then nearly froze when the cargo door opened in Alaska. He told Flora the Army wanted to send him to a military hospital in Georgia but that he had objected and asked to be sent home to Fort Bragg, where his wife and children were living. The plane landed at Pope Air Force Base adjacent to Bragg, and Flora was waiting on the tarmac to greet him. As an attendant picked up the front of the captain's litter to load him into an ambulance for the two-mile trip to Womack Army Hospital, he accidentally bumped Newman's foot, and the wounded patient cried out in pain.

"Goddammit! I knew you were going to do that," Newman shouted at the stretcher bearer. Flora said you could have heard him all over Pope Air Force Base.

"I knew he'd come home," she said.

It was the beginning of a long, difficult convalescence. Newman underwent operations to remove bone shards from his foot, rebuild his shattered ankle, and graft skin from his thigh to close the wound. For a couple of years, tiny pieces of shrapnel continued to work their way out through his skin.

One doctor told him he would probably lose his lower leg. Newman never let himself even consider it. He was more determined than ever to recover. At first, Flo didn't tell the boys how badly wounded their father was. She was afraid of traumatizing them. She told them only that he'd been hurt and was in the hospital, then that he'd been shot in the foot. Eventually, the boys learned details of what had happened and why it was taking so long to heal. After Newman was discharged from the hospital, Roger would watch his father change the bandage on his still-oozing wounds. He seemed to change them a lot. And Roger remembered the nasty smell when his father's foot came out of the cast.

To the boys, then ten and twelve, their father seemed stoic about his war wounds and determined to get back to work, but they also noticed the discipline at home got stricter, perhaps a result of his pain and frustration with the pace of his healing. He lost his temper more often about little things. The whippings grew more frequent, even for minor infractions. Neither son thought their father was abusive. It was just life with a gung-ho soldier. When Newman decided punishment was in order, he would send the offending boy outside to pick out a switch—"and, by God, don't come back with something too small." If he had to go get one himself, Newman would come back with a live tree branch and strip the leaves off.

Newman hobbled around the house with crutches and his cast, then slowly began to venture further. He took the family camping and to the beach. When doctors put him in a walking cast, he went back to work. He couldn't fly and didn't have a command. For a while, he was assigned to help teach a course in unconventional warfare for Green Berets at the Special Forces training center on post.

Newman's disabling wound could have returned him to civilian life, but he was determined to stay in the Army. He vowed to someday walk without a limp. Two-and-a-half years after he was medevaced from Vietnam, the Army sent him to Fort Knox, Kentucky, to go through the armor officers career course, a clear indication the Army still considered him a candidate for a military career. In August 1969, as he was finishing up at Fort Knox, he was promoted to major. Newman was part of the Army's armor branch, whose specialty is sending tanks into combat, which is why he was sent to Fort Knox, Home of Armor. But he didn't want to go back to tanks; he wanted to fly, and he intended to be recertified to fly helicopters.

A bit of a limp proved inevitable. One leg was a half-inch shorter than the other, and his left ankle was partly fused. He had military boots and shoes made with built-up heels on the left side to help conceal the disability, but he couldn't always hide it.

While Newman and his family were living at Fort Knox, he flew down to Fort Rucker, where he had gone through flight school, to try to requalify as a pilot. He was turned over to an instructor pilot who knew about his weakened foot and seemed determined keep him out of the cockpit.

They started in an old H-34, a lumbering, fire-spitting, piston-powered predecessor of the Huey that Newman had never flown before.

"It took all my strength to push in the damn pedal in that son of a bitch," Newman said later. He managed to handle it okay but found the tail touchy to control when taxiing, and he wasn't used to having to control the RPMs of the reciprocating engine manually; the Huey's turbine engine had a governor to do that. As the power increases, the pilot must put more pressure on the left pedal to keep the helicopter "in trim" and prevent the tail from swinging. Like the H-19 he had flown in flight school, the H-34 was known for its strong left pedal.

After Newman convinced the examiner he had the strength in his left leg to control the aircraft, they switched to a Huey, and for the next couple of hours, the tester put the pilot through emergency drills. While aloft, he cut power to the engine without warning, forcing Newman into autorotation in preparation for a crash landing, then turned the power back on as they fell from the sky. Or he pulled a circuit breaker to turn off the hydraulics, making Newman switch to manual control to keep the aircraft flying. It was like flight school on steroids, and Newman hadn't flown since he was wounded. But he won his wings back, just as he said he would.

When he finished school at Fort Knox, Newman returned to Fort Bragg and the 82nd Airborne Division, where he was assigned a staff job as operations officer of the 1st Squadron, 17th Cavalry. The squadron at that time was organized with some elements designated as "sky cav" units, a term adopted in the 1950s by a few senior officers who recognized the helicopter as a natural successor to horses, jeeps, and light tanks. They envisioned using helicopters that could—like the horse cavalry—move quickly with weapons at the ready, seek out the enemy, test him, and pin him down until a stronger force arrived. Those visionaries, however, were largely ignored by the top Army brass and strongly opposed by the Air

Force, which wanted control of the strategically important airspace above the battlefield. The 1st Squadron, 17th Cavalry was a mix of choppers and ground cavalry supporting the quick-response paratroopers of the 82nd Airborne and, on occasion, the Special Forces, whose Green Berets at Fort Bragg were developing counterguerrilla warfare, a relatively new concept suddenly needed in Vietnam.

Newman's experience as a combat pilot in Vietnam and his successful completion of the course at Fort Knox set him apart from other new majors, and after a few months, he was awarded command of C Troop, 1/17th. C Troop was still a conventional cavalry unit with rolling stock instead of helicopters, and it was far from the fighting. But the new commanding officer distinguished himself, collecting a sheaf of letters of appreciation for his unit's performance in command maintenance inspections and field exercises. In the Army, those letters remain part of a soldier's permanent personnel file and are fundamental to promotion. Newman scoffed at them—but they remained in his file.

In the spring of 1970, C Troop got orders to participate in an annual exercise that attempts to simulate unconventional war by exposing troops to a power struggle between the leaders of the mythical country of Pineland and guerrillas fighting for influence and control of Pineland's civilian population. Run for nearly half a century as a sort of final exam for Special Forces trainees, the war game uses local officials and civilian volunteers in a vast rural area of North Carolina to test the skills of would-be Green Berets at Fort Bragg's John F. Kennedy Special Warfare Center and School.

Newman's unit supported the Special Forces, and afterward, his squadron commander wrote him, "There is no question that the exercise was successful as a result of your troop's operations. The aggressive spirit and determination to excel was the mark of the Cavalry trooper."[23]

A few weeks later, Newman learned he was slated to return to Vietnam.

Flo said that until he learned he was going back, Jim Newman was her ideal husband, father, and soldier. But after he got his new orders, she said, he changed.

There is no question Newman could have avoided a second combat tour. He had a permanent disability and, despite his determination to overcome it, a fused ankle with limited mobility was a legitimate reason for staying home. He had talked about retiring from the Army or maybe going back to Texas or Alabama to teach flying, but when his orders came, he refused to challenge them.

He also quit caring about his marriage.

Flo said it started when he was away on a field exercise. One Saturday night, he didn't come home. And when he showed up Sunday, she just knew he'd been with another woman. It turned out the woman's name was Gail, a twenty-something waitress from Virginia, working in a restaurant frequented by soldiers during the exercise. The way Flo heard it from friends, Gail kept flirting with the major, coming on to him. At first, he ignored her advances. Then Newman and a few of his men were at a club one night, and Gail sent someone in to ask him to meet her outside. He went outside to talk to her. That was it. They spent the night together.

Flo said it was like flipping a light switch. He came home and told her he was going to get a divorce. He demanded she give her rings back so he could give them to Gail, and he also gave his new girlfriend one of the family cars. Flora was devastated. She insisted she never had an inkling there was trouble in their marriage.

The fling lasted a few weeks, at least until Newman reported to Hunter Army Airfield near Fort Stewart, Georgia, for training to fly the Army's new helicopter gunship. It is not apparent why he spent a month down there qualifying in the AH1-G Cobra because as a senior officer he wasn't likely to fly one. The Cobra, a hastily designed, slimmed-down Huey with fore-and-aft seating for a two-person crew and heavy armament, was quickly becoming a key element in the U.S. war machine in Vietnam. If Newman got a command in the air cavalry, he could expect to have several Cobras in his unit, but he didn't have to fly them. It was warrant officers and junior commissioned officers who were regularly assigned to fly the fast attack gunships that the men called Snakes. Still, an argument could be made that any commander might benefit from knowing the capabilities and limitations of the weapons systems under his control.

Newman completed the Cobra course at Hunter on August 10, 1970, and was ordered to report one month later to USARV TRANS DET APO SF 96384.

Translated, that meant Vietnam. Again.

TAKING COMMAND

Newman reported to Camp Eagle, headquarters of the famed Screaming Eagles of the 101st Airborne Division, where he would be assigned to the 2nd Squadron, 17th Cavalry Regiment (Airmobile), known in the field as the Second of the 17th Air Cav or simply 2/17. Eagle was a sprawling base, stripped of most of its natural vegetation. The reddish earth turned to dust in the dry season and mud for months during the monsoons. Clusters of identical, low-slung buildings with tin roofs, wooden sides, and giant insect screens in lieu of glass windows were strewn about in patterns someone probably once thought made sense. High sandbag walls surrounded many of the buildings to protect them from rocket and mortar attack. Miles of dirt roads wound everywhere for the myriad jeeps and trucks that rumbled from one part of Eagle to another, carrying supplies, equipment, and men on a million missions confined within the heavily guarded, fenced, and mined perimeter.

Newman sought out the squadron headquarters. He wore the gold-embroidered oak leaf of a major sewn on the collar of his olive-drab fatigues, but he hardly looked the part of a swashbuckling air cavalry troop commander. He was too short by most measures, his hair was already thinning on top, his puckish grin suggested more clown than commander, and despite the lift in his left boot, he walked with a slight but undisguisable limp, the legacy of the wound he got on his foreshortened first tour.

As his orders and military custom dictated, Newman was to report to his new commanding officer, Lieutenant Colonel Robert F. Molinelli. It was destined not to go well. He found the colonel in the fortified, windowless, 2/17 tactical operations center (TOC), where metal-shaded lightbulbs illuminated collections of topographical maps, telephones of dubious utility, dark walls penetrated by constantly humming air conditioners, and squads of crackly two-way radios with a soldier assigned to each. Molinelli, like a caged tiger, was patrolling the room in fatigue pants, boots, and an olive-drab T-shirt. He was, at first, indistinguishable from the enlisted men at the radios, but Molinelli, a square-jawed, picture-perfect model for GI Joe, exuded charisma. Newman approached him and, as per strict military protocol when reporting to a new unit, came to attention, saluted, and introduced himself: "Major James T. Newman reporting for duty, sir." Emphasis on *sir*.

The colonel, unimpressed, snapped something resembling a return salute and barked, "Where the fuck have you been for the last four months?"

Taken by surprise, Newman awkwardly mumbled something about being sent to Cobra school en route.

"I don't need more gun pilots," Molinelli muttered. "I need a troop commander."

They were off to a bad start. Molinelli gave Newman a choice: Charlie Troop over at Phu Bai, which Newman said the colonel called "the sorriest unit in the Army," or another troop based nearer squadron headquarters at Camp Eagle. Newman instantly chose Charlie, figuring it was farther from Molinelli's sight and had no way to go but up. Neither he nor Molinelli had any idea they would soon be engulfed in the deadliest struggle in the brief history of helicopter warfare, a battle that would make them brothers in arms.

Newman's predecessor, Captain John D. Sterrett III, was a staff officer inserted into a major's slot when Molinelli suddenly needed a commanding officer (CO) for Charlie Troop. Sterrett's predecessor had been relieved of his command, a career-ending disgrace, and shipped home. The rumor that came back to the troop had it that he committed suicide, although it apparently wasn't true. Sterrett inherited a demoralized unit but didn't heal it. Not long afterward, someone tossed a fragmentation grenade into his hooch while he was on temporary assignment away from the troop. No one was hurt, and there were indications it was planned that way, perhaps as some sort of initiation rite by a gang of renegade soldiers or, more likely, as a warning to Sterrett not to mess with his men. "Fragging," as it was called, was a growing concern of the top brass, who saw it as one of the most severe signs of plunging morale. Along with increasing drug use, attacks on officers and senior noncommissioned officers were among the sad costs of years of inconclusive war. If battle-hardened soldiers were willing to go to such extremes to punish their superiors for perceived slights or mismanagement, unit discipline must be breaking down. After news stories focused attention on fragging, the White House demanded reports from the field and directed the military to address the problem seriously. In Charlie Troop, at just about that time, a senior sergeant who bunked with the troop's first sergeant was wounded in a second fragging incident during Sterrett's six-month stint as CO. Some of Sterrett's officers interpreted the attacks as indications of poor leadership. Sterrett acknowledged the troop had its share of problems, but he blamed them, at least in part, on the White House and its reluctance to engage the enemy. The war was increasingly unpopular at home, and President Nixon was trying to bring the troops home before he was up for reelection in November 1972. He didn't want more casualties. Some of Charlie Troop's pilots blamed Sterrett. They called him a coward.

Captain Malcolm Jones and Chief Warrant Officer Arthur Edward "Mickey" McLeod arrived at Charlie Troop together, dragging their duffels up the road to the commander's hooch, where they reported to Captain Sterrett. He ordered them to stand at ease and informed Jones he would be the new commanding officer of the aero rifle platoon. McLeod would start out in the front seat of a Cobra. Then he read them a passage from the Bible and dismissed them.

Jones and McLeod looked at each other in amazement. Jones, a Huey pilot, didn't know what an aero rifle platoon was, and McLeod wasn't certified to fly Cobra gunships!

Jones, in a tape recording sent home some weeks later, told his family he was glad Sterrett was being replaced. "You couldn't tell him about things," the Huey pilot said. "He made up his mind, and that was it. He did things one way, and if you thought you had a better idea, he'd just say, 'Well, it won't work because I've tried it.' Evidently, he'd tried everything in the whole world. . . . He was just so doggone unreasonable nobody liked him."[24]

Sterrett was also a strict Christian and a proselytizer who handed out miniature copies of the New Testament to his crews before their first missions. He didn't drink or play cards with the men and earned the resentment of the chopper jockeys when he cut the hours of the enlisted men's and officers' clubs to reduce drinking and encourage the crews to get more rest between missions. For the most part, they weren't drunkards, but the flight crews frequently had a few beers to bring them down from the day's missions and help them face the inevitable dangers of the next day. Sterrett's officers derisively referred to him—behind his back—as Thumper, short for "Bible thumper," and derided their commander for his penchant for running combat operations from a safe distance, preferably high in the sky. Graeme Clark, the pilot of Sterrett's command-and-control ship, was nicknamed Coat because he always showed up at the flight line with a knee-length coat. He said at the altitude the CO flew he needed it to keep warm. Many years later, Clark walked into a Condors reunion wearing the same coat, and his long-ago buddies instantly recognized it and burst into applause.

Soon after Newman arrived at C Troop's headquarters, Colonel Molinelli flew down to hold a change-of-command ceremony in which the unit's small red-and-white flag, called a guidon, is passed from the old commander to the new, signifying the handover of power. Newman wanted to let the men know the change meant more than a symbolic transfer of colors on a stick. He accepted the guidon and announced that beginning that night the clubs would be staying open—and that he would come around that evening to share a drink at both the officers' and the enlisted men's clubs. Message conveyed.

C Troop was headquartered at Phu Bai, an American support base and airstrip about five miles to the east of the 101st's headquarters at Camp Eagle. It was just outside the old imperial capital of Hue, an historic cultural and religious center with a classic citadel, royal palaces, Buddhist temples, and the unkempt remnants of once-grand gardens and tombs. Removed from the hottest combat areas to the north and west, it was rarely attacked, even by long-distance, unguided rockets, and the base motto was painted in huge block letters on the roof of a building: "PHU BAI IS ALL RIGHT"

The soldiers of C Troop rarely, if ever, explored the old city nearby. Their mission was to take the war west into a deep, fog-shrouded jungle valley known as the A Shau, where steep mountains plunged thousands of feet to a river that ran along the Laos border and offered the North Vietnamese Army a choice of supply routes to the more densely populated coastal region around Hue. The North Vietnamese Army saw the A Shau Valley as a critical link in the logistic chain that circumvented the tightly guarded and denuded demilitarized zone that separated the two Vietnams and followed a network of rugged roads known as the Ho Chi Minh Trail that led into South Vietnam. The "trail" snaked through southern Laos, ostensibly neutral ground under the 1954 Geneva Accords that ended French domination of Indochina, and spilled into the A Shau just inside the South Vietnamese border. At the country's narrow northern neck, it was only about thirty miles from the Laos border on the west to Hue and the South China Sea on the east. In 1966, as the United States was rushing men and equipment to the war zone to bolster flagging South Vietnamese forces, North Vietnamese regulars attacked and overran a U.S. Special Forces camp that guarded the southern end of the valley. The North Vietnamese effectively controlled the valley after that, although the Americans staged successive major offensives to drive them out, culminating in the notoriously bloody Battle of Hamburger Hill in May 1969. Overwhelming American firepower, superior numbers, and unchallenged control of the air rewarded the U.S. forces and their South Vietnamese allies with temporary victories each time, but then the allies left, and the North Vietnamese always came back, rebuilt their stocks and communication lines, and soldiered on.

By the time Newman took command, Charlie Troop was spending most of its time flying over the A Shau Valley, monitoring enemy movements and harassing the NVA from the air. It was a dangerous cat-and-mouse game, often played in nasty weather that improved the odds for the troops on the ground. Soon after he arrived, Newman called his platoon commanders together, and they asked if he was planning to fly with them in the AO, the area of operations.

"Hell yes," he said.

"In the jet stream?" they asked. Newman, who had never flown in such mountainous terrain or against well-armed North Vietnamese regulars, told his pilots he would spend his first twenty-five flight hours with the scouts. The scouts flew small, highly maneuverable OH-6 Light Observation Helicopters, universally known as loaches, some aviator's idea of how one could pronounce the abbreviation LOH. Each type of aircraft in the cavalry had a designated color: red for gunships, white for loaches, blue for slicks. The air cav devised a team with a loach to skim over the treetops on reconnaissance with a Cobra gunship following overhead to protect it. The combination, one white and one red, was called a pink team. In areas like the A Shau, where stiff resistance and heavy machine gun fire was expected, two Cobras—one high, one low—were assigned to guard one loach. That was called a "heavy pink team," a standard configuration for Charlie Troop. Since Cobras had no passenger seats or cargo area, a Huey was often assigned as a chase ship to stand by on station to pick up any crews that got shot down.

Zipping over the riverbeds and dirt roads in the valley, an observer in a loach could pick up signs like tire tracks, smoke from campfires, even the smell of human waste from latrines that offered clues to the enemy troops' whereabouts. But to get that close, the pilot had to fly "low and slow" over the area—below the trees, Newman called it—presenting a tempting target to shooters on the ground. When a soldier with an AK-47 assault rifle or a heavier, more deadly 12.5 mm (also called a .51-caliber) machine gun fired on a loach, his tracer rounds could give the Cobra above a target to dive on with rockets blazing.[25] It was a classic cavalry tactic.

Newman always thought the scout platoon leader who flew him out into the AO deliberately whirled and rolled the aircraft, flying out of trim to try to make the Old Man sick. But the CO stuck with it, then made it standard procedure for new pilots assigned to Charlie Troop to fly with the scouts before taking up their regular jobs at the controls of Cobras or Hueys. He said it made them more sensitive to the risks the scouts took—and why it was so important to go in and get them if they went down. It also showed the men he wouldn't ask them to do anything he wouldn't do himself.

They liked Jim Newman from the start.

NOT JUST A PILOT

NEWMAN HEARD COMPLAINTS FROM HIS NEW TROOPS almost from the moment he arrived. The enlisted men said their quarters were too crowded and they had no place to get out of the sun or rain when they were down on the flight line. Some of the officers griped that what little free time they had away from their aircraft was spent doing their own laundry and sweeping out their hooches, jobs done for officers in other units by Vietnamese hooch maids. The Screaming Eagles of the 101st didn't allow hooch maids. Some said it was for security because Vietnamese civilians couldn't be trusted on base and might provide intelligence to the enemy. Others said it was because maid service wasn't consistent with the image of the famed self-sufficiency of paratroopers, who in earlier wars dropped from the sky in chutes and made their own way.

Not long after he got to Phu Bai, Newman located a couple transportable buildings elsewhere on the base that weren't being used, and he arranged to have them moved up to Charlie Troop's area, where one went to the flight line as a ready room for the enlisted men and the other was turned into living quarters with latrines and showers. While he was still finding his way around the base, the major spotted some Vietnamese women in black pajama-like shirts and pants and conical hats.

"What are they doin' here?" he asked one of his officers.

"They're sandbag fillers, sir," came the reply.

"How many hooches you got for officers and warrants?"

"Six, sir."

"Okay," Newman said, "hire six sandbag fillers for C Troop. I can't help it if they wanna spend their time doin' laundry and makin' bunks and sweepin' out hooches." In a tape he sent home, Mac Jones told his family the sandbag fillers were doing "a doggone good job of being hooch maids and a very lousy job of filling sandbags because they haven't filled one yet."[26] The unofficial maids were paid, illegally and off the books, in scrip called military payment certificates, or MPC. The bills looked a bit like Monopoly money and were traded on the black market at about half the value of U.S. dollars, which were prized like gold by Vietnamese and illegal for American troops to spend in Vietnam.

The new troop commander got more popular by the day.

Although the Army is fond of telling young officers that command is no popularity contest, the leaders who won their men's trust were the ones who could send them again and again into difficult, dangerous situations without question or rebuke. Newman had 220 people in his troop and about sixty-five more who answered to him indirectly as part of an attached maintenance unit that kept the troop's twenty-seven aircraft flying. They called themselves the Condors, a nickname the troop acquired before he got to Vietnam and was still used by the troop in Afghanistan more than forty years later. An artistically inclined soldier designed a patch for the unit with two redheaded California condors perched on a dead branch under a full moon and one saying to the other, "Patience my ass, I want to kill something."

It was later amended to show only one condor with the motto removed. Given the aggressive esprit de corps of Charlie Troop, perhaps the creators were unmindful of the California condor's preference for carrion first spotted by other, smaller, birds that couldn't finish their meal.

The Army trained Private First Class Charles Davis to be an aircraft mechanic, but when Davis got to Phu Bai, not long before Newman arrived, he was told he would be assigned to the unit's command-and-control ship as crew chief. The crew chief of a Huey was responsible for keeping the bird ready to fly, knowing when it needed maintenance, and taking general care of the aircraft. In the air, he manned one of the two M-60 machine guns, the principal weapons on slicks. Davis had been trained to repair or replace parts in a maintenance hangar after being told what to do, but he had rarely been inside a helicopter and had never actually flown in one. Newman's predecessor didn't fly in the closing days of his command, and Davis just hung around his helicopter in case he was called upon to do anything. Soon after Newman took command, however, Davis watched the new CO's jeep pull up to the flight line, and Newman got out and walked over to Davis's Huey with the distinctive limp that Davis likened to a waddle. The major asked if the crew chief had done his preflight inspection, and Davis replied, "Sir, I checked the oil levels." He'd never heard what a preflight inspection entailed.

Specialist 4 Charles Davis, Newman's crew chief, who, as a private first class, knew almost nothing about helicopters when he got to C Troop.

"Come on, son," the CO said, "I'll show you what's gonna keep this helicopter in the air." The former wheeled vehicle mechanic who could fix just about anything climbed onto an outboard step and gave the new crew chief a tour of the aircraft, showing him how to check for wear or battle damage and what to look for before letting anyone take the ship off the ground. Davis, who was from a town in Georgia about one hundred thirty miles north of Newman's hometown, soon became the commander's permanent crew chief.

Probably because he had been an enlisted man and certainly from his experience on his first tour when his unit had a scrounger, Newman knew how things got done in the Army. It often wasn't by the book, especially in wartime, where equipment was apt to be damaged or destroyed by enemy fire, and enterprising soldiers looked after themselves and their own units with little regard for the military bean counters' treasured Table of Organization and

Equipment. Charlie Troop was authorized only one jeep, but there always seemed to be several parked in the area, along with a light truck or two. The clubs had refrigerators and air conditioners bartered or stolen from other units, and the men knew the CO wouldn't object.

One day in 1970, a pair of detectives from the Army's Criminal Investigation Division, a military version of the FBI, arrived at Charlie Troop headquarters in search of stolen motor vehicles reported missing by other units based at Phu Bai, Camp Eagle, and nearby U.S. installations. They were driving a jeep. Newman invited the pair into his office to discuss what he acknowledged was a serious situation, and he offered them several suggestions for how they could proceed with their investigation. After a filibuster that went on for some time, the detectives emerged from the headquarters building, walked to the parking area and climbed into their jeep. It wouldn't start. When they got out of the vehicle and opened the hood, they discovered the engine was missing. Newman feigned shock and assigned his jeep and driver to take the gumshoes back to their own headquarters.[27]

He was a compulsive practical joker. During the monsoon season, when C Troop's base at Phu Bai was flooded and oozing mud everywhere, he summoned his top gun pilot, Captain Chuck Vehlow, and told him that since Vehlow had earned a degree in engineering at West Point, he henceforth would serve as the troop's drainage control officer. Vehlow never thought the assignment as funny as Newman did.

Major Newman, left, and Captain Chuck Vehlow, his "drainage control officer."

The commander despised the Army's easing of rules regarding personal appearance that let soldiers grow sideburns, mustaches, and somewhat longer hair in keeping with popular trends of the late 1960s and '70s. His aviators loved their jaunty mustaches, and Newman tolerated well-trimmed ones, but he kept the blade of his boyhood sheath knife razor-sharp and used it on occasion. When he decided one day that Pappy Papin's mustache exceeded its permissible length, he ordered the scout pilot to stand at attention with his heels locked together while Newman shaved one side of the offending growth of facial hair with his knife, whereupon he told Papin to fall out and return to duty. The cocky loach pilot proceeded to shave the left side of his scalp and left eyebrow to match.

Warrant Officer Pappy Papin after his shave.

First Lieutenant Dennis Urick, a slick pilot, had been out on a difficult mission trying to identify helicopters downed in enemy territory. When his ship got close enough for a man with binoculars to identify the tail number, the bird invariably began taking ground fire. Urick determined to try an unconventional maneuver called a "quick stop" in which he approached a desired site, flared the main rotor to bring the craft to a halt, and let the tail drop down and backward until the Huey came to a momentary stop in the air for the observer to get the number. The pilot then tipped the rotor down to regain momentum and hurry away.

He returned from the mission pleased that his crew had identified four downed helicopters. An hour later, Urick got word Major Newman wanted to see him in the operations center. He walked in and years later remembered the chewing out he got from his commanding officer:

"You sorry son of a bitch, Urick. Damn lieutenants, you can't tell them anything." He accused the young pilot of endangering his aircraft and his crew by employing risky maneuvers that could cost him his rank and his wings. Urick managed to interrupt long enough to say he was just doing what he had seen Newman do under similar circumstances. Newman shot back, "You don't do as I do; you do as I tell you, you sorry bastard. Report to squadron!"

On his way to squadron field headquarters, Urick thought he was about to be court-martialed, that his flying days were over. He walked in to report to Colonel Molinelli and saw Newman already there, talking to his boss.

Molinelli turned to Urick and told him he wasn't fit to be a lieutenant in the United States Army—and was therefore being promoted to captain. It had all been a setup.

It was classic Newman, and after he got over the shock, Urick loved him for it. The commander did, however, sometimes go too far. He once wrote a letter to Kate Vehlow telling her that her husband was extending his tour in Vietnam for six months because he was such a great trooper. She told her husband that if he extended for six months she wouldn't be there when he got home.[28]

But he did have his limits. One evening he was returning to Phu Bai by helicopter, and approaching the flight line, he noticed a line of troops queued up outside a hooch he knew was supposed to be unoccupied. He landed and was met by his jeep and driver, as usual. He told the driver to swing by the suspect hooch to see what was going on. The hooch was not far from the MPs' gate and on the periphery of Charlie Troop's territory. Newman walked past the line of soldiers and into the hooch, where he instantly recognized two of his warrant-officer pilots who were running a concession with four prostitutes they had sneaked onto the base. He also spotted several of his own troops waiting their turn.

"How the hell did you get them in here?" Newman demanded of the pilots.

"The same way you just got in here," came the sheepish reply.

"You flew them bitches in here?"

"Yeah."

"Well, you better get them outta here right damn now!"

"We can't fly them out till dark," they said, because the Military Police might see them. No Vietnamese were allowed on the base after 5:00 p.m., not even those with passes. If the women were spotted outside the hooch after hours, the men and women could be arrested by the MPs.[29] Newman relented and ordered them to get the women off base that night and not bring them back.

There's another version of the story. One pilot said the offending warrants offered their CO his choice of the women for as long as he liked, and Newman disappeared into a back room with one of the four and chose to forget his men had been running a flying whore express. Years later at a Charlie Troop reunion, several veterans agreed that either version was credible, and that they weren't necessarily contradictory.

Ricky Miller, the crew chief of a Huey that was affectionately known as Gunky, had a reputation as a master of "midnight requisitioning," technically known as stealing, and Newman happily made use of his skills. Their first encounter, however, hardly endeared Miller to his commander. The CO didn't know it, but Miller had won the respect of every man in the unit the previous August when he had jumped out of his ship and run through murderous NVA fire three times to rescue severely wounded Blues from the jungle.

The major was still new to the troop when Miller met him and didn't know the crew chief's history. The enlisted man was in his usual place at his machine gun aboard "Gunky" returning from a test flight for a captain who was seeking assignment to Charlie Troop as a pilot. As the Huey came in for a landing behind a protective revetment on the flight line, the new pilot made a clumsy approach that Miller said could have killed them all. He shouted at the newbie captain over the intercom, warning they were tipping at a dangerous angle and that the main rotor blade was about to scrape the ground, a potentially deadly error. The pilot—or perhaps the warrant officer copilot—made a last-second correction, and the craft landed awkwardly but safely in its place. Moments later, Newman drove up in his jeep, stalked over to Miller and demanded to know what the crew chief was doing threatening an officer.

"Sir, it wasn't a threat; it was a promise," the crew chief remembers telling his commanding officer.

"Let me tell you if you don't like it here in Charlie Troop I can transfer you out," the furious troop commander upbraided him. "Don't you ever threaten one of my officers."

Perhaps realizing he had heard only the captain's side, Newman gave Miller a chance to explain himself. When the crew chief described the dangerous approach, Newman turned to the warrant who had been flying right seat. The peter pilot nodded his confirmation of Miller's account, and Newman got back in his jeep and left. The captain was never seen around Charlie Troop again. The incident was indelibly printed in Miller's memory, as such an encounter with a senior officer might well be, but when he saw Newman thirty years later at a Condors reunion, the Old Man didn't remember it ever happened, but he remembered Miller well for other things.

One was an incident in the air the next summer when he helped save a loach crew the day they lost three helicopters—including Gunky—in one operation on the Fourth of July. But the story Newman liked to tell was when Miller stole the general's jet engine.

Miller said the boss put him up to it. It was during the Laos operation, and when he landed at Quang Tri to refuel, Newman walked over and told him he wanted to talk.

"Well, crap, what'd I do this time?" Miller thought to himself.

"There's a brand-new engine in a crate up there at the end of the runway in Depot," Newman told the crew chief. "I want it."

"I don't know, sir. That's a big thing."

Newman looked around and turned back to the enlisted man. "I'll give you a case of scotch."

"A case of scotch and a case of Jack Daniel's," Miller countered.

"You know what Jack Daniel's is?"

"Yes. It's gonna be mine. The case of scotch is goin' to the other guys I got to bring in on this."

Miller knew a soldier in the motor pool who could dummy orders for equipment—he was in the Army because he'd been caught doing something similar in Brooklyn and a judge had given him a choice of joining up or going to jail. So Miller had the forger draw up the necessary orders and took a 2½-ton wrecker truck with a driver and headed down to the parts depot. The driver was afraid to talk, so when the sentry flagged them down, he motioned to Miller, who reached down and handed the sentry the orders for a Lycoming L-13 jet engine, the latest improved version of the Huey's power system.

The sentry glanced at the papers and pointed down toward the end of the runway. The soldiers went where they were told, found the crated helicopter engine, and picked up the whole thing with the wrecker's winch. They drove out of the depot to the maintenance area where Charlie Troop's birds were serviced. Newman's helicopter had already been brought in and had the engine pulled out of it. The maintenance men broke open the crate, hoisted the new engine in place, and connected it while Miller's crew loaded the old engine in the crate and took it back to the depot. Miller told the sentry they'd got the wrong engine and was told to return the crate to its proper place. "That's not an L-13; that's one of those small L-11s. I'm just gonna put it back where it was," he said, and that's what they did.

Newman boasted afterward that the new engine had been intended for Lieutenant General James W. Sutherland Jr.'s Huey. Sutherland was commanding general of the Army's XXIV Corps, which had overall responsibility for all U.S. forces in the northern region of South Vietnam. Sutherland had been a colonel when he told a young platoon sergeant named Newman to apply for a direct commission.

Newman actually had great respect for senior officers and was particularly proud to work for strong leaders like Molinelli and then-Brigadier General Sidney Berry, assistant commanding general of the 101st Airborne Division and an outspoken advocate of Army aviation. He liked to tell people he had once cut off Berry's star at the O Club—and got away with it.

The Officers Club at Phu Bai had a peculiar tradition that supposedly entitled any member to cut the rank insignia off the collar of any new arrival to show everyone he was a newbie. General Berry accompanied Newman to the club on Cav Night, any given Friday, and at the bar, the major pulled out a sheath knife and told Berry he was going to cut his collar. The general let him clip the embroidered star from one side, but when Newman started to reach for the other one, the general told him firmly, "You got enough." Berry's star was pinned to the wall behind the bar, and Newman said it was still there when he left Vietnam several months later.[30] Berry later recommended Newman for a commission in the Regular Army, which might have put him on track for a star of his own.

CROSSING THE LINE

SLICK PILOT RICH JOHNSON, THE OPERATIONS OFFICER of Newman's old outfit, the Robin Hoods, was called to a briefing at Group Headquarters outside Saigon in January 1971. No junior officers ever went to Group, except when they arrived in-country and when they were cleared to leave. As soon as he got there, he was told he was to say nothing to anyone about what he learned—not even that there had been a briefing. The Robin Hoods and most other American helicopter units in Vietnam were being ordered to pull up stakes and head north; they'd be told later where to stop.

At the briefing, after being told that everything they were about to learn was absolutely top secret, the assembled officers were ordered to tell their crews only that their unit was leaving Lai Khe and to get all their gear ready to move. Nothing more. Not even the names of other units that were going. The Robin Hoods had pretty good duty, considering it was Vietnam. They were still in the old rubber plantation, and their company area had been spruced up a lot since Newman was there. They had hot showers, separate rooms, furniture. Some had fridges for beer, and there were even a few air conditioners around. Those would be left behind. It was about a hundred degrees down south, so they didn't have sleeping bags, blankets, or field jackets. They didn't need them then, but they'd soon wish they had some. They did have poncho liners, which were featherweight blankets made of quilted, camouflage nylon that GIs used as covers in the tropics or folded up for pillows. Sometimes they were draped over wires for privacy or hung on a bar for decoration. The poncho liners went with them, and somebody scrounged a load of tents to ship wherever they were going.

They sent one of their platoon leaders ahead to serve as a liaison officer and to find out what they'd need and report back, but when he got where they were going, he was ordered not to try to call out; the phones weren't secure. The Robin Hoods could only guess that he got wherever it was.

A few days later, after poring over the field manuals for unit movements and convoys, they loaded up thirty helicopters with all they could, including quite a few bottles of whiskey and several mangy pet dogs adopted by crewmen, and took off. They flew east to the sea, then turned north and started working their way up the coast of Vietnam, stopping every couple of hours to refuel.

By the time they got to Tuy Hoa, about a third of the way up the coast, they were getting cold. The new forward headquarters was to be at Dong Ha, an abandoned U.S. Marine base in the shadow of the demilitarized zone separating the two Vietnams, but the troops weren't told that, just to keep heading north.

Johnson was the leader of the first flight of ten. By that time, he knew their destination and was given the refueling stops along the way, but he wasn't allowed to tell his men. The Army runs on rumor, and when they got to Quang Tri, capital of the northernmost province in South Vietnam, the betting was that they were going to invade North Vietnam. Nobody knew about Laos.

As they took off from Quang Tri, still headed north, the men were shivering, and it looked like snow. Well, it didn't actually snow down that far, and it was probably sixty-five degrees at sea level, but the Robin Hoods were up in the sky and not accustomed to the new climate or terrain. Off to their left they could see high mountains surrounded by gray sky. It would get colder still.

Johnson got on the radio and called the lost liaison officer at Dong Ha, only about five miles away.

"Roger, I've got you coming off Quang Tri, and I'm popping smoke," the officer said, tossing out a smoke grenade to signal where they should land.

"There's nothing there but a field," Johnson told him. It was not even a prepared field. Just dirt.

"Welcome home," came the liaison officer's chipper reply.[31]

The Marines had left three concrete slabs in the earth when they withdrew. The Robin Hoods put their mess hall on one, the operations tent on another, and designated the third for the medics. They laid out an area for each platoon and set up a defense perimeter. They quickly discovered that whoever loaded the tents forgot to pack the poles, so they shivered under their poncho liners and tent tarps the first night.

Dong Ha was at the end of Q.L. 1, Vietnam's main north-south highway. It stopped there because the DMZ that had separated North from South since 1954 lay just outside the city. At Dong Ha, Q.L. 9 turned west toward the mountains, Khe Sanh, and the Laos border. With other units heading west, there were lots of combat engineers with road-building equipment rounding that corner, and the Robin Hoods got out on the two-lane road to ask for help. They brandished bottles of Jack Daniel's to flag down the drivers of earthmovers, front-end loaders, and heavy machines that could build a base a lot faster than a couple hundred men with folding shovels known in the Army as entrenching tools. Within thirty-six hours, they had a level landing zone, a little heliport, and rows of fifty-five-gallon oil drums filled with dirt and lined up as revetments to protect the choppers from enemy artillery fire. The next day, the North Vietnamese started lobbing mortars at the new helicopter base most nights, and the men filled every sandbag they could find to build protective walls around their tents and work areas.

The Robin Hoods didn't know it yet, but they were part of an American helicopter armada being assembled in secret for one of the most audacious offensives of the war.

Newman and his Condors were already up there, settling in on the mountaintop airstrip at Khe Sanh, abandoned more than two years earlier by retreating Marines who held it through a seventy-seven-day pounding by North Vietnamese artillery based in Laos, just to their west. More birds were arriving every day.

For years, the Chinese, Soviets, and North Vietnamese had shipped hundreds of tons of guns, ammunition, food, and supplies to the Cambodian port of Sihanoukville, where they were collected by Communist Vietnamese troops and smuggled through sanctuaries in neutral Cambodia to the war zone in South Vietnam. The U.S. and South Vietnamese invasion of Cambodia the previous year had cut off access to the port by the North Vietnamese, forcing them to rely almost entirely on ferrying supplies overland via a network of truck roads, bicycle, and foot paths that snaked from North Vietnam through southern Laos and spilled out into dozens of offshoots leading into South Vietnam.

The A Shau Valley, the Condors' principal area of operation, was the NVA's second northernmost route to the populated coastal plain.

Similar access routes in the Central Highlands and on south into and through Cambodia gave the enemy multiple ways to reach the southern battlefields around Saigon. American intelligence officers estimated that 90 percent of the North Vietnamese soldiers fighting in the South walked or rode down the trail to get there.

Military people had wanted for years to cut the North's umbilical cord in southern Laos, where it was deemed most vulnerable, but political leaders resisted, largely because they feared that an overt invasion of a neutral nation bordering North Vietnam and China could bring China and perhaps the Soviet Union into the war. The United States instead mounted a "secret war" in Laos, attacking the trails from the air and harassing the North Vietnamese with Special Forces–led fighting units made up of indigenous mountain tribesmen who were culturally distinct from either the ethnic Viets or the Lao. C Troop was one of the aviation units that flew covert cross-border missions to put long-range reconnaissance patrols and supersecret soldiers of the Studies and Operations Group into Laos and southernmost North Vietnam to monitor the Ho Chi Minh Trail.

In late 1967, General William Westmoreland, the longtime commander of U.S. forces in South Vietnam, had ordered detailed plans drawn to invade and seal off the trail at Tchepone, a Laotian town at the top of the supply funnel, about thirty miles west of the border at the DMZ separating North and South Vietnam. The document called for tens of thousands of U.S. troops and South Vietnamese paratroopers to block the trail, destroy supply depots, and hold the territory around the town through two dry seasons in hopes of starving the Northerners in the South of food, supplies, ammunition, and reinforcements as allied troops pounded them inside South Vietnam.[32]

The plan, code-named OPLAN El Paso, was completed after the siege of Khe Sanh and the surprise, countrywide Tet offensive in early 1968 that together demonstrated the seriousness and strength of the enemy. Westy told his bosses he'd need about two hundred thousand more American troops for a broad new offensive, including the attack on the Ho Chi Minh Trail. He never got them.

Americans at home had lost patience with the war and Westmoreland's continuing demands for more U.S. forces, a half million of whom were in the war zone by that time. More than five hundred Americans were being killed in action every month. Not long after the Laos invasion plan was finished, the general was called home from Vietnam and kicked upstairs to the post of Army chief of staff. From the Pentagon, he continued to press the White House and his military colleagues among the Joint Chiefs of Staff to carry out his objectives, but it didn't appear that anyone was listening. One who did—or had his own, similar idea of how to turn the tide of war—was Admiral Thomas H. Moorer, a Navy fleet commander whose involvement with Vietnam spanned more than a decade.

After President Nixon named Moorer chairman of the Joint Chiefs in July 1970, the admiral concluded that the massive military drive into Cambodia in the spring of 1970, while igniting a political firestorm at home, had effectively shut off the North's sea route to the South. U.S. military and CIA intelligence analysts disagreed about the gross tonnage of guns, ammunition, food, and medicine that landed at Cambodia's deepwater port at Sihanoukville and traveled through Cambodian sanctuaries along the border into the southern war zone, but all agreed it constituted a substantial—some said critical—flow.[33]

With the seaport in the hands of Cambodian forces allied with Washington and Saigon, the importance of the Ho Chi Minh Trail supply route ballooned for the North Vietnamese. Admiral Moorer, like General Westmoreland, wanted to cut it and wage a war of attrition against the enemy stranded inside South Vietnam. However, the original plan for doing that envisioned the use of a huge force—a U.S. airmobile division, a U.S. infantry division, and the South Vietnamese airborne division, regarded as that country's elite fighting force. Such a corps would require vast combat and logistical support. Tens of thousands of men with thousands of fixed- and rotary-wing aircraft, heavy artillery, tanks, engineering units, supply trucks, and fuel would constitute one of the largest forces ever assembled in Vietnam for a single operation. But by the time Westmoreland's OPLAN El Paso got dusted off for possible use, the American ground forces that would have been used in the operation were gone or scheduled to go home.

* * *

Richard Nixon had been elected in November 1968 to succeed Lyndon B. Johnson as president, at least in part because people thought Nixon had a secret plan to end the war that had become Johnson's albatross. Nixon didn't actually claim such a plan, but he did nothing to discourage the thought. Two years later, his administration was as bogged down and frustrated by the war as Johnson's had been. Determined to avoid the pitfall that had cost Johnson a second full term, Nixon pursued parallel tracks in search of an end to the war. He stepped up diplomatic and political efforts abroad to push North Vietnam toward a peace agreement while threatening—and executing—massive bombing campaigns against the North to demonstrate the consequences of stalling. To ease political opposition to the war at home and in the Congress, he scaled back U.S. involvement in the ground fighting and increased the pace of withdrawals but vowed not to quit until he won the release of nearly six hundred American prisoners of war being held by North Vietnam. Nixon and his trusted national security adviser, Henry A. Kissinger, tried repeatedly to coax the North Vietnamese to deal at multination peace talks that had dragged on sporadically for years in Paris, but Hanoi was biding its time.

Searching for a new strategy, the administration came up with four options, the last of which contemplated an offensive into southern Laos and adjacent northern Cambodia, but an analyst on the National Security Council staff dismissed that fourth option, noting that it got into the strategy document only "at the insistence of General Westmoreland."[34] A couple of weeks later, in October 1970, Kissinger sent Nixon a CIA memo that he told the president contained no hard intelligence about Hanoi's plans but pointed to stepped-up troop movements down the trail through southern Laos. Kissinger said it could lead to a major attack on allied forces in Cambodia but most likely was part of the Communists' long-term strategy of outlasting their American adversary. Less than two weeks later, Nixon ordered the Central Intelligence Agency and the Defense and State departments to develop some hurry-up contingency plans to deal with the expected buildup of enemy forces in the South. On November 20, 1970—the day the plans were due at the White House—the president told Kissinger he had "worked out [a] new plan for Vietnam at 2:00 this morning," according to Nixon Chief of Staff H. R. Haldeman. Haldeman wrote in his diary that the president "wants to blast talks, give last chance, then pull out . . . take offensive and announce stepped-up withdrawals at same time. Put real heat on North Vietnam."[35]

It was to be one last bold stroke to end the war. The men kept their plan so secret that they held off telling former congressman Melvin Laird, Nixon's own secretary of defense, because they thought he would oppose it and might tell his friends on Capitol Hill, which would stir up a stink.

There were still two years before the next election, but Nixon already was preoccupied with his reelection campaign. He had begun the slow withdrawal of U.S. troops in his first year as president and was actively turning over military resources and combat responsibilities to the South Vietnamese in a program he dubbed "Vietnamization" of the war. Americans were tired of the long, indecisive conflict, and Congress wanted out. On the one hand, Nixon was trying to reduce casualties by limiting the exposure of U.S. troops while he sought a negotiated settlement. On the other hand, he was influenced by Kissinger's desire to strike the North hard to drive the enemy back to the peace table. They tried to do both.

Nixon no longer had the large numbers of troops Westmoreland had contemplated using to go into Laos, and after his surprise strike into Cambodia the year before, Congress wouldn't let him commit U.S. ground forces to any more cross-border operations.

To pull off anything comparable to OPLAN El Paso, he and the Saigon regime would have to assemble the largest South Vietnamese force ever committed to action and ferry it into Laos with U.S. helicopters, protected by America's long-range bombers and tactical jets.

Laos, although technically a neutral kingdom, had for years been the site of a "secret war" in which U.S. Air Force planes and indigenous forces recruited and paid by the CIA bombed and harassed the North Vietnamese forces that used the country as a haven and maintained their critical supply corridor to South Vietnam. The United States enjoyed cordial relations with the royal government, which welcomed the covert help because it simultaneously targeted a Communist insurgency led by the half-brother of the tiny country's ruler. The U.S. Embassy in Vientiane, the Laotian capital, functioned as a tactical headquarters for the cross-border bombing campaign, and the CIA ran a private airline, Air America, that supplied logistical support to pro-government forces. Nonetheless, mounting an overt ground attack into Laos meant yet another escalation of the war, and for South Vietnam, at least, the risk that a defeat of its best and strongest units could spell the beginning of the end. Nixon's plan to "put real heat on North Vietnam" would prove an even bigger gamble than Cambodia the year before.

Hours after the sleepless Nixon came up with his new idea, American commandos staged a long-planned secret raid deep into North Vietnam to try to rescue American prisoners of war they believed were being held in a remote prison camp at Son Tay. The intelligence, however, proved to be dated. The prisoners had been moved months before, and the top-secret strike force landed in an abandoned camp. Nixon, who had approved the mission, at first determined to keep it quiet but then adroitly turned it into a propaganda coup as a demonstration of the bravery and commitment of U.S. troops, who would try anything to save their own and keep the enemy off balance.

A week later, emboldened by the morale boost generated by the failed Son Tay raid, the president told Brigadier General Alexander M. Haig, Nixon's favorite military officer who was then serving as Kissinger's deputy, "I want our top brains and theirs [the South Vietnamese] working in the greatest secrecy to get some plans. If the South is ready to go north, let them go . . . let them go, okay?"

"Yes, sir," Haig replied.[36] The general soon had an opportunity to pursue his commander-in-chief's guidance. But he did not recommend an invasion of the North.

Kissinger had hardly ordered up contingency plans from department and agency chiefs before the U.S. commander in Vietnam, General Creighton W. Abrams Jr., received a top-secret concept plan from his immediate superior, Admiral John S. McCain, that envisioned a U.S.-South Vietnamese offensive to cut the Ho Chi Minh Trail. McCain, whose own son and namesake was a Navy pilot being held prisoner in the North, likely was passing along the vision of his boss, Admiral Moorer. The provenance of the operation grew vague in the months that followed.

Nixon, Kissinger, and others who wrote about it afterward played down their own roles. "Victory has a hundred fathers, but defeat is always an orphan."[37]

Although some documents of the period remain classified more than four decades later, recently opened archival materials clearly show Westmoreland's fingerprints on the elevation of an old idea to a bold new strike plan. With Nixon and Kissinger seriously interested—perhaps even decided—the president dispatched Brigadier General Haig to Saigon on a secret mission to assess support for the invasion plan among top U.S. and South Vietnamese leaders there. Haig was the consummate staff officer, having served as a general's aide and soldier-diplomat and rocketing past other, more senior West Point officers through political favor. He had one tour in Vietnam, earning distinction as a battalion commander with the 1st Infantry Division in 1967. From Washington, Haig traveled first to Cambodia, where he found the situation "serious" and the future unpredictable. As he was landing in Saigon, Colonel Richard Kennedy, a member of the National Security Council staff at the White House, cabled Haig in an "exclusively eyes only" message telling him: "Request you look into status and substance of plan for cutting off supply routes in S. Laos, using a reinforced ARVN division to attack west to Bolovens [Plateau] and operate astride LOC [lines of communication, i.e., the Ho Chi Minh Trail]. . . . This was plan outlined by General Westmoreland at meeting before you left.

"Also request you ask Admiral McCain's views on this and other plans as well as any other suggestions he may have."[38]

Kennedy, like almost all the other key aides at that moment—except Kissinger—is now dead, but he almost certainly was referring to a December 11 meeting of the Washington Special Action Group (WSAG), a panel of key military and foreign policy leaders. Westmoreland sat in for JCS Chairman Moorer at that meeting. Minutes of the WSAG meetings have remained secret for more than forty years while most of the other sensitive documents cited here have been declassified.

Whether Kennedy knew it or not, the primary reason for Haig's trip was to consult the highest political and military authorities in South Vietnam about just that: the prospect of invading Laos to cut the Ho Chi Minh Trail. Hours after the Kennedy cable, Haig messaged Kissinger—also "exclusively eyes only"—that he had discussed the concept of a three-pronged offensive with U.S. Ambassador Ellsworth Bunker and with Abrams and that both U.S. and South Vietnamese leaders were enthusiastic, especially about the Laos part of a Laos-Cambodia operation. "General Abrams describes it as the most significant operation of the war so far and one which he considers as potentially decisive," Haig reported.

Haig had not yet spoken to President Nguyen Van Thieu, a former general, or General Cao Van Vien, chief of the South Vietnamese general staff, but he was told they felt strongly that the objective should be Tchepone, "the decisive target area in Laos which offers the most potentially lucrative results." His subsequent meetings with Thieu, Vien, and U.S. Ambassador to Laos G. McMurtrie Godley added support for the cross-border strike at the Tchepone depot.

While Haig was discussing concepts with the Saigon leadership, General Abrams gave his immediate superior, Admiral McCain, and Chairman Moorer a written plan for a four-phase strike using American forces to open the way to the Laotian border and multiple regiments of South Vietnamese troops to carry the fight from there with full support from U.S. helicopters, jet fighters, and strategic, high-flying B-52 bombers.

Moorer, delighted that Abrams had overcome his reluctance to give the South Vietnamese armed forces responsibility for ambitious operations, recorded in his diary that he was inclined "to go for what Abrams wants us to do . . . exactly like General Abrams wants us to do it *and in no other way* (his emphasis)."[39]

A week later, with Haig back in Washington, President Nixon met with him, Moorer, Kissinger, and Defense Secretary Laird to review the plans. By then, the plans called for a four-pronged attack: west to Tchepone, up Route 7 in Cambodia, a strike at Viet Cong forces in the vast Chup rubber plantation in northern Cambodia, and limited raids into North Vietnam. Nixon, concerned about the political fallout, wanted to minimize U.S. involvement, but having let Laird in on the military's thinking, he asked for the secretary's reaction.

"Let's take a crack at it," Laird said. Nixon approved the Chup operation but held off on going to Tchepone.[40]

The military faced increasing time pressure because the rainy season in the Khe Sanh region and adjoining Laos was drawing to a close, and the generals wanted to hit the North Vietnamese before they regained full mobility as the rain stopped and the mud dried. In early January, Moorer pressed the secretary for approval of the plan as perhaps the last chance for a cross-border operation before U.S. forces were drawn down too low to support one. But even as the planning went forward in Vietnam, Washington appeared to be getting cold feet. Secretary of State William P. Rogers and his deputy, U. Alexis Johnson, objected to a push into Laos. Skeptics in Washington bombarded the U.S. Command in Saigon with questions and what-ifs.

His patience exhausted, General Abrams recommended canceling the operation altogether. Moorer calmed him down. With less than three days to go before the planned launch of Phase I, a road-clearing operation to reopen Route 9 to the border and restoration of the airfield at Khe Sanh, the president gave the go-ahead—but only for that initial part of the operation. As thousands of South Vietnamese troops massed on their side of the border, easily detected by North Vietnamese intelligence, the American command was still waiting for Nixon's signal.

Major Newman (head turned toward camera in foreground) inspecting C Troop's assigned area at the hastily reopened Khe Sanh combat base in preparation for invasion of Laos.

Moorer called Abrams's deputy, General Frederick C. Weyand, one of the most respected general officers in the Army, who told him this could be "the real turning point of the war." Moorer agreed and said he would keep pushing against what he called "explosive" pressure by the Congress and media to get out of Indochina, not go deeper into it.[41] The North Vietnamese quietly prepared to offer only token resistance to an initial attack and draw the allied forces deep into unfamiliar territory before launching a counterattack.

CIA Director Richard Helms phoned Kissinger on January 29, the day before the staging operation was to kick off, and warned him the Americans would take casualties going back into Khe Sanh to repair the airstrip.

"Does everyone know that?" the country's top spy asked. "A lot of NVA troops up there."

"I wasn't aware of that," Kissinger replied. "Thank you for calling it to my attention."[42]

Helms was wrong. The North Vietnamese were there, but they had other plans.

Despite all the U.S. emphasis on secrecy and "eyes-only" communication, the North Vietnamese Army claimed later that it had seen the invasion coming as early as the previous summer and planned for a decisive battle in southern Laos. It boasted of building a new, secret supply road that it hid from U.S. Air Force gunships, and by the time the attack came, the North Vietnamese had sixty thousand troops in position to defend the trail and repulse the invaders. It was the largest force they had ever assembled and included the most sophisticated antiaircraft weapons in their arsenal, as well as tanks rarely seen in battles in the South.[43]

Nixon approved the invasion of Laos on February 4 with the operation set to push off the morning of the 8th, Vietnam time. Ground forces with tanks and armored personnel carriers dug in along the border, and thousands more South Vietnamese rangers, marines, paratroopers, and infantrymen gathered near Khe Sanh to await their rides aboard American helicopters.

Charlie Troop's scouts, gunships, and slicks loaded with South Vietnamese rangers led the way.

C Troop, 2/17 Hueys flying from Khe Sanh into Laos on Operation Lam Son 719.

"Laos 0742 First American aircraft in," Cobra pilot Chuck Vehlow wrote in his pocket daily diary. He reported taking out a truck, two tanks, and "some dinks [NVA soldiers]," plus a "fuel truck (BOOM). What a really really great day!!"[44]

Newman's command ship was characteristically in front, where cavalry officers believed they belonged, and being first to cross the line—even a few minutes before H-Hour—was a source of lifelong pride. He was at the head of what was almost certainly the largest fleet of helicopters ever assembled for a combat operation.

Major Newman at the controls of his command Huey en route to Laos. He is flying right seat, avoiding the customary position for the aircraft commander on the left side, because he was wounded sitting in the left seat on his first tour.

CUTTING DOWN TREES

After the funeral at Arlington, Jim Kane's son Jamie, a thirty-two-year-old Navy veteran, joined his father for a Condors reception at the Old Ebbitt Grill near the White House. Jamie had never met the Condors who gathered for Jim Newman's funeral. Kane introduced his son to Ed Kersey, the man he said had given him a leg up out of Laos. If it hadn't been for Ed, Kane told his son, "you wouldn't be here."

It was an awful morning, the fifth day of the Laos operation, and for Charlie Troop, work started at first light, when a heavy pink team led by gunship platoon leader Chuck Vehlow took off from Khe Sanh and headed west across the border to look for signs that the North Vietnamese Army was preparing to engage the invasion force.

One Cobra would follow the little bird at low altitude with the copilot/gunner, known as the frontseater, noting the scout's position and anything the observer in the loach reported by radio, while the aircraft commander/pilot flew the helicopter and controlled the gunship's principal weaponry, the rocket pods on either side, and a 20 mm cannon. The frontseater kept one hand on the trigger of a fast-firing minigun and frequently scrawled notes from the scout on his cockpit windshield with a grease pencil. A Huey "chase ship" stood by at high altitude to make a quick rescue attempt if the little bird or one of the "snakes" went down.

The choppers cruised over the rolling hills, mostly tan from the semi-arid conditions with large patches of low-growing green shrubs and groves of trees where the plants had found water from a stream or underground source. Farther west, in the foothills and mountains, toward the town of Tchepone, the jungle forest offered dense cover for the North Vietnamese troops using the trail network that snaked south and east into Vietnam. When Vehlow spotted an area likely to be hiding enemy troops and supplies, he directed scout pilot Gary Swift to drop down on the deck for a close look at the terrain. Vehlow followed Swift in, ready to shoot at anything the scout spotted or anyone who fired up at them from the ground. Chief Warrant Officer Mickey McLeod and his newbie frontseater, Captain Clyde Wilkinson, were above them in the high Cobra, keeping out of rifle range but ready to dive on a target.

Swift, who considered himself bait to tempt enemy gunners, spotted a machine gun on a knoll in front of him just as it opened fire on him. He pulled his little bird up and away to dodge his attacker and make room for McLeod's Cobra to dive on the target.

Swift watched the narrow body of the gunship go by on his right, heading straight for its target. It never pulled out. Another machine gun had been hidden down there that none of them had seen, and it picked off the Cobra in mid-dive. Vehlow saw the gunship get hit, too. He radioed McLeod to put the craft down and Vehlow would be right behind him. Smoke belched from McLeod's Cobra, flames streamed out the back, and his buddies watched the craft "auger in," flying straight into the ground with no ability to slow down or pull out. The fuel and ammunition aboard exploded on impact and engulfed the fuselage in flames.

Swift radioed Mac Jones, commander of the Huey chase ship, not to attempt a rescue. There was no way the crew could have survived, nor, with the guns all around, was there any place to land near the crash site. The little bird made a quick 180-degree turn to check out the smoking wreckage below and flew right over another .51-caliber machine-gun pit. Swift, zipping by only feet off the ground, saw the surprised gun crew swinging the weapon around on its tripod to aim at him, but he scooted down the side of the hill to get lower than the gun could point and made his escape.

Vehlow, following the loach, had flown into the same deadly triangle of machine gunners that downed McLeod and Wilkinson. His Cobra took several hits, none fatal, but he didn't know how long he had to get the snake home. He called off the mission and told the scout and chase ship to accompany him back to Khe Sanh to check for damage, rearm, and refuel.

Chief Warrant Officer 2 Arthur Edward "Mickey" McLeod was twenty-five. Captain Clyde David Wilkinson, who outranked him but had been in Vietnam one month to the day and hadn't yet graduated to the back seat of a Cobra, was also twenty-five. Their remains were recovered in Laos in 1997, repatriated to the United States, and identified in 1999.

Captain Jim Kane, flying another Cobra with Warrant Officer Jim Casher in the front seat, received an alert that an aircraft was down, and he was ordered to head for the crash site to provide gun cover. He was only minutes away, but by the time he arrived, all he could see was a bare spot of ground with a smoking pile of wreckage in the center. Jet fighter-bombers were on station about to attack the enemy positions around the site.

Suddenly, "all kinds of shit was happening," Kane recalled. "We took some heavy fire, and something hit up in my rotor head." A .51-caliber machine-gun round, bigger than a man's forefinger, tore through the push-pull tube that controls the pitch of the main rotor. Everything in the Cobra shook violently as Kane fought for control to keep the aircraft flying. He realized in an instant he had to get back to Khe Sanh before the Cobra shook itself apart. Kane reported by radio he was breaking station and returning to base, requesting that ground crews get another Cobra ready for him to take back into the fight.

Gary Swift had taken a couple of hits to his loach as well, one through the aluminum skin, another that took a chunk out of a skid, but the little bird was flying okay, and he got back to Khe Sanh, refueled, reloaded, and headed back toward the crash site to explore the entrenched North Vietnamese positions.

Just then, the ground below erupted with a thunderous roar and a dark cloud of smoke and reddish earth and dust spread quickly over the ground for more than a mile. Based on the air cavalry's reconnaissance report that a large North Vietnamese unit supported by tanks was crossing the area, the Air Force had sent a wave of B-52 bombers—on station so high in the stratosphere they were invisible from the ground—to unleash a devastating carpet of high-explosive horror. More than one hundred 500-pound bombs from each plane tore out the vegetation and cratered the earth in a rectangular pattern more than a mile long and a half-mile wide. Any human or animal standing within a few miles of the Arc Light bombing mission felt the sustained shudder underfoot as steel and high explosives redrew the landscape, pulverizing the soil and pockmarking it with hundreds of deep, barren craters.

With the dust still settling after the massive air strike, gun platoon leader Vehlow and Kane and Casher in new Cobras rendezvoused over Laos not far from where McLeod and Wilkinson tunneled in. Kane was glad to be working with Swift, his roommate and best friend. The two had met right after flight school and roomed together for months at Fort Hood before being shipped to Vietnam on the same plane and assigned to C Troop together. At the Condors' headquarters in Phu Bai, they shared a room at one end of a Quonset hut reserved for officers, and the other pilots knew there was always a beer or a drink available in their "hooch."

Dropping down from about 2,500 feet, Swift made a screaming-fast pass over the newly bombed terrain and saw footprints crossing the fresh dirt upturned by the Arc Light. It never ceased to amaze the Americans that North Vietnamese soldiers somehow survived those fiery attacks, picked themselves up, and kept going.

As he flew past the gun pit that McLeod had targeted when he got hit, Swift saw the machine-gun crew still in place. "If I'd have reached out, I could have grabbed one of 'em by the collar," he said. "I yelled, 'Mark, mark, mark!'"

David "Fuzzy" Fausnight, a chief warrant officer flying another Cobra within radio range, had a portable cassette tape recorder tucked into a small storage area over his shoulder in the cockpit. He plugged a microphone cord into the machine, led the cable to an earpiece in his helmet, then pressed the record button on the machine to pick up the radio traffic between nearby aircraft and headquarters. The static made much of it inaudible, and the tape recording is filled with code names, jargon, the whop-whop of rotor blades, and whoosh of rockets firing just outside the cockpit, but Fausnight captured a terrifying drama in the matter-of-fact tones of aircrews talking to each other.

On the recording, scout pilot Swift is heard radioing his Cobra escorts that he could see evidence the North Vietnamese had been "wandering around down there. They got two holes with trails right through 'em, two fresh bomb holes with trails right through 'em, and they've been running through it. And it looks like, uh, I can't tell—I'm taking fire! I'm taking fire!"

"Roger," acknowledged one of the Cobras.

Swift's loach carried a minigun, a six-barrel, Gatling-type machine gun that spat out more than sixty rounds a second with an ear-shattering, eye-closing burp that startled anyone who didn't know it was coming. Swift liked it because the noise and fiery beam of tracers scared enemy troops back into their holes instinctively, giving him time to get away. This time, though, it jammed.

"My gun doesn't work, and—I'm still taking fire!" he told his gunships.

"Get that little bird out of there," came a voice from on high. It was Lieutenant Colonel Robert Molinelli, the squadron commander.

"Little bird, come on up."

"I'm trying! I'm still taking fire."

Jim Kane, with Casher in the front seat of their Cobra, rolled in on his friend's little bird and spotted where the shooting was coming from. He could see muzzle flashes from two positions and identified the sources as .51-caliber machine guns planted right by a river the Cobra was flying over. It looked like flashlights blinking at him. Swift saw them, too, and dropped a purple smoke grenade to mark the targets telling his guns to head 120 degrees southeast from his mark "right down to the bend there and douche him out; that's where he is."

"I got a mark on him, too, and I'll be back in," Kane radioed back, pulling his ship in a tight arc to make another pass.

"Beautiful firing!" said a voice in the sky as Kane's rockets found their mark.

"I got a fifty!"[45] trumpeted the gun pilot, his momentary euphoria spreading over the radio. What he didn't see was a camouflaged third gun position, now behind him. The Condors were just learning that in Laos, the North Vietnamese often set up their antiaircraft positions in triangles. An attack on one would be answered by the other two in hiding. Kane never caught a glimpse of the third gunner, who opened up on him as his Cobra swooped by.

"Okay," Jim Kane said on the tape, his voice rising with anxiety. "I've got a hydraulics failure."

"Uh, Four-one," Vehlow told him, using Kane's radio call sign, "you got a fire. Put it down somewhere."

"I'm uh, trying to—" Kane said, struggling to control his craft without hydraulics.

"He's on fire! He's on fire!" Swift shouted.

"Four-one," Vehlow repeated insistently, "you're on fire. Put it down." Then he ordered slick pilot Mac Jones, call sign One-five, to "get down there on Four-one." Only a Huey, like Jones's, had room enough to rescue the crewmen if they survived a landing in enemy territory.

"It looks like you blew it out, Four-one," Colonel Molinelli said. Small comfort.

"Put it down," Vehlow told Kane again.

Kane, desperately fighting the damaged controls and looking for a place to land, realized red hydraulic fluid was pouring into the cockpit beneath his boots. What's worse, the flames the other pilots could see outside the aircraft ignited the leaky hydraulic fuel at Kane's feet. He knew he was deep in enemy territory and searched desperately for a place to "prang in," as they called a crash landing. He pushed the stick forward enough to get the nose down and aim for the ground, trying to keep the tail rotor from hitting first and flipping his bird heel over head. He was aware of intense heat filling the cockpit when he spotted a little ravine beside a stream and aimed for it, using both arms and both legs to force the stick forward. It was almost frozen.

Cobras aren't flyable without hydraulic power. He could see the back of Casher's helmet in the front seat and shouted over the intercom to get ready for a crash.

"Okay, God bless," someone said over the radio.

The mortally wounded Cobra sailed toward the earth and crashed into a slight rise with its nose pointing uphill, narrowly avoiding a tail-first touchdown. Kane's body slammed downward in the seat, compressing his spine. Casher's helmet whacked the cockpit, knocking him unconscious in the front seat, his body sagging in its safety harness. The aircraft flipped on its side as the long main rotor blade thrashed the trees and elephant grass before striking the ground. Kane, his boots in flames from the burning fluid, just managed to fling open a canopy door and clamber out. He reached for Casher, unbuckled his harness, and tugged at his limp form in the front seat. Flames engulfed the craft and started to cook the unspent ammunition still aboard, igniting a series of explosions like a string of firecrackers.

"One-five, Four-six." It was Vehlow calling Jones in the Huey chase ship.

"This is One-five."

The shaken pilots still aloft searched anxiously for the Cobra, forgetting to identify themselves as they exchanged clues.

"I want you to get down there on that bird."

"I can't see him."

"Where is he?"

"I've got him!" barked Swift, the scout pilot, spotting the smoking wreckage of his friend's Cobra. "I'm going in. I'm right behind you, Four-six."

"Who's calling?" Jones was confused and still couldn't see the downed Cobra.

"Where is he?" Vehlow asked again.

"He lost him," Jones said.

"I'm going to pull them out," said a voice they recognized as their troop commander, Major Newman. He was somewhere miles away and flying high above, but he headed toward the others when he heard the radio reports.

"Uh, Three-two, Four-six," Vehlow radioed Newman, signaling he wanted to talk.

"This is Three-two. I'm going down to look at him. Get up here."

"Okay, Three-two, uh, I'm coming up on him at this time. I'm gonna check him out."

"See where the smoke is?"

"Okay. Six-zero, are you still on my tail?"

"Negative. I'm down on the blue line," indicating he was close to a narrow river running past the crash site, a blue line on their topographic maps.

"Roger. Okay, I got ya."

"Where is this? This is One-five," Jones pleaded. He had the rescue ship and couldn't find his objective. "Where is he from me? I'm down low here."

"Okay, you got me in sight?"

"Negative," Jones reported. "I don't have a damn soul."

The urgent search was interrupted by a screech on the radio.

"Guys, guys!" shouted Swift from his little bird. "He's on his side. The aircraft is burning!"

There was a momentary silence, then Swift again: "He's upside down. I don't see anybody outside the aircraft."

More chatter as the others tried to find the crash site.

Then:

"He's out!" Swift shouted into the microphone at his lips. "The frontseater is out! He's working his way away from the aircraft."

"Roger that," Vehlow acknowledged. Knowing a man was alive on the ground added immediacy to the emergency. The North

Vietnamese below were certainly looking for the crash site, too. They hated Cobras.

And just then, Vehlow's Cobra got hit, too. Muffled by his helmet, the bullets sounded like people slapping the sides of his gunship.

Swift was getting anxious about his own situation, as well as the snake crew on the ground. He had almost exhausted his fuel and didn't know the condition of his aircraft. He had felt the ground fire hit something on the loach but didn't know how serious it was.

Mac Jones's Huey, One-five, was on station, but he and his crew still hadn't found the crash site.

"Okay, One-five, you got this place in sight?" Swift asked, knowing he had to turn back toward the border soon or crash in Laos when his fuel ran out.

"Negative. I'm, uh—"

"Get your ass down here," the scout pilot barked. "We've got somebody on the ground. Let's go!"

"I'm on the ground," Jones protested. "I'm over to the east of it, I believe. Okay, I've got you in sight."

Vehlow told Jones to stay north of the water because he had just been hit by ground fire coming from the south side.

Newman, flying his heavily loaded command-and-control Huey, radioed that he was about four miles out from the crash site. Swift advised Jones not to land next to the burning Cobra and said he would toss a marker out to show him where to go in.

"I'm, uh, I'm takin' fire," Jones reported. Clearly, the ground was crawling with enemy troops, some of them almost certainly racing toward the crash site. The whoosh of rockets can be heard on the tape as Fuzzy Fausnight's Cobra loosed its missiles at a suspected source of the enemy fire.

Jones reported he was flying at low level about one thousand yards to the north. "If you can get me a place to land where I don't get blowed away, I'm going in," he said.

Swift was still flying his battle-damaged little bird, trying to make sure the others found the crew before he left. He tossed a purple smoke grenade at the spot where he had seen one of the pilots duck out of sight in the bushes. Swift had probably spotted Kane, not Casher, or perhaps Kane dragging Casher and heading for some high grass and nearby bushes on the north side of a small river or creek, but he didn't get a clear enough view to be sure. And he was out of time. His loach was "bingo on fuel," meaning he had barely enough to get back to base before the tanks ran dry. He also noticed the temperature gauge was rising fast, indicating that at least one of the AK-47 rounds that struck the loach had hit the engine, causing it to overheat. Swift reported his problems to Vehlow, who decided to escort him back to Khe Sanh in case the little bird didn't make it all the way. Vehlow's own aircraft was still flying okay, but he knew he'd taken multiple hits and didn't know how serious the damage was.

"Okay, One-five," Swift told Jones. "I put a goofy grape down. No touchdown, but that is it." He meant that he had marked with purple smoke the spot where he had seen the crewman but that there was no good place to land. Jones would have to fly in and hover, possibly putting his crew chief or gunner out to help the crewman get aboard.

Newman had requested jet fighter-bombers from the Air Force to attack the remaining machine-gun positions and the hundreds of North Vietnamese troops known to be in the area and thought to be closing in on the burning Cobra. But with the jets approaching, he held them off while the choppers looked for the surviving crewman.

Jones's Huey finally found the spot and went for it. Swift told him to have his door gunner on the north side "go in hot" with his M-60 blasting to suppress enemy fire but to have the other gunner hold off to avoid hitting the frontseater, who had disappeared into the high growth. Fausnight, overhead in his Cobra, could see secondary explosions bursting from the burning gunship below. The rockets and ammunition aboard were "cooking off," and Jones decided it was too dangerous to stay.

"I'm coming out," he said.

"Roger that," Vehlow acknowledged. "Did you get the front seat?"

"No, I didn't get anybody. . . . The frontseater looked like he was out. Looked like the backseater was in the aircraft burning."

Jones had managed to stick by the crash site for only about thirty seconds before the secondary explosions drove him off without spotting anyone on the ground. He was waiting to make another attempt. More gunships from another unit converged to offer their firepower.

As Newman arrived on scene to take command of the operation, Gary Swift landed back at Khe Sanh and left his little bird with the mechanics. Having heard Jones say over the radio that it looked like the pilot in the back seat was still in the burning Cobra, Swift walked over to the troop's tactical operations center, thinking his best friend had just burned to death in his aircraft.

The TOC was a motley collection of portable steel containers known as Conex boxes, each eight feet wide by eight feet high by ten feet long, where the headquarters types monitored radios, bellowed into field telephones, studied maps, and kept what records they could. Swift asked a soldier at the radio if he had heard anything and was told the search was still going on for the missing frontseater. He found an open Conex with a cot set up inside, closed the door and lay down in the dark. He had watched two fellow Cobra pilots in his platoon die that morning, and two more were out there somewhere on hostile ground, at least one of them probably dead, too. He wanted to blame somebody. He actually thought of lots of people to blame.

Anger surged in him as he thought of what was happening in "that whole bag-of-shit war. We were fed a line of crap about how we're going to save the world from Communism and everything else, and once you get over there, you realize that you've been taken hook, line, and sinker, because it's nothing but politics running the whole stupid thing. And I wanted to blame them; I wanted to blame anybody I could blame. And then, after a while, I just said, you know, it just doesn't do any good. You just have to press on. And go home and forget about this whole thing."

He wasn't angry at his friends or even his immediate superiors. "It wasn't Chuck's fault. It wasn't Molinelli's fault. It was way beyond that. It was the whole scope of the thing that I was blaming. Why are we doing this? What's the point? It's such a waste of money, time, people, and you don't accomplish anything. And that was probably the view of anybody who had been in Vietnam more than six weeks and had seen what a waste this whole thing was. And if they had any perspective at all, they probably shared my views on it."

In the air over Laos, Newman was growing impatient. "You get anybody yet?" he demanded of Jones.

"Negative. I'm goin' to the place now. I'm getting ready to go back in."

Colonel Molinelli, the squadron CO flying high above the others, could see the crash site but no sign of a survivor. "He might have passed out someplace," the colonel guessed aloud. "He must be laying down in there. It's still exploding down underneath me—all over the place." Molinelli was short on fuel and kept saying he had to leave, but he couldn't tear himself away from the search.

Newman was managing the air traffic to protect the man on the ground when Fuzzy Fausnight spotted a light and reported to the others, "It looks like a pen flare." He confirmed it a moment later, saying one of the pocket flares pilots carried in their survival vests flashed from a grove of trees to the east of the burning aircraft.

"There goes another one," said Molinelli, his fuel gauge now on the red line.

One-five, Captain Jones, was down low but couldn't see it. "Okay," said Newman, "lemme look here a minute. Takin' fire! Takin' fire!"

Specialist 5 Richard Frazee, Mac Jones's crew chief, saw the flash in the high grass and told Jones, who headed for it, but the flare went out, and the crew couldn't find the spot again, even as other pilots above said One-five was right over it.

Newman's crew chief and door gunner—like Jones's—were peering out the side doors, looking for any sign of life.

"Okay, where is it from me now?"

"Okay, it's out your, uh . . . seven o'clock."

"Seven."

"Roger . . . right out your left door now. Behind the trees."

"Is it at the trees that's in the little gully there?"

"Roger, just keep on the ground, about eighty meters. You're approaching the area now."

"There goes another one!"

Suddenly, the fast movers and their observer in a small reconnaissance plane came back on the radio looking for bombing guidance.

"Have you got that guy out of there yet?"

"You the ones need some help out here?" another jet jockey asked.

"Okay, I got two down Cobras," replied Newman. "One is already burnt up. The other one—both of 'em are burnt up—but we think we got one man on the ground that's outta one of 'em."

On the ground, pilot Jim Kane had managed to drag Casher up the rise away from their Cobra and into the relative cover of a clump of trees. He pulled an emergency radio from a survival vest and turned it on, but he couldn't hear any voices from aircraft that he knew must be above him somewhere. He figured the radio was broken but sent out Mayday signals anyway, hoping the transmitter was working even if the receiver wasn't. He looked around and realized he was lost. He couldn't tell where the crash site was in relation to his last gun run and just hoped his buddies could see the burning Cobra from above. The underbrush was so thick he couldn't see more than a few feet in any direction. He heard noises that sounded like feet on the ground and bodies breaking through branches, but he couldn't see any movement. He took out his .38 pistol, his only weapon, and waited.

On the radio, there was more talk of where the man might be and who was flying above him.

"We're trying to get a man outta the grass down here. We can't find him again right now."

Newman had summoned a flight of four Hueys with a platoon of crack South Vietnamese rangers, called Hac Bao (Black Panthers), to land and scour the tall, thick elephant grass for his lost crewman. He directed the choppers to follow each other one at a time into a landing zone he marked with a violet smoke grenade.

"Okay, y'all fired up?" he asked the Hac Bao commander. "Yer people know where to go?"

"Roger that."

Newman advised Jones the Hac Bao were right above him and heading for the landing zone. Then he picked up a beeping sound coming from the downed Cobra's survival radio. The crew was trying to use the radio, but the signal was too weak to carry a voice clearly enough to understand.

"Okay, now I got a real live beeper down there," Newman reported. "I heard his voice, but he's too garbled."

Just then, Frazee told Jones on the intercom that he saw a man on the ground. Jones dropped to within ten feet of the ground but couldn't land in the high, flat-bladed elephant grass. He ordered the door gunner, Gary Schuler, to jump out and make his way to the downed man on foot. Schuler, small and thin, looked at Frazee in disbelief. He didn't even know which way to go. The moment still haunts him. His throat tightened up, and he thought of the hundreds of enemy troops he knew were nearby. They had been shooting up at his Huey. Schuler realized he would be alone down there and surely was about to be killed or captured. He hoped they would kill him and not take him prisoner. He has relived that moment endlessly since and still wonders if he could have survived by himself.

Frazee, seeing the desperation on his buddy's face, decided instantly they would jump together. They grabbed their M-16 assault rifles and pocketsful of grenades and ammunition magazines as they went.

Once on the ground in the elephant grass, Frazee couldn't see where he was. He had spotted some pen flares from the air, but the sun was in his eyes, and he wasn't sure where they had come from. The grass was taller than Schuler in places, and he didn't know which way to walk. The two men set out on foot, hoping they were going in the right direction and stopping now and then to listen for some sound from the downed pilots—or enemy troops. Schuler had another fear. He was afraid they would run into poisonous snakes in the high grass. He hated snakes.

Mac Jones, having just put his two machine gunners on the ground, felt naked with no one manning the door guns. He told his copilot to take the .38 pistol out of his shoulder holster and be ready to fire if he spotted any NVA. They would laugh about the futility of that later, but at the time, it wasn't funny.

The aircrews above focused on a clump of trees near the crash site where they thought the pen flares came from.

"One-five, Three-two," Newman said, calling Jones as their two Hueys circled, keeping within sight of each other to avoid a collision.

"One-five," Jones responded. ". . . Go!"

"Roger. Do you see the man?"

"Roger. We saw him in the bush."

"Okay. Roger. Hac Bao's coming right up above you now. Soon as they get in there—"

Jones: "He's coming out! Okay, I've got him in sight. He's in a clump of trees. I've got my crewmen out." But Jones couldn't talk to his crewmen. They didn't have a radio. Realizing his men weren't close enough to reach the downed pilot and couldn't take his directions, Jones dropped down to bring them back aboard. As he hovered above the grass, Frazee and Schuler tried to jump for the skids, but the aircraft was just out of reach. They dumped the ammunition and grenades out of their pockets and anything else weighing them down. Jones dipped his aircraft a bit more. Frazee, the larger of the two, heaved Schuler up over his head and onto the ship. The door gunner, sprawled on the floor, reached down and, with strength he never knew he had, hauled his crewmate up beside him.

Newman, talking to a Cobra flying high above them and other helicopters nearby, decided the Hac Bao were in the wrong place and ordered them back to the landing zone to be picked up in order to clear the area for the bombers that were still on station somewhere above them. With the North Vietnamese troops nearby, Newman was trying to get everyone else out of the target zone and direct the bombing runs to proceed—without hitting the area near the burning Cobra.

First Lieutenant Ed Kersey, commander of the Blues platoon, was aboard Newman's command ship because his ground unit was barred by law from going into Laos. Kersey was basically along for the ride, designated as an observer. As the Huey passed low over the downed gunship, he could see both canopy doors open and no one inside. It was the first indication that both pilots had escaped the fire. Two North Vietnamese soldiers popped up and started shooting at the Huey, but Kersey said Newman never flinched. The crew chief and door gunner opened fire and silenced the enemy soldiers. The chopper got close enough for its crew to see footprints leading away from the burn spot, and Newman followed them in a slow hover. Suddenly, someone in the Huey spotted one of the wounded pilots. The survivor was standing in a clump of trees surrounded by elephant grass too high to land in. As the downdraft from the main rotor blade parted the grass on Kersey's side, the lieutenant saw both men. Kane was standing, but Casher appeared too badly hurt to get up. Newman told his crew chief, Specialist 4 Charles Davis, to watch the tail rotor and guide him clear of the ground or trees as the pilot held the aircraft in a hover and inched downward, shearing the leaves and branches off the trees with his main rotor blade. Davis would say, "Tail to the left," over the intercom, and Newman would put pressure on his right pedal to ease the tail over. "Tail to the right," and he stepped harder on the left pedal. Kersey climbed out on one of the skids, squatting to reach down as far as he could while clinging with two fingers of his left hand to a cargo ring mounted in the floor of the Huey. Kane boosted Casher's limp form over his head, and Kersey grabbed the armored chicken plate on his chest and part of his shirt and heaved him aboard. Then he reached down and locked arms with Kane, pulling the pilot up as well.

Kersey recalled years later that Newman was dead calm as he pulled pitch and eased the helicopter back into the air, turning for home. When he got the speed up to about forty knots, the whole aircraft shook like a wet dog. The Huey lumbered home just above the treetops, a slow-flying target for any soldier below with a gun.

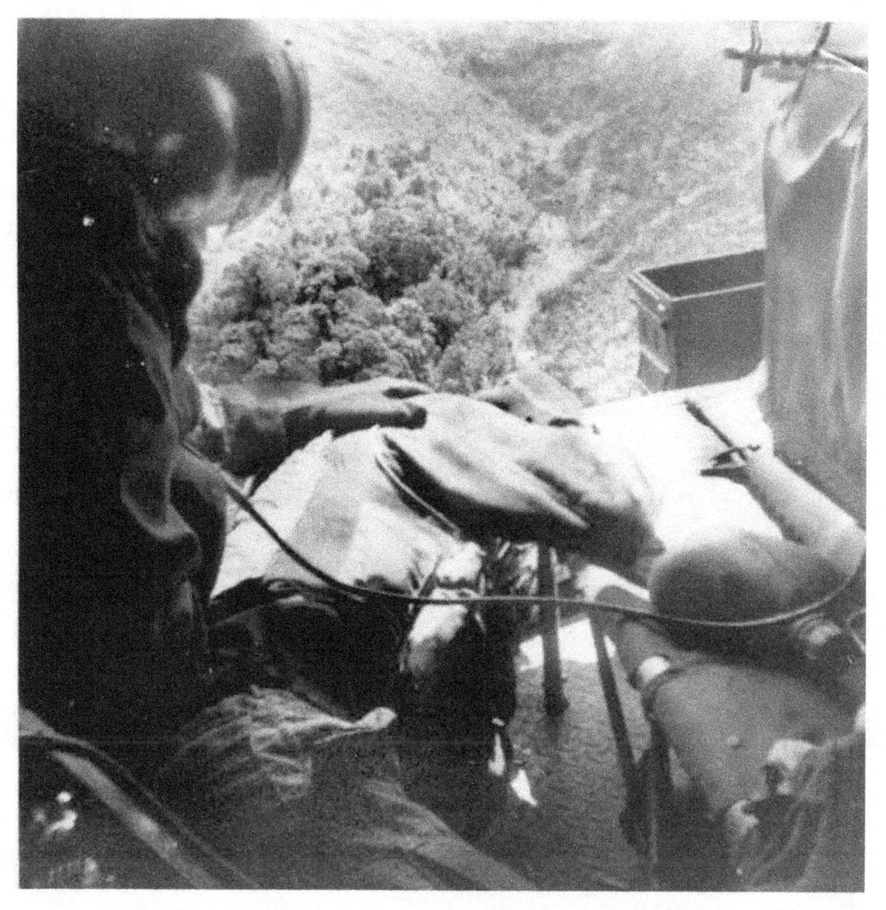

Newman's forward observer, First Lieutenant Kastysis J. Miller, comforts Jim Casher with a hand on his shoulder as the Cobra pilot lies wounded on the floor of Major Newman's helicopter after being rescued in Laos.

"I have Four-one and his frontseater aboard," Newman announced over the radio. "I'm takin' 'em back now to the medevac pad. They appear to be in shock. And my aircraft will be unflyable once I get it on the ground. I tore up my rotor blade."

He ordered Jones and the other slicks to get their troops off the ground and let the bombers and gunships go after the NVA.

* * *

Back at Khe Sanh, Michael Horsch, a crew chief from another Huey, was standing on the flight line of the former Marine combat base that had been scraped out of a mountaintop. He picked up a noise unlike anything he had ever heard in Vietnam. It sounded like a thrashing machine on the farm where he grew up in Alabama. He and several other crewmen listened as the sound grew louder and closer, but they couldn't see anything in the distance for what seemed like a couple of minutes. Finally, a Huey helicopter, clinging to the air just above the treetops in the valley below, pulled itself barely high enough to clear the mountainside and limp toward the aid-station landing area. Newman set his ship down near the medevac pad as softly as he could manage. Horsch could see the main rotor blades were shredded and the tail boom had pulled away from the forward part of the fuselage. He saw daylight through the tear in the skin and wondered what was holding the ship together.[46]

A crewman walked around the aircraft later that day with a stick of chalk and circled seventy-eight holes, yet no one aboard had been wounded. A civilian engineer from Bell Helicopter, the manufacturer, was summoned to survey the damage, took one look at the rotor blades stripped down to their honeycomb core for six feet at either end and promptly declared the aircraft unflyable.

"Hell," Newman said in his Georgia drawl, "I flew it in here."

The battered main rotor blade of Newman's Huey after he used it to cut down trees to rescue Kane and Casher in Laos.

As it turned out, Jim Kane was more seriously wounded than Jim Casher. Both men were ferried to the Army's 18th Surgical Hospital in Quang Tri, then on to a larger facility at Danang. Casher had a concussion and was battered and bruised in the crash, but he recovered and returned to the unit before the Laos operation ended. Going back into battle after being wounded can give a soldier the jitters. Vehlow took Casher on his first combat mission back into Laos and let him fly the entire mission from the front seat of the Cobra to let him get his confidence back. Casher soon was promoted from the front seat to the backseat of a gunship and finished his tour a seasoned aircraft commander. The lasting impact on him would not be known for decades.

Kane's injuries were more complicated from the outset. Both his arms and legs were pushing on the stick with all his might at the moment of impact, forcing his back hard against the stiff, armored seat when the Cobra smacked down. The downward force compressed three lumbar vertebrae together as one at the base of his spine. Several of his back teeth were crushed to the gum line and had to be pulled later. His boots and his helicopter flight suit, which was made of woven Nomex flame-retardant fiber, protected most of his body from the burning hydraulic fluid. Per military regulation, however, he had used a twisted elastic cord with metal hooks at each end to "blouse" his trousers, tucking the bottom of his pants legs under the elastic just above the boot line. The blousing makes it appear as though his trousers were tucked neatly into his boots. The heat of the fire melted the elastic and burned its twists deep into his legs at midcalf, leaving a permanent reminder of how he had bloused his boots that day.

With Kane's extensive back injuries, it seemed impossible that he could have boosted Casher up to Kersey aboard the command ship. The fact that he did is one of those battlefield mysteries that cause doctors to shake their heads and murmur about the power of necessity, the effects of shock, and adrenalin. It was weeks before Kane could walk again.

In the military hospital at Danang, headquarters for all forces in the northern region, he was placed in a Stryker frame that holds a body firmly sandwiched between two rigid metal structures suspended in the air. The contraption makes it possible for nurses to rotate the body without moving the spine. The upper sheet can be raised or removed when the patient's body is lying flat. Kane, in his Stryker frame, was loaded aboard a C-130 air ambulance with about seventy other wounded soldiers, the less severely disabled in seats up forward and those in litters stacked three or four high in row after row crowding the cavernous cargo bay from side to side and back to front. The

C-130 Hercules, workhorse of air forces around the world for more than fifty years, has four turbo-prop engines whose roar fills the fat belly of the plane, drowning all but the loudest screams.

Kane's flight out of Vietnam took him first to Camp Zama, the former Japanese Imperial Military Academy being used as a rest stop by the U.S. Air Force, then lumbering across the Pacific to refuel in Anchorage, where Newman himself had stopped en route home as a war casualty on his first combat tour. The Stryker frames were lined up in the rear, and Kane would always remember the whoosh of the wind as the aft cargo door, big enough to load trucks and helicopters, dropped open and let in Alaska's frigid February air. He also remembered the nurses walking the aisles between stretchers, encouraging the troops, asking where they were from and tending to their wounds for some twenty-four hours in the air. He slept a lot. There was another refueling at Fort Lewis, Washington, where many of the litters were carried off the plane, bound for military hospitals in the West.

The final airborne leg took Kane across the country to Washington, D.C., where he was welcomed by Red Cross workers at Walter Reed Army Hospital and transferred to a bed in the Officers' Ward. It was the first real mattress he had felt in days. For Kane, the Vietnam War was over; his battle to get back on his feet had not yet begun. The first time he tried to walk on his own, he collapsed and sprawled on the hospital floor and was dragged in agony back to his bed by fellow patients, some of whom were missing limbs. When he was well enough to get around, he was transferred to Walter Reed's convalescence center, a whimsical nineteenth-century estate that served as a finishing school for girls in a woodsy Washington suburb. After several months there, he got recertified and flew Cobras again, but this time at Fort Hood, Texas. Jim Kane would not see combat again. The Army gave him an early out in 1974, but his private war had not yet begun.

MEDEVAC RESCUE

WHAT AMERICAN HELICOPTER PILOTS LEARNED in the opening days of the battle, the South Vietnamese soldiers on the ground discovered in the second week. The allies had stuck their arms deep into a hornet's nest.

A battalion of several hundred South Vietnamese rangers, among the best fighters their country could field, had been flown into Laos a few days after the main force crossed the border. The troops set up a base they called Ranger North on high ground about five miles inside Laos. It was the northernmost of some two dozen landing zones and firebases the South Vietnamese hastily constructed as they pushed into Laos to cut the enemy supply lines. On February 18, 1971, after several days of skirmishes, a North Vietnamese regiment of perhaps a thousand men attacked Ranger North at first light. Infantrymen backed by mortars and artillery inflicted heavy casualties on the rangers. The South Vietnamese fended off the initial assault, appealing for artillery support from other bases nearby and firing their rifles at point-blank range as the enemy penetrated the perimeter of the base. The defenders' crude network of ditches and bunkers dug out of the red earth around the hill's highest point proved a better target than it was a sanctuary. At midday, the rangers radioed for U.S. medevac choppers to come get their wounded. Probably fearing the Americans wouldn't come if they knew how dangerous it was, the exhausted defenders lied, saying they had not been in shooting contact with the enemy for two days.

The call was relayed to Chief Warrant Officer Joe Brown, commander of a Huey helicopter rigged as an airborne ambulance with a red cross painted on its nose and medical corpsmen aboard in place of door gunners. The red cross, internationally recognized symbol of noncombatant status, was ignored by the North Vietnamese. Brown, nicknamed Easter Bear—all helicopter pilots had nicknames—had been flying since he was a kid. His father, owner of a wilderness ranch in Oregon, taught him the controls of the family's Stinson Voyager, forerunner of the Army's single-engine Sentinel used extensively during World War II. The Browns used their old plane on elk-hunting and trout-fishing expeditions. Joe's parents were determined that all six of their children go to college, but Joe, the third born, just wasn't cut out for school. His brothers and sisters thought of him as something of a rebel, and having knocked around for a while after high school, he volunteered for the draft in 1966, when the Vietnam buildup was gobbling up most new recruits and sending them into combat as grunts, lowly infantrymen. Joe Brown managed to convert his flying prowess and aptitude into a flight-school slot, earned promotion to warrant officer, and became a pilot. On his first tour, he had flown a Cobra gunship, but when the Army offered him an early out if he would go back to the war zone for an abbreviated six-month second tour, Brown said he'd had enough killing. He would go, but only to fly a "dustoff," a medical evacuation helicopter that carried no guns.[47] Dustoffs were beloved by the grunts because their crews flew into notoriously dangerous situations to evacuate the wounded and get them to the nearest surgical hospital, where doctors struggled to save the lives of soldiers who certainly would have died on the battlefield in earlier wars. The nickname, picked from a list of call signs by an early medevac commander in Vietnam, was a good fit for the powerful, debris-scattering whoosh of a helicopter landing and taking off in the chaos of combat.[48]

Brown, now twenty-five, and nearly four months into his second tour, had dark hair long enough to blow across his eyes, a mustache, and sideburns that gave him the jaunty look cultivated by helicopter pilots who flew their Hueys as if they were sports cars. Described by his sister Sally as "the fearless one" growing up,[49] Joe Brown made a pass at Ranger North, but the eruption of rifle and machine-gun fire from the North Vietnamese surrounding the base drove him off. Speaking to each other by intercom and looking down at the dangerous ground, peter pilot Darrel Monteith, crew chief Dennis Fujii, and medics Paul Simcoe and James Costello—a newbie learning the ropes from Simcoe—could tell where they were going by the pall of black smoke hanging over the base. It was the residue from dozens of mortar shells and artillery rounds that had exploded on the hill during the intense attack.

Simcoe, who had been in-country for four months and was the senior medic aboard the aircraft, dubbed the "Ship of Fools," could see many wounded on the hill as they flew by. All agreed to try again. Their second approach was the same, with rifle and .51-caliber machine-gun fire coming at them from all directions. Brown decided to try a high-speed, low-level approach from the south, hoping to zip onto the landing pad before the enemy gunners had time to react. That time he succeeded, perhaps because the enemy let him land to get a better shot.

As the aircraft pulled pitch and slowed to a hover just over the landing zone, the crew could see rangers holding up their wounded in ditches, ready to rush for the Huey. Before the aircraft could land, some of the soldiers dropped their wounded companions and raced toward the chopper on their own. North Vietnamese gunners "walked" their mortars in, correcting their aim a bit each time to get closer to the target. A round exploded right under the nose of the dustoff as the craft neared the ground, sending searing shrapnel in all directions. Brown was hit in the chest, Monteith in the spine, Fujii in the shoulder. The aircraft fell the last few feet and hit the earth, but the pilots managed to keep it from flipping onto its side, and the crew bailed out and ran with the rangers back to the comparative safety of their ditches.

Mortars can be devastatingly accurate when the firing crew has a forward observer close enough to watch the shells land and relay adjustments back to the firing team. The NVA clearly had Ranger North and its landing zone within range of several mortar crews and had people watching and correcting after each shot, which is how the explosions seemed to "walk" toward their target.

Simcoe looked back to see the dustoff shredded with bullet and shrapnel holes. He and Fujii found a shallow ditch dug by the diminutive South Vietnamese defenders. It offered little cover to the larger Americans. The medic checked crew chief Fujii's wound and determined the shrapnel fortunately had gone in and out without causing extensive damage, but they were caught in a rain of fire with no apparent escape. Simcoe spotted a South Vietnamese soldier in a small bunker and asked him to find a radio. The soldier was reluctant to move, but Simcoe was forceful. They ran to another bunker, where Simcoe found both pilots severely wounded. Brown was worse off than Monteith, who could barely walk. There was a military radio in the dirt. Simcoe grabbed the telephone-like transceiver, squeezed the talk button, and reached an American on a base somewhere nearby. He reported his position and the status of the crew, then waited with the others for about an hour until they finally spotted a chopper coming toward them. He helped Brown and Monteith hobble toward the approaching rescue ship, but when they were within about fifteen yards, enemy fire poured in from all sides. Simcoe watched as the pilot, his eyes like saucers, shook his head to signal he couldn't stay, and the aircraft flew off. Another mortar crashed near the grounded crew, now caught in the open. Brown, hit again, fell to the ground, and this time Simcoe was wounded as well. He and Monteith, who could no longer use his legs, crawled to another bunker, but it offered little protection. Instead of sandbags for walls and a roof, the South Vietnamese rangers had covered the opening in the ground with bamboo. The medic tried to get to Brown, but every time he started out of the hole, the shooting erupted again.

"I had some kind of a beacon device, or Monteith had it," Simcoe recalled, "so we placed that at the bunker entrance and waited. Another dustoff tried to get us, but he didn't even approach the hill. He was about three hundred feet up and took off."[50]

They waited some more. Then suddenly, all hell broke loose.

* * *

Major Jim Newman had gone out with a heavy pink team that was looking for a North Vietnamese fuel pipeline and enemy troops in the area where they had lost the two Cobras six days earlier.

Captain Chuck Vehlow, the troop's gunship platoon leader and Newman's most trusted "gun," was flying one Cobra, and he had brought First Lieutenant George "Doc" Schopfer back to fly the other. Schopfer was a short-timer, not just a "double-digit midget," but counting down the last days until the end of his hitch. In GI lingo, he had "sixteen days and a wakeup" before he would board a civilian charter and go home to "the World," as GIs called anyplace but Vietnam, especially the States. It was customary to leave short-timers in the rear to reduce the risk of their being killed at the end of their yearlong tour of duty. But Vehlow had approached Schopfer at Khe Sanh that morning and said he didn't have anyone else left to fly Cobras. He'd lost McLeod and Wilkinson in one ship, and with Kane and Casher wounded the same day, C Troop was short of gun pilots. Vehlow decided he had no choice but to tap the short-timer.

Major Newman and Captain Vehlow hardly seemed a natural pair. Newman, the barely educated ex-enlisted man from a backward town in Georgia might have felt threatened by the arrival in his unit of an all-American boy from the Wisconsin heartland who had played football at West Point and had "career officer" written all over him. Newman was deeply suspicious of the officer corps in general, particularly of officers who did everything by the book. Vehlow, always eager to please, especially his commanding officer, went to great lengths to show he was a good pilot and an ideal subordinate. Newman was short, walked with a limp, and had thinning hair that revealed he was considerably older than his men. Vehlow stood erect, the clean-cut product of a Wisconsin Lutheran upbringing, careful never to step out of line. The Old Man saw something he liked in the junior captain the first time he saw him and put Vehlow in charge of the guns. He frequently picked Vehlow's Cobra to protect him on dicey missions.

They were about fifteen minutes from Ranger North when they heard an emergency signal on the "guard" channel indicating crewmen were in trouble on the ground. The signal came from the emergency beacon that dustoff crewmen Monteith and Simcoe had turned on.

"It wasn't my people, but I was close to them, and I had Chuck Vehlow covering me," Newman said years later, explaining his decision to attempt a rescue. He was known among his men for his coolness under fire, his steady voice, and deliberate action. He said he wasn't afraid.

"I figured when my time came I's going to go," he drawled. "I already figured I's one ahead because I didn't go the first time," when he was hit in 1966.[51] After he recovered and went back to flying, Newman always commanded from the right seat, the one usually occupied by the peter pilot; and he always put an armored chest protector, a chicken plate, in the curved Plexiglas chin bubble beneath the pedals on a Huey. Sometimes he tossed in a second one, because that's where the AK-47 round had come through to tear up his leg. On that first tour, he was flying left seat, the aircraft commander's position, when the bullet that hit him shot up through the chin bubble.

Newman told the Cobras to follow him toward the source of the emergency signal. As the three choppers approached Ranger North, the pilots could see the crashed medevac in the landing zone and fighting going on around and on the hilltop base. Schopfer saw soldiers standing up in the concertina wire surrounding the base and thought they were South Vietnamese until he realized they were shooting up at him. It was jaw-dropping to see enemy troops so brazenly out in the open.

Vehlow saw tracers and puffs of smoke coming from a ridgeline to the northwest, indicating the NVA were firing their mortars and .51-caliber machine guns from hidden positions across a small valley.[52] He radioed Schopfer: "There's a lot of fire off the ridgeline to the northwest. Basically, what I wanna do, I want you to hose down that area" with his ship's 20 mm cannon to keep the enemy's heads down and suppress their mortar and machine-gun attack on the landing zone. "I'll stay behind Three-two [Newman] and cover him all the way in. I'll put a high cap on him, and I'll cover him all the way out. I want you to work on the ridgeline."[53]

They spotted a plume of yellow smoke from a signal grenade tossed onto the landing zone by the medevac crew.

"That's it," Vehlow told Newman. There are several ways to approach a landing zone under fire; Newman chose the most direct, heading straight in as fast as possible at low altitude, hoping to catch as many enemy gunners as possible off guard.

"Okay, roger. I'm gonna go in there. Now, the friendlies I've got plotted to the right side . . . , the yellow smoke on top. Now, I'm gonna go in there shootin'," meaning he would have his crew chief and door gunner blazing away out the sides with their M-60 machine guns to keep the surrounding NVA soldiers' heads down.

Vehlow: "Roger that." He told his commanding officer he would have Schopfer working the ridgeline, well out of the way of Newman's gunners, and "I'm going to be right behind you, so go ahead and fire either way."

Newman: "Okay, I'm ready to go in. You ready to go in?"

Schopfer: "This is Two-three. . . . Roger, I'm ready."

Vehlow to Schopfer: "Okay, start hosing down that area."

Then to Newman: "Whenever you're ready."

Newman: "Okay, I'm goin' down. You got me covered?"

"Yeah, we gotcha."

"Okay."

Short-timer Schopfer thought to himself it was "really turning into a shit mission." If the commanding officer went down, C Troop would have to mount an even bigger operation to get him out.[54]

At that moment, the world around Simcoe and his fellow crew members trapped on the ground seemed to explode. Lying as low as they could in their too-shallow cover, they heard the rapid rat-tat-tat of the Huey's machine-gun bursts. The shots were coming closer. The whoosh and explosions from Vehlow's rockets aimed at the perimeter mixed with the sudden increase in firing from the NVA attackers, who would do anything to get another American chopper. In the distance, Doc Schopfer was pumping 20 mm exploding incendiary shells from his three-barrel autocannon into the nearby hillside where mortarmen and machine gunners were firing toward the base. Exploding mortar rounds flashed and kicked up clouds of dirt and gunpowder smoke on the landing zone as heavy machine guns hurled their bullets at the firebase.

Through the roar of guns, the dustoff crew caught the familiar whop-whop-whop of a Huey coming for them. Simcoe and Costello decided to make a run for it. Simcoe, weakened by blood loss, half dragged, half carried Monteith, the peter pilot, to the chopper. Costello ran to where Brown had fallen and pulled him to the open helicopter, lifting the bleeding pilot onto the floor of the aircraft. Nobody noticed Fujii wasn't with them.

"Three-two, which way are you gonna come out?" Vehlow asked anxiously from above as he watched exploding mortar rounds advancing toward Newman's aircraft. Ninety-eight seconds had elapsed since Newman entered the kill zone, and they were running out of time. Shells smashed into the ground all around them, hurling white-hot shrapnel in all directions.

"Get outta there, Three-two," Vehlow insisted, commanding his own commander.

"Okay, I'm comin' out," Newman replied as his Huey lurched off the ground, dipped forward and churned the air into a dust cloud, clawing for altitude and enough forward speed to get airborne. It was a helicopter's most vulnerable moment. The awkward bird, heavy with radio gear and extra people, lifted straight up off the ground, presenting a clear target for the enemy, but it couldn't stay in a hover or get away until it gained enough lateral speed to build lift under the rotor and begin to fly.

"Takin' fire, takin' fire!" Newman shouted into his radio mic, pulling the collective and pushing the cyclic to dip his main rotor blade, raise the tail, and slip forward fast enough to soar over the concertina wire strung all around the outside of the base. Vehlow figured the Old Man wouldn't try to head off to the north because that's where the big guns were waiting for him, but he wasn't sure which way the Huey would attempt to escape. He saw Newman take off toward the east, and Vehlow tucked his Cobra into a tight right turn to concentrate his fire on the perimeter and keep out of the escaping Huey's way. He fell in behind it, firing cover all the way out. It took another thirty seconds for the loaded Huey to get through the hail of bullets before Newman could take stock and report.

"Okay, I got three U.S. aboard," Newman announced.

"Roger. Okay, we're right with ya, Three-two."

"Okay. Roger. Stay with me. Still workin'."

A minute later Newman asked for the frequency of the dustoff detachment, then reported he could see artillery going off over to his right and .51-caliber machine guns, too.

"Three-two, did you take any hits?" Vehlow asked, but Newman didn't reply. He was still worried about the artillery fire aimed at the base he just left behind. Gun pilots assured him they were attacking the source of the fire.

Newman, concerned that he had only three of the four crewmen normally on board a dustoff, asked again for the medevac frequency. He made contact with the crew's headquarters and reported directly: "It's a three-fer. I got three U.S. I got, uh, lemme see—"

"Say again?"

"Uh, this is Three-two. I got four U.S. aboard!"

"I got one that slid in with my gunner that I didn't see."

"Roger that. Good to hear."

On their way back to Vietnam and the tiny, underground hospital at Khe Sanh, Newman learned about Fujii.

"Okay, one of the people back here tells me there were five on that ship, and one's still there," he told Vehlow. Newman's own crew chief heard the report and was horrified at the thought that the Old Man would turn around and go back in, but Newman realized it was too late. They had to get the wounded already on board to the hospital.

"We're headed back," Three-two reported. "We're just to the east of the smoke on the ridgeline there."

The radio traffic turned to discussion of a scout helicopter that had been over Ranger North and took a hit in the engine. The pilots arranged to escort him back to Khe Sanh with one ship flying on either side in case he didn't make it. Newman headed straight to the makeshift hospital. Corpsman Simcoe, who himself had been hit by shrapnel in the back, arms, and buttocks running for the chopper, tried to tend to his gravely wounded aircraft commander, but both of Brown's lungs were punctured. He was still talking, but there was nothing the medic could do for him but hold his hand. Joseph Gordon Brown, chief warrant officer, the two-tour pilot who flew dustoffs because he didn't want to kill people anymore, died as the Huey landed at the aid station.

Paul Simcoe, who hadn't even graduated from high school when he joined the Army and was trained as a medic, went home to California, graduated from college and medical school, and eventually became an emergency-room physician. "I suppose my experiences in Vietnam propelled me that way," he wrote nearly four decades later. "I seemed to have a natural ability for medical stuff."

Dennis Fujii, the crew chief who missed his ride out, became a celebrated, if reluctant, hero, the best known of any of those involved in the incident.

He has retold the story many times.

Dennis Fujii, reluctant hero.

The young specialist 5 was in the bunker with Simcoe and Costello when they heard Newman's chopper coming in and decided to make a run for it, but the entrance to the bunker was tiny, and they had to crawl out one at a time. Costello went first, then Simcoe. As Fujii emerged from the bunker and stood up, a mortar round exploded nearby, and the concussion threw him backward, a tiny bit of shrapnel piercing the skin at his right eyelid. It stung like hell as he lay at the entrance to the bunker, temporarily blind in that eye. With the other, he could see his crewmates pick up the two wounded pilots and clamber aboard the Huey.

"You're not gonna make it," he told himself. "You're not gonna make it." He watched the chopper take off, flying through a blizzard of fire. When his ride somehow got away, he turned his attention to his fresh wound, squeezing the skin around his eye to force the metal sliver to the surface. It actually wasn't the first time he had found himself alone in Laos that day. Fujii's ship had crossed the border in the blackness before dawn on its first rescue mission of the day, but the pilots got lost in the unfamiliar territory and Brown abruptly put the bird down on a hilltop to figure out where he was. Fujii jumped out a side door to see what he could, and Brown—unaware his crew chief was on the ground—lurched back into the air, snapping the intercom wire that led from the aircraft to Fujii's flight helmet.

"I could have been captured right there," Fujii said, remembering how he stood all alone in the dark on a Laotian hilltop, outraged at being left behind. Within moments, Simcoe realized what had happened and told the pilot, who circled back and picked up Fujii, but the crew chief was badly shaken and angry. He was hardly over it when he found himself left behind for the second time that day. He went in search of the South Vietnamese rangers his ship had come to help. They were desperate and welcomed an American who could communicate by radio with the gunships and fighter-bombers overhead.

Fortunately, Fujii was not new to ground combat. A Hawaiian of Irish and Japanese descent, he had enlisted in the Army in Hawaii to get away from an unhappy family life and was sent to Vietnam in 1968 as an infantryman—a grunt—with the 2nd Battalion, 35th Infantry, a unit raised in Hawaii and attached to the U.S. 4th Infantry Division in the central highlands of South Vietnam. Watching the helicopters come in to get him and his fellow foot soldiers, carry their supplies, and evacuate their wounded, Fujii began to envy the lives of the aviators who didn't have to hump the boonies. They got to sleep in beds at night and ate hot food in a mess hall. They drank at the NCO and officers' clubs on base and even took showers. He hardly ever got a real shower. Near the end of his first twelve-month tour, he volunteered to stay in 'Nam if he could be a door gunner on a Huey. A fatalist by nature, he figured if he was going to die in Vietnam, at least he wouldn't be going to sleep wet every night.[55] He was assigned to an assault helicopter company and worked his way up to crew chief before volunteering for yet another combat tour, this time with DMZ Dustoff, the medevac unit up north that took him into Laos.

On Ranger North, the commanding officer of the beleaguered battalion, who spoke excellent English, told Fujii, who spoke practically no Vietnamese, to take over the radio they were using to call for artillery and air support. He was awed that the senior officers of the unit treated him, a lowly spec 5, with respect and even sought his advice. Fujii took it as a measure of their hopeless situation. The North Vietnamese were barely outside the wire surrounding the camp, and more seemed to arrive all the time. He said when the South Vietnamese would radio targets to their own artillery units in Laos, the North Vietnamese would come up on the same frequency and change the map coordinates to redirect the firing. The rangers needed a good English speaker to talk to the Americans. Fujii settled into the command bunker with the radio. With little or no hope of a rescue bird, he stayed up all night and into the next day, carrying the portable PRC-25 radio with him when he went outside to take a piss. He was furious that someone stole his shirt with a gold necklace and a ring in the pockets when he took them off to have someone change the bandage on his shoulder. After dark, Fujii made contact with the crew of a C-130 Spectre gunship, a flying minigun platform the Air Force used to provide withering close air support to troops on the ground. Painted black on the bottom to make it less visible from the ground in the night sky, the Spectre, one of the American weapons the North Vietnamese most feared and hated, circled the surrounded firebase hosing down the hillside approaches with deadly streams of bullets from its fast-firing 20 mm Gatling guns. The aircrews were so impressed with the trapped American guiding their fire that the military started talking to the press about the bravery of an American soldier inadvertently trapped on the ground in Laos. UPI, the feisty, headline-grabbing No. 2 American wire service, called him a "one-man army."[56] He felt more deserted than honored. Fujii's disabled medevac chopper was still sitting where it had slammed into the landing zone, and the commander asked how much fuel it had aboard. Fujii replied that the tank was nearly full; he had topped it off just before leaving Khe Sanh. The officer thought it dangerous to have so much jet fuel close to his men's bunkers and trenches. The crew chief knew where the emergency release valve was on the outside of the aircraft. He just didn't know how to get there and back alive. The commander offered Fujii a few men to cover him, but Fujii thought he was safer going alone in the dark. He made a run for it, threw the fuel release handle, and sped back to the bunker under fire, leaving the jet fuel to drain onto the ground. He didn't realize it wouldn't be his last trip to the crashed machine.

"Shit was just hitting the fan so bad," Fujii recalled. Despite heavy casualties inflicted on them from the air, the North Vietnamese were determined to thwart the allied invasion of their supply corridor, and they focused on Ranger North first. The defenders held out through the night and the next day, but by the following night, they were running low on ammunition and supplies. Fujii could see enemy bodies littering the hillside, but the attackers didn't back off.

By the night of the 19th, Fujii's second with the rangers as the lone American soldier on the ground in Laos, the fingers on his right hand were numb from pressing the talk button on the radio. The enemy was closing in, and the rangers had run out of pen flares to tell the gunships overhead where they were. Fujii remembered he had a strobe light in the helicopter that would be a good signaling device if he could get to it. A new Spectre was coming on station, and Fujii told the crew he could hear the plane right overhead but couldn't show the crew his position. He asked them to make a 180-degree turn and come back toward the base while he got his strobe. "I had no choice. Do or die. I took the radio with me in case I got wounded really bad, and I dragged the radio because if I stood up, they'd see me." He worried the South Vietnamese might shoot him inadvertently in the dark. When he got to the chopper, he found the door open and the cargo area already ransacked by rangers. The water, C rations, and ammunition were all gone, but he had hidden a pistol belt with a .38 Smith & Wesson revolver, some pen flares, and the strobe in a compartment the scavengers hadn't found. He grabbed them, ran back to the command bunker, and called the gunship on the radio.

"Are you still close by?"

"Yeah, just circling."

He propped the light on top of the bunker, and the moment he turned it on and ducked, a barrage of rifle fire shot toward the flashing light from closer than ever. Fujii crawled back into the bunker, and the commander sent one of his junior officers outside to check the defenses. About two minutes later, the lieutenant came flying back through the hole in a panic, his face peppered with shrapnel. No one said anything, and Fujii could barely make out what was going on. They had only a candle for light inside the bunker, but he realized the wounded officer was ripping the rank insignia off his uniform. Then he saw the man take out his wallet and tear up and burn his identification in the flame. Clearly, he was preparing to be captured. The foe was notoriously unmerciful to officers.

"What the fuck is going on?" Fujii shouted at the commander.

"They've broken through," he replied. "I think they're looking for you."[57]

Fujii panicked and told the commander he wanted the gunship to fire directly on the hill. The rangers passed the word to others in the camp to keep down, and Fujii told the Spectre to open up directly on the strobe. He knew the command bunker was relatively secure because the roof had taken two direct hits from 81 mm mortars without serious damage. The carnage outside was awful. Hundreds of North Vietnamese lay dead or wounded, some having got through the wire to within a few yards of the bunkers. The blazing minigun assault stalled the North Vietnamese attack, but the South Vietnamese had already paid a price. The ranger unit was devastated.

The next morning, Fujii pleaded on the radio for help. "We cannot hold out any longer. We need help now!"

A major he hadn't spoken to before replied in a deliberate, calming voice, "Hang on. Help is on the way. You get your ass on the first bird that comes in."[58] Fujii needed no encouragement to take that direct order from a superior. Within minutes, several helicopters from Charlie Company, 158th Aviation Battalion, which called itself The Phoenix, swooped in to the landing zone. The American soldier threw away his empty weapon as he ran for the first chopper and heaved aboard. A moment later, several South Vietnamese, including the battalion's executive officer, dived in on top of him.

"Let's get outta here. Let's go! Let's go! Let's go!" Fujii shouted to the crew chief. The bird lifted off, and as it flew out over the perimeter of the camp, directly above the attacking North Vietnamese, Fujii could feel bullets hitting the belly of the chopper and hoped they wouldn't come through the floor where he was spread-eagled with a half-dozen Vietnamese on top of him. In moments, the chopper spouted a white vapor trail and belched a black smoke ring. It was going down. Using autorotation to control his descent, the pilot managed to glide onto the next firebase, Ranger South, less than a mile from the lost hilltop they had just abandoned. The aircraft crashed onto the landing zone, and the crew leaped out and ran for cover before it burst into flames. Fujii and the South Vietnamese scrambled out, too, and when Fujii saw a South Vietnamese ranger standing nearby, he concluded they had crashed back onto the base where he'd just been. He stood there, next to the burning helicopter as the tail boom melted and fell to the ground. A Vietnamese ranger grabbed his shirt and dragged him to the nearest bunker.

Following the unwritten code to leave none of its own behind, another Phoenix helicopter came in for the downed crew, but it left the pilot behind by accident. Yet another chopper came in to get him. Fujii missed both. When he emerged from the bunker about twenty minutes after his crash landing, there was just the burned outline on the ground of the helicopter he had flown in on. The crew chief watched through an officer's binoculars as American bombers pounded the abandoned hill that had been Ranger North. It was crawling with North Vietnamese occupiers. Fujii was stuck for two more days as Ranger South came under fierce attack, and when one more helicopter finally came in and flew him toward safety, he marveled that no one was shooting at him.

He figured the enemy wanted him off that hill.

The next day, Ranger South was overrun.

Fujii, put on display by the military as a hero, was awarded the Distinguished Service Cross and flown home to Hawaii for a motorcade through Honolulu with speeches and a band playing patriotic tunes. He was bathed in honor and public admiration. But he was miserable for the rest of his life—ruined, he said, by the war, or maybe by the Army that celebrated his exploits.

Jim Newman was nominated for the Medal of Honor, his country's highest award for combat valor, but the decoration was downgraded to a Distinguished Service Cross, the nation's second-highest award for valor, the same one given to Fujii. Newman always figured, perhaps uncharitably, that if Fujii had come out of that bunker and got on his chopper, Newman would have worn the Medal of Honor's distinctive five-pointed gold star on a pale blue silk ribbon at his throat. Thirty-five years later, his men were still trying to get it for him.

TAR BABIES AND BEANS

SAVING KANE AND CASHER AND THEN THE MEDEVAC CREW a few days later made Jim Newman a hero among his own men, and his fame spread quickly through the squadron and other units involved in the invasion force. After the division put him in for the Medal of Honor, he was temporarily grounded for fear he'd be killed before the president could hang the medal around his neck. Eventually, the Army decided to downgrade the award and gave Newman the Distinguished Service Cross instead. However, the idea of pilots risking everything to rescue their buddies, no matter how popular among the troops, had its influential opponents in the U.S. command structure.

Major John A. G. Klose called it the "tar-baby syndrome," a reference to the popular Uncle Remus story retold by Joel Chandler Harris in the nineteenth century. Tar baby was a pitch-soaked doll that Brer Fox placed in the road to lure Brer Rabbit into a trap. When Brer Rabbit approached and couldn't get the doll to answer him, he hit it with his fist, which stuck in the tar. In trying to escape, Brer Rabbit got all four paws stuck and was held there at the mercy of Brer Fox.[59] Klose, the operations officer of the main lift unit that carried thousands and thousands of South Vietnamese troops into Laos, ordered his flight crews not to try to rescue comrades who got shot down. He tagged the downed birds "tar babies" and spent the rest of his long military career defending the rule he formulated during that battle.

"If a bird goes down out of the lift, the lift must continue," Klose argued. "You don't go down with him, because where you have one down, you might have two or three before you get that tar baby out." In a videotaped oral history interview thirty years later as he ended his career, Klose told an official Army historian, "When you listen to these tapes, you might say that sonofabitch has no feeling at all. The feeling was you had to keep the lift going. There was no alternative."[60] Klose argued it was the job of the air cavalry and South Vietnamese Hac Bao to recover his downed helicopters and their crews in Laos. Indeed, Newman's C Troop was assigned those missions, and Klose learned to admire the Cav during that operation. He even forgave them their "funny hats," a favorite target of soldiers who hadn't earned the privilege of wearing black Stetsons to the officers' and enlisted men's clubs on base. But Klose would have frowned on Newman's risking his own neck—and leadership of the troop—to pull off rescues himself, and he objected to units being sent in to recover crews they'd lost. "We never sent a unit to get their own dead," Klose said of his operation. "It's demoralizing." That's not the way Newman and his men felt about it. Like Lieutenant Kersey, the neophyte platoon leader rescued with his exhausted men in the A Shau Valley only to be dropped back in to recover the remains of a loach crew, C Troop's officers and men never questioned orders to go back into the jungle to bring back their own, alive or dead.

There were limits, however. Only hours after the medevac rescue, a Condor scout crew was lost in Laos. Warrant Officer Gregory S. Crandall was the loach's pilot on a recon mission that afternoon eight miles east of Tchepone. Specialist 4 Walter Lewellen, the crew chief, was such a short-timer he could have skipped the mission, but he wanted one last flight before heading home. He was scheduled to hitch a helicopter ride down to Phu Bai to get some rest, pack his gear, and turn in his weapon before returning to the States in two weeks. Lewellen was nineteen. So was Specialist 4 Robert Joseph Engen, a trained Cobra repairman who went along as the observer. They had left Khe Sanh about a half hour earlier, and Crandall took the little bird down to about thirty feet off the ground[61] to get a close look at possible enemy positions. Captain Chuck Vehlow, whose Cobra had protected Newman earlier that day, was again part of a heavy pink team, flying low snake to cover Crandall. As the scout zipped across his path from right to left, Vehlow heard Crandall key his microphone and say, "Taking . . ." That was it. The aircraft exploded, and Vehlow watched it tumble the short distance to the ground. Vehlow figured it was hit by a rocket-propelled grenade because there was no plume of smoke, the signature of a heat-seeking missile. The little bird just blew up in the air. Crandall must have seen something coming at him, but he had no time to get away. Gary Schuler was the door gunner on the chase ship, as he had been days before when Kane and Casher were shot down. His Huey flew over the crash site, and Schuler could see the charred bodies of the crew in the wreckage, but intense enemy activity in the area made it too dangerous to land to recover the remains. Vehlow also circled the wreckage. Some of the chopper's parts were still burning, but there was no evidence at all of survivors. Stunned, he and his frontseater returned to Khe Sanh and filled out the required witness statements describing the loss. It was late in the day, and light was fading, but Newman went to Vehlow's quarters to figure out how to stage a night recovery. Flying through mountainous, enemy-held terrain in the dark was dangerous, and navigation instruments were comparatively primitive, but they asked the airfield at Quang Tri to set up radar vectors to guide them to and from the crash site.

Newman and Vehlow lifted off from Khe Sanh but soon encountered clouds and fog descending into the valleys and merging with smoke from the many fires burning in the combat zone between them and the crash site. When air traffic controllers at Quang Tri informed the recovery team it could not provide radar support, Newman aborted the mission.

"What a day," Vehlow wrote in his pocket diary that night. He mentioned Newman's medevac rescue, then added, "Crandall crashed and burned. IFR [instrument flight rules] at night attempt." Newman decided it was too dangerous for the little birds in Laos, that they were no match for the massive, well-hidden, sophisticated antiaircraft weapons dug in there. He ordered the scouts out of the fight. What a day, indeed.

Napping in a war zone. An unidentified trooper rests on his pack on a hillside near Khe Sanh as two Cobra gunships approach in a low pass over his position.

Crandall and his crew were declared missing in action, a standard first step when no remains were recovered, and some weeks later, after the Laos operation had ended and there was no reasonable chance of another recovery mission, the Army declared the men killed in action, bodies not recovered. Crandall's family sent a letter to the troop expressing hope that somehow the pilot might still be alive. Schuler wanted to write back to say he had seen the bodies in what little remained of the aircraft. But he worried he would only complicate things for the family. He didn't know what the Army might have said that left any doubt. He was a low-ranking enlisted man and not authorized to deal with the family, but he wasn't concerned about getting in trouble if he spoke out. Rather, he feared Crandall's relatives wouldn't know whether to believe him or whatever the Army had told them. So he let it go. Then he fretted for years that the family still held out hope that Crandall was alive when Schuler was certain he couldn't be. To this day, the thought still contributes to the anguish about the war that he has never been able to shake.[62]

After the war, the Crandall case became emblematic of the military's efforts to resolve as many of the two thousand MIA reports as it could. A joint task force was established to search for and recover any possible remains and close the military's books, even while some families refused to let go of their last shreds of hope. The families organized themselves into a politically powerful interest group that for decades kept the focus on the fate of the men who didn't come home. Twenty years after Crandall's loach went down, a U.S. and Laotian search team located the crash site and recovered a handful of evidence: four human teeth, Crandall's dog tags, a name tag from Robert Engen's uniform, and a piece of the helicopter's painted aluminum skin with identifying information on it.

The military's identification lab in Hawaii used old dental X-rays to determine that one of the teeth was Crandall's, and the Army decided the tooth would be buried with full military honors at Arlington National Cemetery. The ceremony took place on September 17, 1993. The minuscule remains of the other two men were buried separately. Crandall's sister, Nancy Gourley, refused to accept the tooth as sufficient evidence of his death. She, her mother, and two other sisters attended the funeral, but she publicly protested that the Army was insisting on burying a single tooth in a full-size coffin as if it were her brother's body. Nancy Gourley said a dog tag and a tooth did not constitute sufficient evidence of death, and before the scheduled ceremony, she walked up to the secretary of defense at a prisoner-of-war remembrance event and asked him to stop the funeral. He didn't.[63] Many years later, following the declassification of some records related to the case, she called Vehlow to question him about his witness statement.

"I know she wanted me to say that there was a possibility of him being alive," he said afterward. "I couldn't do that."[64]

The March 15, 1971, issue of *Newsweek* featured "The Helicopter War," and on the cover was a color photograph of a C Troop little bird and Cobra preparing for takeoff from Khe Sanh. Atop the story inside was a half-page, black-and-white photo of four litter bearers carrying the facedown body of First Lieutenant Morris Alfred Simpson, his lifeless arms hanging almost to the ground as the soldiers bore him to the underground aid station at Khe Sanh. "Butch" Simpson, twenty-seven, of Richland Hills, Texas, was a slick pilot who had been trained to fly scouts and was tapped during the Laos operation because C Troop was running out of loach pilots. He was flying a reconnaissance mission looking for enemy tanks with his crew chief/observer, Specialist 5 Don Wilson. They were about 150 feet off the ground, looking down at the jungle. They could see areas of open ground covered by tall elephant grass and trails visible in places through the jungle tree cover. They saw signs of recent enemy activity below.

Wilson was an experienced crew chief, nearing the end of his tour of duty. He had flown with several C Troop pilots, but only once or twice with Simpson.

"Maybe we ought to pick up the speed a little bit," he suggested to the pilot over the intercom.

"Don't worry," Simpson said, turning to look his crew chief in the eye. "I'll take care of you."

At that moment, a spray of ground fire from an AK-47 peppered the little bird, and Wilson saw Simpson knocked back in his seat, a single bullet hole piercing the plastic flight helmet in the center of the pilot's forehead. The stunned crew chief tossed a smoke grenade he'd been holding in one hand out the door of the aircraft, let go of his M-16 with his other hand, and grabbed for the controls in front of him. Wilson, like a number of seasoned crew chiefs, had learned the rudiments of flying from his pilots but had no formal training in how to handle the aircraft in flight.

By his own description, he was scared shitless. He tried to key the microphone to tell the crews in the two Cobra gunships escorting him what had happened, but all he could hear was burps of static as everyone attempted to break in and talk at once. Break. Break. Break. Break. He realized his M-16 was between his legs and interfering with his hold on the cyclic stick between his knees. He grabbed the weapon with one hand and threw it out the window. He knew the little bird had taken multiple hits—fourteen holes were found later—but he was relieved the instruments were all in the green.

Between the radio static and questions from pilots, Wilson managed to tell them what had happened. They tried to ask how badly Simpson was hurt, but finally a gruff voice came over the airwaves that he recognized as Major Newman, flying somewhere above in his command-and-control ship. He told everyone to shut the fuck up and listen to Wilson, who reported what had happened and that he had to get the bird back to Khe Sanh. A pilot asked how Simpson was doing and Newman barked at him to let the kid alone, that he knew what he was doing. Newman told Wilson to divert to a new heading that would take him to a nearby South Vietnamese firebase, where the Huey could pick him up. He found it and headed for the dirt helipad inside the wire.

Just then, a giant H-54 Flying Skycrane, the biggest lift ship in service, cranked up its seventy-two-foot rotor blades to take off from the landing pad. The base disappeared in a dust storm of red powder, and Wilson realized there was no way he could get in there to land. He turned and made a loop back to a dirt access road that led from the base down to Route 9. As he dropped toward it, the dust swirl swallowed the little bird, and he descended the last fifty feet with practically no visibility. He hit hard, but the aircraft didn't crash or turn over. He shut the engine off and jumped out.

Wilson could smell the pungent odor of nuoc mam, a Vietnamese sauce made from fermented fish that he associated with the presence of enemy troops. He was unarmed and figured the NVA troops couldn't be far off. He ran around to the right side of the loach, unstrapped Simpson's body, pulled it out of the seat, and dragged it away from the aircraft in case the fuel caught fire or the ammunition exploded. Newman's Huey swooped in from somewhere, and a crew member jumped out and helped Wilson load the body facedown on the floor of the cargo compartment. They jumped in, and Newman took off for the now-familiar aid station at Khe Sanh.

What Wilson already knew quickly became apparent to all: Simpson was beyond help. He never knew what hit him. Stretcher bearers carried his body to the bunker. When the medics spotted Wilson's blood-soaked flight suit and blood on his hands and face, they rushed to help him, but he assured them he wasn't hurt, that it wasn't his blood. Newman and his crew returned to the air, and Wilson walked back along the flight line alone to C Troop's area. He got some clean clothes and went down to the river to wash Simpson's blood off his body. Two weeks later, he was on his way home, but he never got over the nightmares.[65 66]

Blood-spattered console and windshield of Butch Simpson's little bird after crew chief Don Wilson landed the dead pilot's aircraft.

The Laos invasion turned into a rout for some of the crack South Vietnamese troops sent in to cut the trail and destroy the enemy supply centers in and around Tchepone. No one seemed to anticipate the tenacity—or deadly accuracy—of the North Vietnamese defenders, whose leaders knew they were protecting the last lifeline for their troops fighting in the South. Although they never controlled the air above the battlefield, the NVA units engaged in the fight were better armed and more experienced than any single force the U.S. and South Vietnamese allies had encountered in

THE WAR IN INDOCHINA

From hunter to hunted: The body of a U.S. helicopter pilot returns to Khe Sanh

C Troop pilot Butch Simpson's body is borne by fellow Condors to the aid station at Khe Sanh after he was shot aloft over Laos. When this photo appeared in Newsweek magazine, some Condors were infuriated that the media would show the body of a dead comrade, even if it was not identified. This clipping shows the writing of Captain Mac Jones's mother, who drew an arrow on the picture to point to her son accompanying Simpson's body.

more than a decade of fighting. Fighting close to their own soil and supplies, the North committed heavy tanks never used in South Vietnam, long-range artillery, and radar-guided antiaircraft guns. By the time all their reinforcements were in place, the North Vietnamese outnumbered the 17,000 South Vietnamese ground forces in Laos by more than three to one.

Then-Brigadier General Sidney Berry, an aviator and the senior U.S. commander aloft over Laos, told his superiors five weeks into the battle that the Americans were up against "an extensive, sophisticated, well-integrated, highly mobile air defense system." On the ground, North and South Vietnamese "divisions, regiments, and battalions have opposed each other. Both sides have employed tanks, artillery, rockets, mortars, and a complete family of infantry weapon. NVA forces have opposed Allied air and airmobile operations with heavy antiaircraft fire from an extensive, sophisticated air defense system equipped with a wide variety of modern AA weapons ably supported by fires from infantry weapons." It was nothing like the guerrilla war the Americans had been fighting in the South. Berry and other generals likened it to a "mid-intensity conflict" that NATO forces would expect to encounter in a conventional war in Europe or perhaps North Africa. One level higher would involve battlefield nuclear weapons.

The North Vietnamese were not alone in marshaling the best forces they could. The helicopter armada assembled for the attempt to cut the Ho Chi Minh Trail was larger than any deployed before or since, and it faced the most intense ground resistance Army aviators ever endured. The cost in lives and machines was devastating, but defenders of the operation have argued for decades that the losses were small when compared with the hours flown in combat. In 1995, fifteen years after his retirement as a three-star general, Berry gave *The Washington Post* his own numbers for the air war: 107 U.S. Army helicopters "lost to hostile action" during 134,861 hours of flying. Retired Lieutenant Colonel Mike Sloniker, a dogged researcher who spent years studying details of the operation, added two big U.S. Marine CH53 Sea Stallions to Berry's list. Sixty-five helicopter crewmen were known killed, and forty-two were declared missing or "body not recovered." Records show 818 crewmen were wounded. Only one of the MIAs made it home alive. He was a door gunner, Specialist 4 Paul Lagenour, aboard one of four helicopters shot down trying to extract South Vietnamese troops from Landing Zone Lolo on March 19, 1971, as ground troops of the Army of the Republic of Vietnam (ARVN) sought to disengage nearly six weeks into the battle. After the crash, he walked back toward South Vietnam and into an American armored unit's temporary outpost thirteen days later.[67]

Casualties were even worse on the ground for the South Vietnamese, who committed their three best divisions to the fight: the 1st Infantry, the Airborne Division, and the Marines; plus thousands more, including the Hac Bao rangers who flew with C Troop, artillery and tank crews, and support troops of many kinds. The North Vietnamese, who had put up restrained resistance at the beginning, closed on the battered ARVN troops to the end, chasing them down with fierce determination.

On March 9, 1971, a month after the invasion began, President Nguyen Van Thieu was told that elements of the South Vietnamese 1st Infantry Division had reached Tchepone. He quickly approved the operation commander's request to withdraw from Laos. Many units in the battered invasion force were still engaged in fighting, some of them surrounded by North Vietnamese. Getting them out demanded more care and daring than putting them down there in the first place.

Klose, who was fond of turning observations into tactical rules for others to follow, often told students and younger aviators, "There is no mission more difficult than the extraction of troops in combat." It was a corollary of what he called Klose's Law: "Once you start an air assault, all of your options are bad. You're gonna go back in there, or you're gonna write off the landed force, and that is not an option." A helicopter unit that puts troops on the ground is committed from there on out to feed them, resupply them, reinforce them, and—almost always—get them out again.

The American helicopter fleet was losing aircraft faster than they could be replaced, and for many units, the worst was yet to come. The North Vietnamese Army had let the invasion force land with little resistance, but now it knew just where the South Vietnamese were and where the American chopper pilots would have to go to get them out.

The plight of one unit was told and retold by American pilots, including some from C Troop, who tried to save it. The 4th Battalion, 1st Regiment, 1st Infantry Division, landed in Laos with 420 men. When the regiment's first three battalions started to withdraw, the 4/1 was ordered to remain behind and fight a rearguard action to enable the other battalions to escape. At that point, it was the unit deepest in Laos, and Lolo, the firebase it was trying to hold, was surrounded by enemy troops and being hammered incessantly, day and night, by North Vietnamese artillery dug into an escarpment a few hundred yards away. The battalion commander, his deputy, and most other officers were killed the first night the battalion was alone, and the ragged band of survivors, led by a sergeant and linked to the outside by a single field radio, was desperate for ammunition—or a ride out.

American aircrews tried but couldn't penetrate the heavy fire. An ad hoc C Troop crew and a Huey borrowed from another unit were sent out with a mysterious "Sergeant Keith," who was to pinpoint the enemy gun positions and direct a team of Cobras to knock out the guns long enough for U.S. lift ships to extract the remnants of the battalion. The Condors had seen Keith around the troop before, but he wasn't part of the troop, and some said he wasn't really a sergeant, perhaps not even in the military. C Troop was sometimes picked to fly deniable "black ops," cross-border intelligence missions such as prisoner snatches or secret sensor readings performed by Special Forces troops, and the shadowy Sergeant Keith was thought to be associated with those. He was known to be a friend of Major Newman's, and was said to be on his fifth or possibly sixth yearlong tour in Vietnam, which made him one of the longest-serving Americans there.[68] The day of the search he was wearing camouflage fatigues that weren't regular issue and was carrying some sort of special gyro-stabilized binoculars that weren't regular issue either. He was, apparently, attached to the 101st Division's intelligence staff.

Dennis Urick, who had just been promoted to captain, was flying the Huey, seeking to draw fire and give his Cobra escorts their targets. Sergeant Keith was lying on his stomach in the cargo bay behind Urick and the copilot, training his glasses on the long escarpment. Specialist 5 Richard Frazee, the crew chief, was manning a machine gun mounted in the left rear door, behind an aluminum and canvas bench seat that ran the width of the helicopter. The door gunner was behind Frazee on the opposite side of the aircraft, pointing his machine gun out the right side of the ship.

On the third and lowest pass over the ridge, Keith got up and crouched behind the pilot and copilot with one knee on the floor and told them over the intercom to go around again for another look. Just then the cliffside lit up with green and yellow tracers and other colors Frazee had never seen before. Six rounds from a .51-caliber heavy machine gun smashed into the Huey. A white-hot incendiary shell tore up through the floor into the sole of Keith's foot, came out through the top of his knee, went through his wrist and shoulder, and cut his mic cord before it smashed into the helicopter's transmission assembly that controlled the main rotor over their heads. Frazee's first reaction was to return fire. He heard someone yelling, "Who's hit? Who's hit?" and looked down to discover his flame-proof uniform and chicken plate were soaked in blood. At first, he thought he must have been wounded, although he didn't feel anything. Then he turned and saw through the seat webbing that Keith was on his back in the cargo bay with most of his leg missing, except for some tendons still attached to his foot inside his boot. The long bench seat, not usually installed on a "slick," prevented Frazee from going directly from his gun position to the cargo area. Instead, he had to unbuckle his harness and climb outside around the seat into the strong wind and swing back into the bay, a short but difficult maneuver in a shot-up bird. The round that hit Keith was so hot it had melted the fat in his leg, and the floor was slick with fat, blood, and bone fragments. A chunk of his leg had landed in the copilot's lap.

As he reached Keith, Frazee saw that the sergeant was still conscious and looking up at the confused, horrified crew chief. The wounded observer smiled, and both men reached for the rotor tie-down strap, the most obvious and available equipment they could use as a tourniquet. Frazee wrapped it around the sergeant's leg above the knee and tied it tightly to stanch the bleeding. Captain Urick saw Keith's blood splattered on the windshield. Warning lights flickered on the dashboard. The aircraft shuddered, and parts began to vibrate as the damaged transmission slowed the rotor. He descended to low level, knowing it made him an easier target but also giving him a better chance of putting the bird on the ground in one piece if it lost more power. Urick radioed the Cobra pilots to break off the engagement and accompany him back to Khe Sanh.

The gunship escorts swooped down, loosing rockets and cannon fire to make gunners on the ground duck and—they hoped—miss a shot at the wounded Huey. About halfway back to the border, still about fifteen miles from Khe Sanh, Frazee saw a .51-cal open fire below them, and he watched Fuzzy Fausnight's Cobra roll in on the machine-gun pit to distract the enemy gun crew. Fuzzy was out of ammunition, but he used his gunship as bait to draw fire away from the bigger, slower Huey and perhaps intimidate the machine-gun crew enough to keep their heads down. Several warning lights were flashing on Urick's instrument panel, and the ship was vibrating severely as he approached the medical aid station at Khe Sanh, where dustoff pilot Joe Brown had died a month earlier. He made what he called a "controlled crash" onto the landing pad, and soldiers from the aid station dashed out with a litter to lift Sergeant Keith out of the aircraft. Urick saw him flash a thumbs-up at the chopper as attendants carried him into the underground aid station. There, medics worked to stop the bleeding and stabilize him with intravenous fluids before loading him on another aircraft for the short hop east to the 18th Surgical Hospital at the U.S. base at Quang Tri. Doctors at the hospital amputated Keith's mutilated leg and treated his other wounds to prepare him for evacuation back to "the World."

Before nightfall, Major Newman sent Urick and his crew to Quang Tri for some rest, hot food, and drinks at the on-base clubs before returning to Khe Sanh and more flights into Laos the next day. They went to see Keith at the hospital and gave him a Cav hat and a .51-caliber round they found in the helicopter. They had drilled a hole through the bullet and put it on a dog-tag chain for Keith to wear around his neck. The tough sergeant started to cry, making Urick feel worse about the ill-fated mission, but Keith said it was because he was so affected by the camaraderie of the Condors who made him feel like part of their unit. His only complaint, he said, was that his left leg felt cold. Urick glanced down and saw that was the one he had lost.

The part Frazee remembered was getting the ship back to Charlie Troop's landing area and stepping out onto the skid, still covered with Keith's blood and practically immobilized by the trauma of the day. He sat down on the skid pad, the little step that pilots used to climb into their seats, and wondered if he could go on. He'd seen a lot in recent weeks, but this time, he couldn't face going back to work to deal with the awful mess inside the aircraft. As he sat, Condor Six walked by, paused, and gave him an order:

"Get off your ass, Frazee. Clean out that helicopter, and let's get on with it."[69]

Newman knew, instinctively, that the crew chief did not need sympathy, a pat on the shoulder, or the prayer that might have come from the previous troop commander, Captain Sterrett. What Frazee got was not a nudge over the edge into self-pity but an order to keep going. A few minutes later, a couple of enlisted men came by and offered to take over the gruesome task of washing Keith's blood and severed tissue off the floor, dashboard, windshield, and seats to get the Huey ready for the overnight maintenance guys to put it back in flying condition.

He declined to turn the job over to them but agreed to let them help.

Years later, having relived the incident endless times, Frazee recognized that Newman had said exactly what the crew chief needed to hear to keep from losing it on that horrible afternoon.

Studies have shown for years that combat stress is cumulative and that almost all soldiers will break down if they aren't given occasional rest away from the shooting.

Even without hard evidence, U.S. policy in Vietnam was to limit tours of duty to twelve months, broken midway by a week of rest and recuperation in the soldier's choice of several Asian capitals or Hawaii. Bangkok was favored, especially by unmarried soldiers, for the ready availability of bars and female companionship, facilitated and regulated by authorities.

Most divisions also had their own in-country R & R camps, where soldiers could be rewarded with two or three days of rest in a secure rear area. The brief rest periods were to show appreciation for meritorious service, as well as give exhausted troops a break from the fighting. But that weeklong trip outside Vietnam was the stuff of seemingly endless longing before and oft-repeated tales of conquest after. Sex and alcohol were the stuff of legends.

Mac Jones was C Troop's operations officer by the time the unit moved to Khe Sanh to lead the charge into Laos. His R & R was coming up just then, and he had selected Bangkok, a popular destination for unmarried soldiers, but once the operation began and the troop took severe losses, he assumed he wouldn't be spared to go on holiday. The day before the Cobra shootdowns, he had narrowly survived a free fall from five thousand feet after an enemy shell smashed into a control rod leading to the main rotor. He had been flying chase when McLeod and Wilkinson were killed, again when Kane and Casher got hit, and yet another time when they were shot down and rescued, all within a couple of hours. The next day, he was chase again on the first-light mission, and scout pilot Bob Pascoe's loach with a crew chief and another officer aboard got hit by a .51-cal that broke its back and took out the radios.

Jones thought he'd lost another aircraft when he couldn't raise Pascoe on the radio, but the little bird was heading for home, losing airspeed and altitude. Pascoe made it to Khe Sanh and safety, but Jones wondered if he had become a jinx after five ill-starred missions in a row.

Sitting in a Conex box that served as the operations center, Newman asked Jones if he didn't have an R & R coming up.

"Yessir, but we have this battle . . ."

Newman didn't need clinical studies to know the value of that break. He told Jones there wasn't a man in his unit who had spent his whole tour in Vietnam without an R & R and ordered Captain Jones to take his as scheduled. The young officer was so overwhelmed with gratitude that he went back to his own quarters in another Conex a few yards away to think of some way to say thank you. Atop an upturned ammo box that served as his only shelf in the cramped sleeping space were Jones's most precious possessions: two cans of C-Ration Beans w/Frankfurter Chunks in Tomato Sauce.

Helicopter pilots lived better than grunts, but at Khe Sanh, they had little to treasure. There were no showers to wash the powdery red earth from their pores and clothes. Their liquor-stocked clubs and movie nights were left behind in Phu Bai. The days were for flying and getting shot at, the nights for fitful sleep between shelling by North Vietnamese artillery.

Soldiers in the field did their best to tolerate the random, multicourse meals they got in small brown cardboard boxes stamped in black with the words MEAL, COMBAT, INDIVIDUAL. Inside each C-Rats box were four olive-drab tins. They were of varying size and substance, but one thing did not vary: they were always bland, never delicious. The largest can contained one of a dozen main course selections, each with some sort of meat product. Ham and Eggs, Chopped was about the worst. Beef, Spiced with Sauce wasn't much better and practically indistinguishable from the more optimistically named Beefsteak. Pork steak, boned chicken, and turkey loaf may never have made anyone's list of favorites. The smaller tins held bread products such as crackers or hardtack and perhaps cocoa powder or jam, cheese spread, and a dessert that could be fruitcake, fruit cocktail, pudding, or some other sweet.

A plastic spoon was slipped inside the box with an accessory pack that held four American-brand cigarettes and small quantities of matches, chewing gum, toilet paper, instant coffee, sugar, salt, and a powdered cream substitute. That completed each 1,200-calorie meal. Troops quickly learned to save a brilliant little folding can opener known as a P-38 that they could wear on their dog-tag chains and use to deftly open each tin. They cut out air holes on the side of the cracker can to make a stove fueled by a heat tab or a little piece of C-4 plastic explosive. That warmed the meat course and heated water for coffee or cocoa.

Beans w/Frankfurter Chunks were the undisputed favorite main course, and some soldiers were known to squirrel them away to trade later on an informal black market. Mac Jones had saved two.

An individual meal of C-Rats containing the beans and franks prized by Mac Jones and other troops who hoarded or traded for them.

He picked up both cans and walked back to the operations shack.

"Here, sir, I want you to have these," he told Newman.

The commander accepted the offering, knowing how much those two cans meant at a time when even small comforts were few. Jones thought he detected a bit of a tear in the major's eye. Well, he couldn't be sure. But for years to come, even in the last months of Newman's life, an unmarked package would arrive in the mail every now and then at Newman's house in North Carolina or Jones's in Florida. The contents were always the same: two cans of Van Camp's Beanee Weenees, the closest civilian equivalent of Meal, Combat, Individual Beans w/Frankfurter Chunks.

Jones flew to Danang to catch the charter jet that would take him and about three hundred other soldiers to Bangkok for their treasured R & R. While waiting for the flight, Jones tried to rid himself of the Khe Sanh dirt that had dyed his skin red. He would take a shower, go outside, and lie in the tropical sun to work up a sweat, then take another shower. He figured he'd had about a dozen of those before the plane took off. When he got to the Happy Happy Club in Bangkok, he picked girl number thirty-nine from a lineup as his companion for the week. In their hotel room upstairs, she took one look at his naked body and announced: "You dirty." The earth was still oozing from his pores.

"You washy," he ordered.

Back in Laos, the American fliers were dodging every way they could to get in and rescue the beleaguered survivors of the 4th Battalion. There were said to be eighty-eight infantrymen still alive from the original four hundred twenty who had landed in Laos. Most were wounded, and they were out of ammunition, holed up in a huge bomb crater that offered some protection from the guns up on the escarpment. An English-speaking voice on the radio told the gunship the unit was surrounded, and he was throwing out a smoke grenade to show the Americans where to aim. Just put the ordnance on that smoke, the voice said; the ARVN would stay in their holes.

Minutes later, with helicopters already in the air and standing by, a flight of B-52s soaring five miles above the earth dropped hundreds of tons of explosives, some of the bombs falling within a few hundred yards of the embattled 4th Battalion.

A Cobra pilot with the call sign Music One-Six and his frontseater had been flying all afternoon trying to suppress the enemy fire pounding the battalion. When the slicks arrived to extract the troops on the ground, the area was still dark from the smoke of the Arc Light bombing run and Music One-Six offered to guide them in through the haze. The lift birds were led by Captain Rich Johnson, the twenty-three-year-old operations officer from Newman's old unit who had brought his Robin Hoods north from their rubber plantation to join the invasion force. With his commanding officer out of action after being shot down the first day of the operation, Johnson was acting commander of the helicopter company and the first ship going in to pick up the beleaguered South Vietnamese.

"Follow me," Music One-Six told him, "and I'll lead you to the friendlies." The gunship got hit on the way and lost both its hydraulics systems, a fatal wound for a Cobra. "We're going in," the Cobra pilot reported, saying he would try to put it down in a nearby river. Johnson—ignoring his superior officer Klose's tar-baby order—told the stricken pilot to go for it, that his Huey was following right behind him and would pick up the two crewmen as soon as they got out of the aircraft. But Music One-Six couldn't control his ship and realized it was hopeless. He was heading for a stand of tall trees, unable to steer away.

"Good-bye. Send my love to my family. I'm dead."

Johnson watched as the Cobra went in. He could see Music One-Six and his frontseater still inside the chopper. Then it exploded.

"I was ready to go home," Johnson said, sickened by what he had just witnessed. But he got into the landing zone, and desperate soldiers swarmed onto his slick. Johnson told his copilot to lock in his harness and get his hands lightly on the controls in case the aircraft commander couldn't manage. He figured he could take ten or eleven of the Vietnamese soldiers because they were smaller than Americans and had lost their heavy packs. A soldier opened the door to Johnson's cockpit but couldn't climb in. He just clung to the doorpost. Others grabbed onto the skids.

Johnson had developed great respect for the South Vietnamese fighters during the previous month in Laos. Unlike the troops he had seen in the South who seemed to avoid every opportunity for a fight, those in Laos performed as well as or better than American units he had seen. They showed themselves to be superb soldiers, whether forced to be for their own survival or because they were better trained than other units. But their discipline ended at that landing pad. They wanted out.

Johnson cranked up the RPMs on his engine, trying to lift straight up out of the hover hold with trees directly in front of him and no place to turn for ground speed and lift. He watched the torque meter go past the red line at fifty and climb to sixty, but he couldn't maintain altitude. His gunners couldn't fire their weapons because wounded soldiers were clinging to their guns. They were about one hundred fifty to two hundred feet in the air and beginning to fall back down.

The young captain ordered his crew chief and door gunner to kick four people off the aircraft. It was them or everyone. Four men plummeted from the helicopter, falling fifteen to twenty stories to almost certain death. Johnson regained control of the bird and landed at Khe Sanh a few minutes later with twenty-one ARVN soldiers and his own four-man crew.

The second slick into the landing zone picked up the remaining troops but got shot down on takeoff, killing three of the wounded aboard. The crew pulled the two M-60 machine guns out of the downed Huey and set up firing positions on the ground. They had the only working weapons with ammunition, but they couldn't hold out very long. A third Huey from Johnson's lift tried to get in almost immediately after the second was shot down, but it, too, was stitched by enemy ground fire, lost its hydraulics, and had to return to Khe Sanh. Gunships from Molinelli's 2/17 Air Cav rocketed the escarpment, trying to take out a 23 mm antiaircraft gun and suppress other North Vietnamese weapons that were zeroed in on the landing zone. After a few minutes, a fourth lift bird slipped in to pick up the downed American crew and the rest of the Vietnamese on the ground. That one made it out.[70]

Of the four hundred twenty members of the 4th Battalion, 1st Infantry, who went into Laos, thirty-six made it back to South Vietnam. All were wounded, all of them enlisted men. No officer survived.[71]

A BAD HELICOPTER DAY

STEVE KARSCHNER, A NEWBIE SCOUT PILOT, was flying in the observer's seat in Warrant Officer E. W. "Pappy" Papin's little bird. Karschner had celebrated his twentieth birthday two days earlier and had been in Vietnam barely two weeks. Papin was on his third tour flying scouts in Vietnam and, in the vernacular of some of his fellow pilots, was "cleared for weird." He was there to find a fight—and usually did. For Pappy, it was all about locating targets for the Cobras to shoot at, and he fearlessly used himself as bait. Karschner had been working last-light missions and routine reconnaissance with veteran Condor pilots since arriving in-country straight out of flight school. Captain Bob Newman, no relation to the troop commander, sometimes let him fly to practice being aircraft commander. But on this day, July 4, 1971, he was assigned to fly with Papin into the notorious A Shau Valley, and Papin always took the controls. The two men were the eyes, ears, and noses of a heavy pink team—a loach and two

Cobras. Gunky, an oil-slicked old Huey, was the chase ship, following the others and keeping them in sight, ready to swoop down to pick up the crew if one of the aircraft went down. Warrant Officer 2 Michael R. Sherrer, the team leader flying the lead Cobra, was on his last combat mission after eleven months flying snakes in Vietnam and Laos without a scratch. He had survived the Laos campaign, crediting his perfecting of a weaving flight pattern that he believed made his aircraft hard to hit. Now, the twenty-three-year-old team leader had only thirty days left, and it was an unofficial rule that pilots didn't go on combat missions when they were that short unless no one else was available. His frontseater, Warrant Officer Ross Eliason, had been in Vietnam barely six weeks.

The team had just crossed into the valley when Karschner saw the first airframes, crashed and burned on the ground. The little bird was still up pretty high, but he picked out four or five burn spots right away. It was sobering. This was for real. One skeletal airframe was identifiable as a large, fixed-wing plane; the others were helicopters. As soon as he and Papin hit the deck to begin their recon mission, Karschner noticed a cluster of three tubes, about eight feet long, tied together and leaning against a tree. They were dull and silver gray. He reported the sighting to Papin, who swung the little bird around to have a look for himself. Karschner popped a smoke grenade out the window to mark the spot, and the low Cobra in their heavy pink team rolled in and fired a pair of white phosphorus rockets at the marked target. There was no response, but as the choppers followed the road up the valley, Karschner saw lots of evidence of enemy activity: communication wire—commo—stretched along the roadside, sticks in the ground used as road markers, truck treads, footprints, and muddy water, indicating it had been recently disturbed, mostly likely by trucks crossing the stream. He even saw a bridge and heard someone on the radio say it had been rebuilt since they had knocked it out several days ago. Pappy was reporting their findings to the Cobras following them, then abruptly pulled up from only a few feet off the road to altitude—1,000 or 1,500 feet—to prepare for another pass. Papin thought he saw something, maybe a machine-gun nest, and decided to take a closer look. Newbie Karschner's eyes bulged as Papin put the aircraft into a dive. The air speed indicator passed 100 knots in the chopper's gut-wrenching fall, and he heard Papin's voice over the intercom say, "Get ready. We're gonna take fire." They had just leveled off back down on the deck, and Pappy swung into a defensive left turn when the whole world broke loose. Papin saw a trapdoor drop open, and two enemy soldiers opened up on the loach with their .51-caliber heavy machine gun. Suddenly, the place lit up. Pappy said it looked like the Fourth of July. In fact, it *was* the Fourth of July.

Karschner heard the first shot come from behind him and shouted, "Taking fire!" into the microphone at his lips as he tossed another smoke grenade with his left hand. In a split second, gunfire of every description erupted from the brush around them. Looking straight out in front, he could see North Vietnamese soldiers pointing their guns up at his helicopter. He grabbed an M-16 rifle beside him and returned fire, but it took only seconds to empty the clip, and he heard Pappy say, "We're hit."

Karschner was reloading when he looked over at Pappy and saw him maneuvering the aircraft with only the collective. The cyclic was disabled, and he couldn't turn left or steer forward. The pilot pulled the nose up as the little bird slowed down, losing what little altitude it had, and heading for a patch of elephant grass next to a bomb crater with dead tree trunks up through the high grass. The trees had been denuded by Agent Orange.

"Brace yourself," Pappy said. "We're gonna crash." Following his training, Karschner reached down to his left and locked his shoulder harness. He stuck his rifle out the door and emptied another magazine, then pulled it back to pop in another clip. He waited. There was nothing else to do. Peering straight ahead, he saw the sky and realized the little bird's tail must be pointing straight at the ground. They couldn't fly that way.

The aircraft shook some as it fell backward and came down on the tail. It hung there for an instant, then toppled over on its left side—Karschner's side. Dirt came through his doorway as he watched the spinning rotor blade smash itself to pieces in the ground. Karschner's memory of the incident is so acute he could replay it in his head decades later. It was always the same.

The loach's electrically operated minigun, mounted just outside the left door, went off, its Gatling-like barrels pouring bullets uncontrollably into the dirt right under him. The roar was deafening. Karschner tried to cover his face to protect himself from the stones and debris bouncing up at him as the minigun tore through its ammo at four thousand rounds a minute. It could have lasted about a minute. He heard Pappy shouting for him to get out as the pilot himself unbuckled his harness and climbed toward the sky to escape through his open door. Pappy was standing on Karschner and jumping up to get a higher foothold. The newbie shoved him upward and started throwing stuff out the door after him: magazines, first aid kit, anything loose, as he tried to find a way out himself. He could hear shooting outside as he tried to kick out the Plexiglas nose bubble. His leg seemed weak; the plastic wouldn't give. He decided to climb up through Pappy's door, but just before he stuck his head out, he remembered his flight-school emergency training and reached out to pull the fuel valve shut. Then he dove out the door, caught a glimpse of enemy soldiers nearby, and crashed head first onto the ground.

Toting his M-16, Karschner rolled over and crawled to the lip of a bomb crater, where he fired what rounds he had left toward the enemy troops. He maneuvered around to the other side of the downed chopper to get to Pappy, who handed him some more magazines, and they both went back to shooting at the soldiers slowly closing in on them.

From just above and behind him, perhaps fifty yards away, Karschner heard the unmistakable whop-whop-whop of a Huey and looked up to see a machine gunner on the left side of the aircraft pointing the barrel right at him. It was Specialist 5 Ricky Miller, Gunky's veteran crew chief, firing his M-60 barely over Karschner's head at the enemy troops just beyond the downed scout crew.[72]

Miller had been talking to his aircraft commander, Warrant Officer 2 Royce "Crash" Grubbs, on the intercom as they followed the loach and snakes into the valley. Grubbs had been riding Miller for not adjusting his seat properly. The experienced and sometimes obstinate crew chief told his commander sarcastically that when they got back to Phu Bai he'd get a tape measure and record the pilot's height in order to set the seat the way he wanted before the next mission. Grubbs chuckled, and just then Miller heard a loud "voom" as something big shot past the ship. Shoof! Another shot just in front of his face.

"Oh my God," he said, sitting up in his seat and looking out through a sizable hole in the windshield. "You all right, sir?" he asked Grubbs. Grubbs nodded. "I heard this whizzing noise," the pilot said. Miller thought it sounded more like a roar. The bullet from a .51-caliber machine gun had punctured the soundproofing and disappeared into the engine compartment.

"We got any fire lights comin' on?" the crew chief asked in a Texas drawl. He was firing back with his M-60, swinging from front to back to direct his weapon through its full field of fire. A burst of AK fire from the ground went by him as he swung around without letting go of the trigger.

"Takin' fire!" he shouted, tossing out a red smoke grenade to mark the spot for Mike Sherrer's low Cobra. The gunship rushed in to cover the downed loach and suppress the fire aimed up at Gunky. Miller heard a strange sound coming from Gunky's engine.

"Sir, we got any lights on up there?" he asked again and looked over the pilot's shoulder at the instrument panel. He didn't see any warning lights, but he could tell the dash itself was shot up. Nor did he hear any answer. Miller kept shooting. Karschner appeared in his line of fire with as many as twenty North Vietnamese soldiers making their way toward the downed crew and crash site. Miller popped the rarely used gunsight of his M-60 into position to give him more accuracy and aimed just over Karschner's right shoulder, expecting the flyer to get down and give him a chance to take out some of the oncoming enemy.

With no time to pull up and dive on a proper gun run, Sherrer dropped his gunship to about a hundred feet and loosed his rockets and cannon fire, firing explosives at random to distract the enemy and give Grubbs a few seconds to pick up Papin and Karschner. The Cobra zoomed past between Gunky and the valley wall, the NVA soldiers dropped down to escape the shelling, and Sherrer broke to the left, knowing the high snake flown by Captains Bill Childers and Rick "The Mayor" Daly would follow him in with guns blazing to cover Gunky's escape.

Miller, aboard the Huey, realized he couldn't hear the radio anymore. He reached up to change the frequency and saw a big hole in the bottom of the radio.

"Can anybody hear me?" Nothing. Grubbs brought the Huey to a hover with its skids about three feet off the ground as Miller and the door gunner kept shooting from opposite sides of the ship. With no radios, the racket from their two machine guns was all they could hear. Suddenly, an AK-47 round slammed into the cocking mechanism of Miller's weapon and silenced it. He tried to clear the gun, but it wouldn't shoot. Another incoming round hit something and shattered, spitting pieces of hot metal that pierced both of his hands.

He grabbed an M-16 and started to fire above Karschner and Papin as they ran toward him. One man went down in the elephant grass, but the other kept coming until he got to the ship. Miller grabbed him and pulled him in as he fired off a burst from his rifle. Memories differ as to which of the scout's crewmen got aboard first, but Miller helped pull both of them in.[73]

Grubbs tipped the nose down and took off. Old Gunky shook and shuddered as it rose toward the trees. Karschner thought it might fall apart trying to gain altitude, but Grubbs kept the wounded ship low and negotiated between the treetops just above the valley floor.

As the second Cobra dropped into position to cover the escaping Huey, Daly saw from the front seat that Gunky was trailing smoke. The Cobra crew tried calling the slick on the radio but got no response, then called Sherrer's gunship, but nothing came back. The Mayor couldn't tell whether his radios or theirs had been knocked out. He and Childers switched to the emergency guard channel and called for a medevac chopper to come rescue Gunky's crew if they made it to a landing spot in one piece. They hoped someone could hear them.

Major Newman, who was listening to the radio traffic at C Troop headquarters in Phu Bai, picked up broken pieces of a transmission and concluded the team was in some sort of trouble. He grabbed his helmet on his way to the flight line, called for Captain Vehlow, who by then was his operations officer, to go with him as copilot, and barked an order to stand up the Blues in case a ground force was needed. The command ship was in the air in minutes and headed for the valley.

Childers and Daly closed on Gunky to keep the shot-up Huey in sight, and Daly tried to signal Miller from his front seat, pointing back at the smoke pouring out the back of the Huey. When Miller didn't appear to understand, the Cobra pulled up alongside, and

Daly used his grease pencil to fashion a sign that said "FIRE" and held it up in the cockpit window to signal Miller. The crew chief first took it as an order to fire his weapon and said to himself he was already firing the only weapon he had left after the machine gun was disabled. Then he saw Daly pointing toward the tail, and he tapped Grubbs's shoulder to let him know they apparently had a fire in the tail. The pilot, who had lost the hydraulics controlling his steering, already was searching desperately for a hole in the trees where he could put the ship down.

Gunky made it over the east wall of the A Shau and headed north as Grubbs looked for a path through the densely jungled mountains. He made it about five miles when he spotted an abandoned American firebase on a ridge overlooking a valley the Americans called Tennessee. Grubbs went for the firebase as his best option. Karschner was propped on the passenger bench, a fold-down, tubular aluminum frame with canvas stretched across it to make a seat. Ricky Miller leaned over and shouted into his helmet to strap himself in because they were going down.

It wasn't like this in the movies, the newbie said to himself. "Crash" Grubbs fought for control of his aircraft as its power slacked and the hydraulic system failed. The nickname, he pointed out later, came from a door gunner who teased him about returning from a combat assault with a tree branch stuck to the bottom of his aircraft. Grubbs was careful to note he never actually crashed his Huey. But with no hope of getting back to the coast, Grubbs put Gunky on the ground at the old firebase, and Papin, Karschner, and the four-man crew jumped clear of the stricken Huey. Karschner's leg collapsed under him, and he tumbled to the ground next to a row of old foxholes. He had some cuts and bruises but didn't think he'd been hit. The others hastily spread out to form a defensive perimeter around their downed aircraft in case they had stumbled onto an enemy unit again.

Someone found a survival radio in the Huey and called the Cobra orbiting above to let people know they were alive and needed to be picked up.

A C-Troop Huey that usually carried riflemen from the Blues platoon was dispatched to rescue the beleaguered Gunky crew and scouts Papin and Karschner.

It was when Childers and Daly heard the survival signal from Gunky that they realized their own radio was working and that they should have heard Sherrer's Cobra. It must be down out there somewhere. No one had heard from the second gunship for several minutes, and everybody was getting low on fuel. When Childers reported what little he knew, Newman ordered the Childers-Daly Cobra to return to refuel and said he would go looking for the missing gunship in the area where the loach had been shot down.

No one had seen Sherrer's snake since Gunky dropped down to get Papin and Karschner off the ground as the NVA closed in on the downed little bird and its crew. Sherrer shot past Gunky on his gun run, and as he pulled out to the left to make room for the second Cobra to go in, a .51-caliber machine-gun round nailed his transmission. The engine RPM dropped abruptly, then stabilized as oily smoke poured into the cockpit. Sherrer keyed his mic and reported his trouble, but no one heard him, probably because Crash Grubbs was already transmitting his problems on the same frequency.

Sherrer, who was shorter, thinner, and lighter than most pilots, struggled to control his aircraft for a couple of miles, cruising unsteadily above the valley floor. Then the transmission froze, and the RPM dropped to zero. The pilot couldn't pull pitch to get the nose up and had no way to autorotate to soften his landing. The Cobra dropped like a brick. The skids hit first and absorbed some of the shock, but the impact knocked Sherrer's helmet off. Frontseater Eliason fell forward, and his face smashed into the gunsight in front of him, breaking his jaw and knocking him unconscious. Sherrer realized the aircraft was on fire and pulled the break-out knife from its holder and smashed the Plexiglas window beside him. He climbed through the hole and got out.

Short as he was, he was able to reach Eliason's cockpit window because when the skids collapsed the Cobra's fuselage came to rest in the dirt. Sherrer broke the window and looked in to see his copilot's head thrown back in the seat and his face covered with blood. He was barely conscious. Sherrer unclipped Eliason's harness and tugged on him to try to free him from the cockpit. The diminutive team leader weighed a hundred thirty pounds at most. His wounded crewman was at least thirty or forty pounds heavier. As Sherrer pulled from under his arms, Eliason began to kick his feet and tumbled out on top of Sherrer. They sat there for a moment, Eliason asking what had happened, as Sherrer took off his crewmate's helmet and started to crawl away from the burning Cobra before the ammunition started to cook off. A moment later, the aircraft exploded, and fiery pieces rained down on the two men, who did their best to douse the flames closest to them.

Eliason was still groggy and kept asking what happened. Sherrer realized he had lost his .38-caliber pistol in the crash and reached over to take Eliason's sidearm. Eliason also had the Cobra's only survival vest. Sherrer knew the smoke from the wreckage would draw enemy troops, and he started crawling north through the elephant grass to get away from the aircraft with the dazed Eliason following him. They moved slowly at first. Then Sherrer heard voices, faint at first, but getting closer to the burning helicopter. They picked up the pace, and when the enemy started firing into the bush to scare them into giving away their position, both men took off up the valley as fast as they could run. Sherrer found a small animal trail and followed it with Eliason running right behind.

They came to a knoll big enough to hide behind in the elephant grass, and Sherrer paused to go through Eliason's survival vest. The radio was gone, but he got out a flare kit and signal mirror and used his knife to bury the fishing tackle and anything else he figured they wouldn't need. They had been told the North Vietnamese hated Cobras more than anything, so he tore the snake insignia from their flight suits, then realized they had left their helmets and chicken plates behind, a dead giveaway that told the enemy they were alive and probably on the run.

The pursuing troops fired a rocket-propelled grenade every now and then, and Sherrer could tell they were getting closer. Then he heard the sound of a helicopter somewhere off to the north. It had to be a Huey. He caught sight of it and realized it wasn't headed directly toward them but would pass off to the west. He fished the signal mirror out of the survival vest and held it up, reading the instructions in red letters on the back as he held the rectangular device out in front of his face, and tilted it toward the sky:

> "1. Reflect sunlight from mirror onto a nearby surface, raft, hand, etc.
> "2. Slowly bring mirror up to eye level and look through sighting hole. You will see a bright light spot. This is the aim indicator.
> "3. Hold mirror close to the eye and slowly turn and manipulate it so that the bright light spot is on the target.
> "4. Even though no aircraft or ships are in sight, continue sweeping the horizon for mirror flashes may be seen for many miles, even in hazy weather."[74]

Sherrer stepped onto the top of the knoll and tried to hold the mirror steady to let the pilots know it was a mirror and not a muzzle flash.

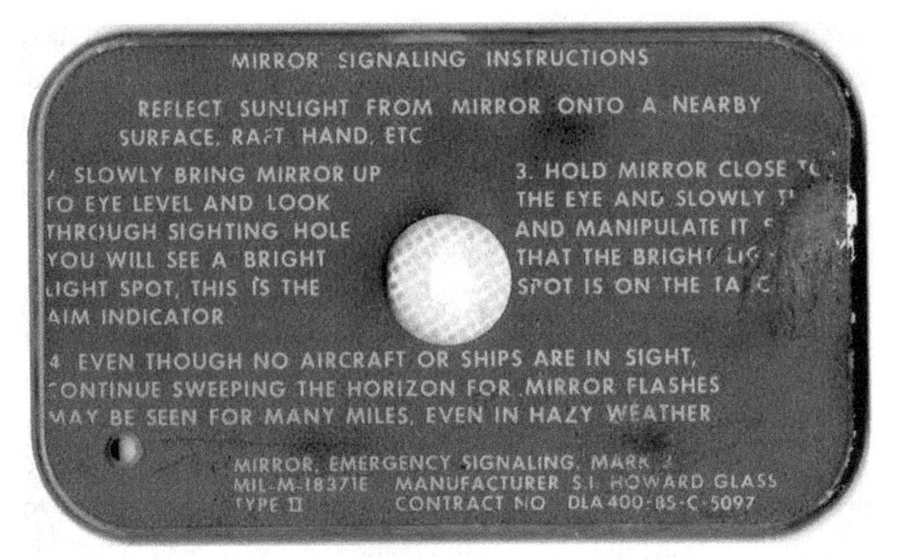

Vietnam-era emergency mirror like the one downed Cobra pilot Mike Sherrer used to signal Newman's passing helicopter.

The Huey started to roll, then leveled out and headed straight for them. Sherrer hoped the crew had spotted his signal and wouldn't start shooting at him. But as it approached and was about to pass overhead, the enemy troops opened fire at the chopper, and the Huey's gunners started shooting back. Sherrer dove off the mound and crouched in the dirt with Eliason as the firefight swirled around them and over their heads. A couple minutes passed with the Cobra pilots keeping their heads down. Suddenly, the elephant grass parted, and Sherrer saw Newman and Vehlow through the windshield, their faces obscured by helmets and dark visors, as the Huey bore down on the knoll where Sherrer was standing. He helped Eliason scramble up the rise, and the helicopter's crew chief reached out and pulled them aboard.

C Troop had just lost three helicopters in a matter of minutes—but not a single man.

Sherrer and Eliason were hospitalized with back injuries at the Army's 85th Evacuation Hospital in Phu Bai. Eliason's broken jaw was wired shut until it could heal, and he was shipped home. Sherrer followed a couple of weeks later when his tour was up.

Pappy Papin, the scout pilot, was propped against the firewall on the floor of the damaged Gunky when he looked down and saw he was sitting in a widening pool of red liquid. He thought he must have been severely wounded, and when he looked for the source, he found a bullet hole through the right shoulder of his chicken plate. The round had gone through, and some small pieces of shrapnel had penetrated his skin, but what he first thought was his own blood on the floor was red hydraulic fluid leaking from the chopper's damaged drive system. Pappy finished three tours in Vietnam and was starting on a fourth when the cav unit he was with at the time was called home in April 1972. A few years later he disappeared into the secretive world of black operations, Delta Force, SEAL Team Six, and what he called "a unit that didn't have a name."

Some of his former colleagues said his exploits included stealing a couple of Russian helicopters for U.S. intelligence and other adventures Pappy would never talk about.

Steve Karschner, the newbie, had a sore back the next morning, and Newman sent him to the hospital for X-rays. The doctors found bits of grit and metal the size of pinheads beneath the skin and cleaned out what they could. He thought the little pieces of shrapnel probably came from the minigun going off or maybe an explosion in the mayhem of the crash. He was picking out pieces of the stuff for years. But Karschner returned to duty and was flying with Papin again over the Rung Rung Valley the next week when a round came up through the floor of the little bird, tore off Karschner's heel, and severed his Achilles tendon. He went through surgery in Danang, then was sent home to Valley Forge General Hospital, an Army medical center in

Phoenixville, Pennsylvania, the closest military hospital to his parents' home. He spent thirteen months there because the wound refused to heal. He underwent more surgery and skin grafts and was released at one point to return to duty. He wanted to take a flight physical and go back to flying, but the flight surgeon just laughed at him. Eventually, while back in the hospital, a new wound broke open and bled in the night. Doctors found an intact bullet lodged behind his knee that had gone unnoticed for months. The X-rays taken earlier had stopped an inch short of the knee.

On August 24, 1972, more than a year after he was wounded the second time, Karschner was discharged from the hospital and released from the Army against his will. He was told he was too physically disabled to serve. Leaving the Army was a bitter disappointment. By his own account, the young aviator got drunk when he was discharged and stayed that way for six months.

He kept the bullet the doctors cut out of him and wore it around his neck for years. What he really wanted to do was to fly again—and he did—but not for the Army.[75]

COMING HOME

AFTER THE NEAR-CATASTROPHE ON JULY 4, C Troop kept fighting the war as other units stood down and packed to go home. To blunt the sting of the failed Laos adventure and consumed by polls showing his popularity slipping at home, President Nixon ordered 100,000 more Americans withdrawn from the war zone before the end of the year. As more units disengaged, U.S. casualties plummeted to their lowest levels since the buildup began five years earlier, but troop morale slid, too. No one wanted to be the last man killed in Vietnam. Drug use, mostly marijuana and heroin, was endemic in many units. Alcohol was cheap, easily available on or off post, and was a growing problem that worried commanders and their top sergeants charged with maintaining discipline. Nor were senior officers and noncoms immune. Enlisted men generally knew which of their officers did dope, sometimes because they shared it. Powerful, locally grown grass was easy to buy and readily smoked by troops alone or in small groups. Soldiers said it gave them the courage to go into combat—or at least made them nonchalant.

Even in Charlie Troop, soldiers openly expressed their opposition to what was more and more obviously a futile fight. A twenty-three-year-old scout pilot, Robert Newman of Fresno, California, told a reporter there was no longer any reason for American involvement in Vietnam. He kept flying because it was his job, but he sympathized with his younger brother, who had applied for conscientious objector status when he registered for the draft. "No family owes the government more than two tours over here," Newman said, "and I've done them both."[76]

The North Vietnamese, emboldened by their rebuff of the South Vietnamese invasion of Laos, resumed operations in the Condors' old stomping grounds, the fog-shrouded mountain walls and twisting river runs of the A Shau and Rung Rung Valleys west of Hue. It wasn't clear yet to U.S. intelligence, but the North was already preparing for a major offensive that it hoped would rout the weakened South Vietnamese forces in the early spring of 1972, when there would be few U.S. ground forces left to stop an onslaught. The cav pilots were among the first to notice the buildup along traditional supply routes like the road through the A Shau and in an area they called the Warehouse, a hidden enemy supply depot. The 2/17 Air Cavalry Squadron went after its usual targets and got into quite a few skirmishes that later analysis showed were the first signs of the coming offensive. Jim Casher, who was a frontseater when he was shot down in Laos with Jim Kane and rescued by Major Newman's tree-cutting chopper, had returned to flying and was promoted to the back seat, the aircraft commander's position in a Cobra. Newman worried that the gun pilot was still in pain from the back injury he got in the shoot-down, but Casher never complained, and however much he hurt, it didn't affect his flying. Pursuing his old enemy with the coolness his comrades would remember for years, Casher knocked out three

.51-caliber machine guns in three consecutive days. That netted him hero status among his fellow flyers, who counted the 51 as the most dreaded antihelicopter weapon in the enemy arsenal. It had been just such a gun that brought down Kane and Casher and probably McLeod and Wilkinson, too, that awful day in February. Rick Daly, "The Mayor," a captain fresh out of flight school and Cobra training when he got to Charlie Troop, flew frontseat for Casher as he learned the territory. What he remembered most about the young warrant officer was that Casher kept a puppy, one of the mongrels soldiers were always rescuing from Vietnamese villages, where dogs were frequently raised for their meat.

The war was far from over, but the Americans were leaving. Newman and the Condors who served under him had seen the hottest fire they would ever know. It was customary in Vietnam for U.S. commanding officers to serve only six months at the head of a unit, then be brought into headquarters and given a staff job, which was safer and less likely to burn them out. It also gave other officers a shot at command, a key ticket to punch on the Army career ladder. Molinelli approached Newman after the Laos operation and offered him a chance to come inside, but Condor Six wouldn't hear of it. Leading C Troop was the best job he'd ever had. He was doing what he was trained to do; he loved it and thought commanding human beings in battle was among the greatest honors he could be given.[77] Molinelli and General Berry agreed to let him keep the troop. He would have volunteered to overstay his twelve-month tour and bring the troop home when it was withdrawn from the war, but he didn't know when that would be. Top military planners wanted to keep the air cavalry in-country as long as they could to gather intelligence and back up South Vietnamese ground forces. In mid-September, Newman and Vehlow left Phu Bai together, but not before the impertinent Six got in a final practical joke for his troops to remember.

With the unit's freshly shined helicopters lined up nose to tail on the tarmac and the troop standing in formation to observe the passing of the guidon from one commander to the next, Newman faced his replacement, Captain Thomas P. Barrett, and stuck out his right hand, as if to welcome Barrett. Barrett, thinking Newman was offering to shake hands, put out his hand to meet the major's, and Newman poured a handful of Vietnam sand into Barrett's palm. Then, with his own hand empty and open, he quickly popped a salute, which military rules and custom dictate must be returned with a like salute. Barrett, uncertain whether to drop the sand or salute with a closed fist, stood awkwardly and embarrassed in front of the men while Newman looked at him with an impish grin. Newman's admirers in the ranks were delighted—but weren't supposed to laugh.[78]

Newman left Phu Bai the next day, September 10, 1971, to fly south to complete the paperwork for leaving the country. But rather than wait for the usual military flight, he bought a ticket on Air Vietnam, the republic's civilian airline, and took a seat among more than 120 Vietnamese passengers on the country's only Boeing 727 jet, the pride of its fleet. The airplane, crowded not only with people but also with their live chickens and all sorts of odorous food and possessions, probably immersed Newman more deeply in Vietnamese society for that ninety-minute flight to Saigon than he had experienced during his two tours of duty.

Vehlow got a thirty-day drop as the drawdown progressed, and he left the troop a day after Newman. They met up at the Bien Hoa Air Base outside of Saigon for a couple of days of paper chasing, drinking at the O club, and reminiscing about the most amazing, dangerous, and exciting time either of them would ever experience. Vehlow, the promising young West Pointer, was headed off to be a general's aide at Fort Belvoir, Virginia, outside Washington. Waiting for him were his wife Kate and a baby boy he hardly knew. Their child was born while Vehlow was in flight school, shortly before the young officer was sent to Vietnam.

Newman could have rejoined Molinelli at Fort Hood, Texas, where the tough, square-jawed commander was putting together an experimental unit with thousands of men and hundreds of helicopters to apply the lessons of Vietnam and devise strategy for the next generation of helicopter warfare. But Newman wanted to go home to Fort Bragg, although it wasn't clear what he would find there. His fling with Gail, the waitress from Virginia he had met before returning to Vietnam, was long over. Flora, his wife of nineteen years, hoped they could put their marriage back together, but she didn't know what to expect. He hadn't written her in months.

His boys, Roger and Ronald, were still living with their mother in the split-level house on Inverness Drive that the Newmans bought new in 1963, when an Army-friendly developer started building houses a few minutes' drive from the military base. It had a carport that they extended to fit two, sometimes even three, family automobiles. Roger had just turned seventeen on September 11, 1971, the day before his father left Vietnam for home. Ronald was fifteen. Both boys were in high school and working part-time jobs to earn spending money. All they remember of the homecoming is that their father didn't stay long. While he was away, he had sent them and their mother star sapphire rings like one he wore himself on his pinky finger. He had bought them at a PX, where soldiers got great discounts on jewelry, cameras, TVs, music players, and lots of consumer products they shipped home for practically nothing. He also sent the boys Seiko watches that were a popular Japanese import at the time, a notch below the Rolex many pilots wore.

Flora and the boys drove to the airport to pick up Newman and rode back to the house with him, but there was no homecoming ceremony because Flo was so uncertain of his plans. They spent the night together, but the next day Newman got a phone call, took it, and left shortly afterward without saying when he would be back.

Flo was pretty sure the affair with Gail was finished—she and Roger had retrieved Newman's car from Gail's driveway in Virginia after he left for Vietnam—but she also knew he had said before he left that he wanted a divorce. He hadn't taken that back. The boys, aware of their parents' fights before their father's departure, weren't sure what to expect either.

During an earlier tour at Fort Bragg, Newman had been friends with a fellow airborne officer named Ken Fogelquist. Fogelquist and his Korean-born wife Kim knew the Newmans socially and had had dinner at their house. It turned out the phone call had come from Kim, supposedly to ask Newman about her husband, who was nearing the end of his Vietnam tour. Major Fogelquist was a top military adviser to the South Vietnamese Airborne Division, which was mauled during the Laos invasion, but like other American ground troops, he was barred from going into Laos with his unit. Given the military bureaucracy and the difficulty of communicating inside Vietnam, it is unlikely Newman and Fogelquist were in regular contact with each other during their combat assignments in different parts of the country.

Newman returned home about midnight and stayed in the house intermittently but hardly interacted with his family. He and Flo drove all the way to Fort Rucker, Alabama, for the flight school graduation of one of his good friends, but they barely spoke to each other on the long trip. Then one afternoon, two weeks after he came home from the war, everything changed in an instant. Newman returned from watching Roger play football, stormed upstairs to the bedroom where Flo was on the phone, and slapped her in the face. He accused her of talking about him to her friends and ordered her never to do that again. Flo, who said her husband had never struck her in all their years of marriage, didn't know what he was talking about. Frightened for what he might do next, she screamed for fifteen-year-old Ronald, who raced up the stairs and got between his parents to separate them. Flo, steaming with anger, stalked down the seven steps to the living room of the split-level and sat down on the sofa. Her husband, still furious, sat in a chair across from her, looked her in the eye and ordered, "Don't you ever say that I hit you, and don't you ever drag Ron into it." She stood up, got her pocketbook, and walked out the door. His words rang in her head for years.

Flo called a lawyer she had consulted about a divorce during Jimmy's fling with Gail, and he told her to report the assault to police. When she hesitated, he told her if she didn't, she would have to find another lawyer.

Fayette County court records show that on September 24, 1971, Newman was formally charged with assault on a female. The boys told their mother that when the sheriff's deputies came to the house the next morning to serve the warrant, they got to chatting with Newman about having served as paratroopers in the 82nd Airborne, as Newman had. It was the early '70s and a classic good-old-boys connection. Instead of taking Newman into custody, the law enforcement officers told him to come to headquarters when he was ready and fill out some paperwork. The record shows only that the case was "NPWL," an abbreviation meaning it was "nolle pros'd with leave," or dropped at the request of the prosecutor. Flo didn't return to the house for months, choosing to stay with various friends while she sought a divorce.

She kept an eye on the boys and the house from a distance and learned from friends that her husband was spending most of his time in a rented house with Kim Fogelquist and her four children while Kim's husband was still in Vietnam. Flo asked her attorney when she could go back home, and he told her she was free to return at any time, as long as she and her husband didn't sleep together if she intended to pursue a formal breakup of the marriage. That was not an issue.

The four Newmans shared the house through the fall, but the major and his wife slept in separate rooms and barely spoke to each other. In November, Newman was appointed executive officer of the 269th Aviation Battalion, a unit comparable in size to the 2/17 Air Cavalry Squadron that Molinelli had commanded in Vietnam. On paper, it was a promotion from commander of a troop to the No. 2 officer in a much larger battalion, but for Newman, it was just a staff job. He wasn't commanding officer anymore, and his job was essentially to manage paperwork and the headquarters staff. Frontline officers described the XO's job as keeping the tent poles lined up. Even in peacetime, when the Army focused on shuffling paper and shining boots, the executive officer wasn't the leader and got none of the glory. Newman regarded it as an assignment with nothing to do.

"I couldn't go kill somebody every day," he lamented years later. "I didn't have a mission of no kind."[79] Not to mention he despised his CO, whom he called "as sorry an officer as ever lived." He would get one more bright moment when the commanding general of Fort Bragg and the XVIII Airborne Corps personally presented Newman with the Distinguished Service Cross he had earned in the rescue of the medevac crew from Ranger North in Laos. The citation described Newman's "indomitable courage, complete disregard for his safety, and profound concern for his fellow soldiers." To Newman, however, it was a consolation prize. From his point of view, the formal military ceremony with its speeches, spit-shined boots, and troops passing in review simply meant he had been passed over for the Medal of Honor that is customarily draped around a hero's neck by the president of the United States. His superiors' recommendation had been reviewed right up through the commanders at every level in Vietnam and by

Admiral John S. McCain Jr., commander-in-chief of the Pacific, and they had unanimously agreed: his feat, brave and skillful as it was, did not rise to "conspicuous gallantry and intrepidity at the risk of his or her life above and beyond the call of duty while engaged in an action against an enemy of the United States," the legal standard set by Congress for the Medal of Honor.

It was about that time Newman stopped coming home at night and permanently moved in with Kim. He never said good-bye to his boys.

Chuck Vehlow, by then an aide to Brigadier General Winfield Scott III at Fort Belvoir, Virginia, outside Washington, D.C., had wanted to go down to Fort Bragg for the presentation of Newman's DSC, but his general had other plans, and Vehlow had no choice but to go along. A couple of weeks later, he took his wife, Kate, to meet the man he revered and followed throughout his tour in Vietnam. Vehlow had never seen his former commander in a peacetime environment, and Newman seemed changed in ways the captain did not understand. The two couples went to the Officers Club on post that afternoon and stayed for dinner. Newman seemed uneasy, nervous. The confidence Vehlow had so admired under fire was gone. Vehlow thought he looked agitated about something, and Kate thought he treated his lady, Kim, like a second-class citizen. Even in the early '70s, when the women's movement was in its infancy and the Army had not yet discovered it, officers and gentlemen weren't expected to be rude and dismissive of their women. The foursome spent some time together the next day, again at the O club. The Vehlows considered it odd that they were not invited home or somewhere else, but there was no talk of that or of Kim and Jim's future. Again, Kate was put off by her husband's hero. Vehlow had always spoken so highly of him, worshiped him even, but she couldn't see it. She was the wife of an Army officer and knew something about discipline, but she refused to accept her husband's attempts to explain about Newman. "Look at the way he treats his wife," she said, unaware that Kim was not his wife. She saw a different person than her husband did and thought he was a scumbag. Newman was consistent, though: he treated all his women like that.

Neither of the Vehlows realized they were seeing Newman as his life was imploding. Despite the clues they picked up in his behavior and loss of confidence, they didn't connect the dots, and he told them none of it.

Two weekends later, on February 6, 1972, not quite five months after he returned from the war, James Taylor Newman, thirty-six, and Kimberley Ann Fogelquist, thirty-seven, were married in Dillon, South Carolina, a notorious marriage mill. Known as "Little Vegas," Dillon was an hour's drive south of Fort Bragg and made itself a favorite stop for soldiers in a hurry. A Sunday wedding before a probate judge took about ten minutes with few questions asked, even important ones. Neither Newman nor Kim had bothered to get a divorce first.

Instead of a fresh start, however, the major's life quickly spiraled downward as if his tail rotor had been severed in flight. On March 3, he and Kim were arrested by North Carolina authorities and charged with bigamy. A few days later, two agents from the State Bureau of Investigation showed up at the Newman house on Inverness and asked if Flo had a photograph of her husband. Her whole family from Georgia was staying with her because an older sister had died in Fayetteville, and the family had come up for the funeral. The detectives warned Flo her life could be in danger and offered to take her and the boys to Fort Bragg to keep them safe while they investigated an allegation that Newman intended to burn her house down. Armed with the photo she gave them, they arrested him later that day on a charge of conspiracy to commit arson.

The *Fayetteville Observer* reported that a taxi driver named Willie Douglas Elliott told police that Newman and an unidentified second man approached him and offered to pay him "a large sum of money" to kill Major Fogelquist, Kim's husband, and burn down the house where Flo and her two sons were living."[80] The newspaper identified Kim as "a Korean who married her first husband in the office of the mayor of Seoul." Flo said the cabbie told police he was instructed to take a five-gallon can of gasoline to the house, pour the liquid on the living room floor above the furnace and set it afire. The day after Newman's arrest, agents added a charge of conspiracy to murder Fogelquist. The arson supposedly was to take place while Flo and her family were attending the funeral to avoid injuring them, but the cabdriver was told to go from there to a house where Fogelquist was staying and finish him off. Fogelquist had returned from the war by that time to find his marriage ended and his children living with his ex-wife. The man said to be with Newman during the attempt to hire the taxi driver was never identified.

By the end of the month, a grand jury handed up an indictment charging Newman with two counts of conspiracy and one of bigamy, all felonies under North Carolina law.[81] In a plea agreement with the local prosecutor, Newman admitted to the bigamy charge, and the conspiracy counts against him were dropped. He was sentenced to serve between two and three years in state prison, but the sentence was suspended on condition he complete three years' probation without violating the judge's terms, one of which was that "he not threaten, harass or otherwise abuse his present wife Mrs. Newman." He was ordered to pay a $500 fine and court costs.[82] Kim Fogelquist also pleaded guilty to bigamy and was sentenced to probation as well.

Ron Newman, the major's younger son, had turned fifteen the summer before his father came home from the war. Ron missed him, and when he heard that Newman was staying in a house on Shasta Street, decided to go over to see his father. Ron knocked on the door. Major Newman answered the knock, but when he saw Ron standing on the stoop, he told him they had nothing to talk about and closed the door in his son's face. Ron turned away, hurt and bitterly angry. He encountered his father inadvertently once several years ago, but he never went to see him again—until he watched the burial at Arlington, forty years later.

MOVING ON

NEWMAN'S CAREER AS AN ARMY OFFICER SHONE AT FIRST, despite the turmoil in his personal life.

Before they left Vietnam, then-Brigadier General Sidney Berry, who had steered U.S. operations during the Laos invasion, told Newman he had a good shot at eventually earning a general officer's star, perhaps even two, because he had so distinguished himself as a leader in combat. There was, however, a big stumbling block. Newman had not gone to the U.S. Military Academy at West Point and was technically a "reserve officer." Reserve officers, who obtained their commissions through ROTC, Officer Training School, or directly from the enlisted ranks, as Newman had, rarely got promoted that high. Despite his having been on active duty his whole career and having impressed his superiors at every level, Newman wasn't part of the Regular Army. The RA fraternity protected its own, and its members regarded themselves as the keepers of Army tradition and culture. They were also protected from personnel cutbacks and filled practically all the slots in the rarified, star-studded world of the generals. The distinction between reserve and regular officers has since been abolished, but in those days, to make Regular Army, Newman had to win the approval of a special selection board at the Pentagon. That could be arranged.

Newman's last Vietnam-service OER, the obligatory Officer Efficiency Report completed by every officer's superior, gave him perfect marks and noted that "he is applying for a Regular Army commission." Lieutenant Colonel Archie A. Rider, who had succeeded Molinelli as commander of the 2/17 Air Cavalry Squadron, noted in the report: "He is the type of young officer the Army needs to retain. I strongly recommend that he be integrated into the Regular Army immediately and that his career be carefully monitored to insure optimum development of his potential, which is great." The report was endorsed by Brigadier General John G. Hill Jr., a decorated brigade commander who had followed Berry as assistant division commander of the 101st Airborne Division. The recommendations reached Army headquarters after Newman got home. In January 1972, the Army approved Newman's request for certification that he had completed the equivalent of two years in college, helping patch another hole in his résumé. On February 29, 1972, General Berry—having won a second star and been promoted to chief of Army personnel, wrote the president of the Regular Army selection board to recommend Newman. The major could hardly have hoped for a better patron. Berry, an expert aviator himself, quoted his own earlier evaluation of his former subordinate: "Major Newman is one of the two most outstanding air cavalry troop commanders I know. He leads by personal example; coordinates fire and maneuvers with rare professional skill and effectiveness; and accomplishes with calmness, poise, skill, and efficiency the most difficult mission. He is a soldier, fighter, leader, officer, individual of the highest quality. Recommend he be integrated into the Regular Army and given civil schooling and sent to CGSC," the Army's Command and General Staff College, which trains officers for senior leadership posts. In a quick, more personal "Dear Jim" letter written the same day, Berry told Newman, "I am happy to recommend you for commissioning in the Regular Army. . . . Should you pass through Washington, stop by to see me." Newman's path seemed blessed.

On March 8, the Army's adjutant general wrote that his Regular Army application had been received and would be considered. That was the day the major was arrested and charged with conspiracy to commit arson. Newman's career stopped dead in its tracks.

Army bureaucracy moves as slowly and deliberately as its funeral caissons, but six months later—after he had struck his plea deal and been put on probation—Newman was notified he would be involuntarily retired from the Army. No reason was given in the pro forma letter to the post commander that put him and three others on the cut list. Even if the Army hadn't been shedding officers in its post-Vietnam retrenchment, Newman's felony conviction for bigamy was reason enough to strip him of his uniform.

Available records offer few clues to what happened to Newman in the ensuing months, but he spent part of that time in Womack Army Hospital on the base, where he was a patient when orders came from the Department of the Army to release him, retired from active duty. He had managed to stave off being cashiered while he qualified as "permanently unfit for duty by reason of physical disability" due to the combat wound he suffered more than six years earlier. He was classified as 40 percent disabled, which entitled him to collect veterans disability benefits as well as his retirement pay. That percentage of disability would rise in subsequent years as new health problems arose that could be traced to Vietnam. Shortly before orders were cut placing Newman into the retired reserve, his commanding officer at the

269th Combat Aviation Battalion wrote him a "To Whom It May Concern" letter attesting to Newman's more than twenty years of service to his country. "His performance of his duty during the entire time that I have been associated with him has been singularly outstanding and that of a true professional," Lieutenant Colonel Richard L. Lincoln wrote in a canned letter that followed Army form. "He exhibits those traits of leadership and character that the rest of us try so hard to emulate. I have complete confidence in Major Newman and it is without hesitation or qualification that I strongly recommend him for any position of trust or great responsibility that he might seek."

Armed with little more than that paper, James T. Newman drove out of Fort Bragg and into civilian life on February 23, 1973, after twenty-one years, one month, and twenty-five days of service. Within a few weeks, he landed a job as an insurance salesman after a private investigator told his prospective employer he "found no reason why your applicant would not train favorable in this line of work. He is [described] as an individual endowed with ambition, well groomed, meets the public well." The private eye learned of the bigamy case but not the other charges and accepted Newman's story that he had been separated for "several years . . . and was under the opinion that the divorce had been finalized through litigation action taken while overseas."

John Hancock Mutual Life Insurance Company was satisfied. Newman took a quick course in selling insurance and was hired as an entry-level agent. He was good at it, boasting in a résumé that he sold more than one million dollars in policies every year for three years. He was promoted to sales manager, hiring, training, and sometimes firing young agents for the office, as well as continuing to sell policies on his own.

In a curious addition to the written intelligence about him, Newman had his handwriting analyzed, probably at the behest of Hancock, by a specialist who was well known in the insurance business for helping salesmen overcome fear. The late Frank G. Budd of Phoenix, Arizona, called himself a certified master graphoanalyst and believed that by analyzing someone's handwriting, he could evaluate the person's personality and determine the person's ability to succeed in a particular line of work. Budd dictated his findings into a tape recorder and sent them to Newman on an undated cassette that wished him well. Budd apparently never met Jim Newman, and whatever Newman wrote to him or gave him for analysis is lost. "Emotionally you are fine, very normal," the analyst assured him. "Your feelings are highly responsive to stimulus, meaning that you feel quickly, you pick up signals from others quickly, and you send signals of your own quickly. Your feelings are consistent. They are deep and lasting. You are emotionally stable, and to some extent you are emotionally motivated; you are a plunger, you get involved with the people to whom and with which you respond. You're not always verbally spontaneous, and sometimes there is a conflict between the signals that you're sending and what you're saying. And the reason we care is that these scared kids you're gonna be contracting are going to require some reassurance and when you send conflicting signals, they find that very distracting, very rattling. That's not reassuring to 'em. So it'll be important, Jim, that as a general agent, you feel comfortable with going ahead and expressing your honest feelings, even when you're afraid. . . . In the area of mental processes, your mind is good, you're sharp, you catch on quickly, and you analyze pretty well. You're receptive to the ideas and opinions of others without being easily influenced. You do pay attention. You're not detail oriented per se. There's a lot of restlessness. And you get impatient. You are articulate. You do show imagination. You probably train without repetition. . . .You like to get up and get out there and get your feet wet. And you learn more by doing than you do out of books. Your judgment's basically sound, notwithstanding the fact you're a little bit impulsive at times, and that's fine. That has to do with emotional commitment.

"In the area of capacity for achievement, your drive level is high. Your goals are practical. Your self-motivation's above average. Your determination's good. I want to add here you do have a tendency to try too hard to control your environment, to control what's happening to you, and I would build a case right now for developing a little more trust in your own mentality before you take on a General Agency... [B]e awfully careful that you don't assume responsibility for other people. Don't try too hard to control everything that's happening to you. You control what's happening directly to you. You control your choices and try to avoid controlling theirs. In the area of defenses, your integrity is very much intact. I do not identify any hostility characteristics. I think you're well socially adjusted. You certainly have been honest with me in your written correspondence, but from a verbal standpoint, you have a tendency to check what you think people want to hear. In other words, uh, if your boss is the person, supervisor, whoever you are working for, asks you how you feel about something, you have a tendency to find out how he feels about it before you tell him how you feel about it. You're gonna have to develop more directness with your agents. They are gonna wanna know what you think, and you're gonna have to be able to just tell 'em, right or wrong, and that goes back to being willing to be yourself. So, a little more confidence in your own mentality, a little more willingness to be yourself, and I think the desire to control everything that's happening around you will, if not disappear, at least dissipate. Your drive level's good, your integrity's intact, your judgment is sound. You are emotionally capable of commitment, and I don't see any reason in the world you can't run a successful General Agency. My very best personal wishes to you. If you have any questions, give me a call, Jim. My number's on the label of this cassette. For our purposes at this time, this will be the end of this tape."[83]

Records at John Hancock, since absorbed by Manulife Financial, the giant Canadian insurance and financial services company, show that Newman worked for John Hancock for about six years.[84] He spent most of that time in Fayetteville, but in 1979, to take advantage of a promotion to a larger market, he moved his family to Stone Mountain, Georgia, to sell insurance in the burgeoning Atlanta metropolitan area. It may have been more lucrative, but it was an awful move that took a toll on his marriage and bred powerful resentment in his fifteen-year-old stepson, John Fogelquist, who hated leaving his high school buddies and a girlfriend in North Carolina. John's older sisters had grown and moved out by that time. John and Jay, who was then five, were the only children still at home. The experiment lasted only a year or so, and the family moved back to Fayetteville, where Newman decided to try pushing products he loved. He went to work for a Buick dealer. He had a lot of cars over time, but he had a special thing for big, sporty Buicks.

Not long afterward, his younger brother Jack drove through Fayetteville on his way to Washington, D.C., for a family vacation because Jack wanted to show his brand-spanking-new Pontiac to his big brother. Jack had grown up worshipping Jimmy, who joined the Army the year Jack was born. The godlike figure he remembered from boyhood was a tough, no-nonsense soldier who jumped out of airplanes and usually wore a uniform when the family got together at Fort Campbell or Fort Bragg. Then Jimmy went off to war and got shot in his helicopter, and Jack didn't see him until he was healed and had a built-up boot on one foot. Jimmy, as Jack and the family knew him, came home to Newnan—and brought along a woman Jack's age. That was Gail, just before Jimmy went back to Vietnam, and it was the first time Jack noticed a change in his brother. The tough disciplinarian who, Jack remembered, whipped his own boys for the tiniest infractions, was acting light-hearted and happy-go-lucky with his pretty new girlfriend half his age. He was funny, full of quips that made people laugh, not as serious and aloof as he had been before. Jack liked the new, good-humored brother, but the family was nonetheless scandalized that he brought that woman who wasn't his wife home to Georgia.

The stop on the way to Washington came years later, after Jimmy had returned from Vietnam the second time, was married to Kim, and had gone into the automobile business. Kim was cooking dinner and didn't have some ingredient she needed. Jack jumped in his new car—just four hundred miles on the odometer—to run to the store. On his way out of the supermarket parking lot, another car bashed in the side of the Pontiac. Jimmy was sales manager of the Buick dealership at the time and told his disheartened little brother not to worry, they'd take the car down in the morning and get it rushed through the body shop. The two General Motors brands were in the middle of the GM lineup, although Buick occupied the higher rung, just below Cadillac, while the Pontiac (since discontinued) ranked one step above the more affordable Chevrolet. The next day, Jack climbed in from the passenger side because the caved-in driver's door wouldn't open, and Jimmy slid in next to him. They stopped at a red light behind a truck rigged to carry huge sheets of glass, and while they were waiting for the light to change, they heard tires screaming behind them just before a moving truck caromed into the rear of the Pontiac and sent it crashing into the glass truck. The truck's load exploded into a million shards that scattered across the road. The Newman brothers surveyed the disaster around them, got back in the Pontiac, which was still drivable somehow, and drove to the Buick dealer. With three insurance companies now involved, they got Jack's wreck of a car declared a total loss, and Jimmy sent his little brother home with a brand-new Buick. It was the car Jack had wanted to begin with but couldn't afford.[85]

The brotherly relationship eventually dissolved in a long-running dispute that began over a personal debt traceable to the time Jimmy got in real trouble and Jack helped bail him out. When Jimmy was arrested during the tumultuous end of his first marriage, he was released on his own recognizance the first time, but the next week, when the conspiracy charges were filed against him, bail was set at $10,000, and he was held in jail. He called his father, who had always adored him, forgiven him, and boasted of his accomplishments. His father said he would go to the bank and borrow the money on the family house, which was paid for. Jack thought it was too big a risk for his parents to take when they no longer had much income of their own, and he and his sister Elaine went to a bank vice president they knew and borrowed the money instead on their own signatures. They agreed to make the payments until Jimmy could take them over. Jimmy's father, who hadn't had a drink for at least six months before his favorite son called for help, went straight to the bottle. Jack remembered that the experience sent the old man on a bender that kept him blotto for days. He finally landed in the hospital to dry out. A few months later, Elaine's husband lost his job, and Jack, who was working as a computer operator at the Playtex factory, got stuck paying off the loan by himself. For years, Jack tried to get his brother to pay him back, but he said Jimmy went on with his new life and ignored Jack's requests, even the written appeals. The brothers remained friendly for several years, and Jack gave up trying to recoup the money. They visited each other several times in North Carolina or Georgia, and Jack watched Jimmy's marriage to Kim degenerate into shouting matches and fury. Eventually, after their parents died in the mid-1990s, Jimmy cut Jack out of his life as he had done with his two oldest sons.[86] He claimed he had only one sibling, Elaine, and pretended his sister Patricia and brother Jack didn't exist, just as he denied having had any children born before the Vietnam War.

Elaine brought up Jack's name once to Jimmy, and he cut her off. "He's your brother," Jimmy said. "I don't have a brother."[87]

THE BOYS

When Newman remarried Kimberley Fogelquist—legally—after their divorces were final, he walked into a custody battle over his new wife's four children by her first husband, Major Ken Fogelquist. The three oldest children were girls; the youngest was a boy, John, who was eight. At first, John liked the new arrangement. His stepfather made his mother laugh, in stark contrast to her frequent angry outbursts at his father, and John and his sisters had a peaceful, happy home. But not for long. One day a couple of deputy sheriffs showed up at the door with a court order, John's mother put his clothes in a suitcase, and the officers whisked him away and took him to live with his father in Virginia. The little boy was plopped down in a strange house already occupied by his father's new girlfriend and her two children. He was confused, sad, and lonely, but he saw no way out when his new family enrolled him in the local elementary school, seemingly for good. He didn't know that, back in Fayetteville, the

Newmans had hired a lawyer and went to court to fight the judge's order giving John to his father. About three months later, the boy was sitting in the living room when he heard a knock on the door. It was his mother and Jim Newman, waving court documents authorizing them to take John back to North Carolina. He and his new father figure bonded instantly. John was glad to go home. Jim spoiled him from the start. As arranged in the Fogelquists' divorce settlement, the girls went off to California with their father, who retired from the Army and was starting a new business, and John became the center of attention in the home of his mother and stepfather. Jim taught him to ride dirt bikes, gave him a motorized minibike, and showed him not only how to ride it but also how to fix it when something went wrong. They did lots of boy stuff together, and John loved it. Those happy times were cut short, however, just when they seemed the best.

Kim was pregnant, and while she could still travel, Jim rented a Winnebago motor home to take the family to Disney World for a vacation. John could hardly believe his good fortune. Disney World was a nine-year-old's dream of Nirvana. But on the way down, the muffler fell off the vehicle, and the family had to stop for repairs. The setback triggered a stressful outburst in John's mother, who started fussing at her husband in an unrelenting, escalating attack that turned into arguing, then shouting, even screaming. It was the first time John saw them fight, and it reminded him of his mother's bad days when she would light into him without warning or provocation. He felt sorry for Jim because she was just giving him hell, and the little boy couldn't see that he'd done anything wrong. It was destined to get worse, but John couldn't have known at the time that his mother's episodic tantrums were an inevitable symptom of the bipolar disorder that plagued her the rest of her life.

When they got to Orlando, Kim was still struggling with her mood swings and pregnancy, so Jim took John around the vast theme park. John loved that part and started thinking of himself as Jim's new son.[88]

On March 3, 1974, John's status as No. 1 son ended in an instant. At Cape Fear Valley Medical Center in Fayetteville, Kim gave birth to her fifth child, the first by her second husband. The father named him James Taylor Newman Jr., and in that moment, the retired Army major, war hero, and combative, trouble-making returnee James T. Newman changed again. The whipping belt that Roger and Ronald knew so well as little boys never came out again. The military discipline that had taught them right from wrong disappeared. The distant father who grew so remote from his first two sons that he came to deny their existence formed a bond with his third son that lasted the rest of his life. Jay, as the boy is known, grew up in an angry, emotion-fraught household, but to his father, he could do no wrong—and he worshipped his father for it. John, who had just turned ten a few days earlier, sensed immediately he had slipped from the catbird seat. Baby Jay was Jim's focus from then on. He could do no wrong. John thought Jay was spoiled beyond spoiled, got every new toy and unlimited doses of his father's attention. John doesn't remember feeling jealous or angry about being displaced; Jim included him, too. But there was no question which kid came first in his father's eyes.

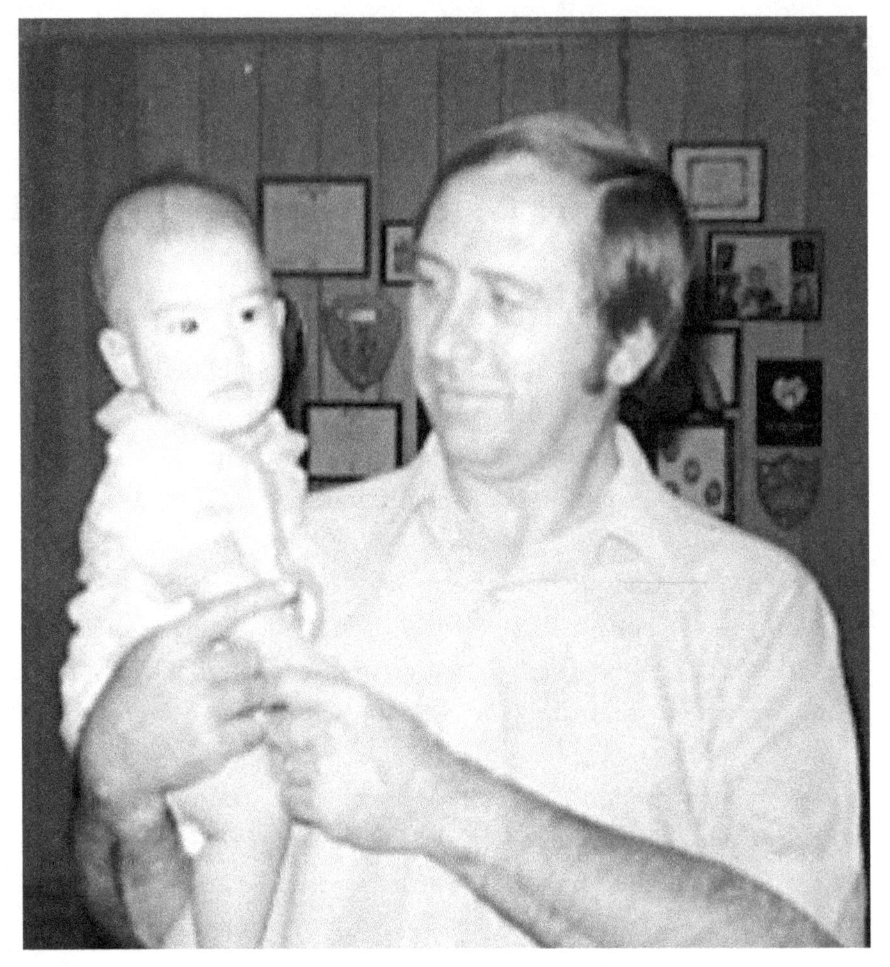

Jim Newman with his last-born son, Jay, in 1974.

John did learn mechanics from his stepdad, something Jay never cottoned to, and Jim instilled in him a lifelong love of fixing whatever broke. Like Jim, he assembled a tool collection that filled a sizable shed; he prided himself on having a tool to meet any need. For John's sixteenth birthday, Jim gave him an ancient Oldsmobile Starfire he bought from his sister in Georgia for five hundred dollars. John adored the relic of a car and especially the hours and hours he and Jim spent together over several months rebuilding the engine, replacing the interior, and restoring the body. Jay was getting most of the attention by then, but John basked in having Jim working beside him on that car. It meant everything to John. One Friday night, when the car was about finished, Jim took John down to a local electronic appliance store "just to look around." John desperately wanted a car stereo for his new wheels, and Jim told him to pick one out. Newman pulled a wad of cash out of his pocket, paid for it, and gave the unit to John, who installed it in the Olds the next morning. The teenager spent the rest of the day driving around Fayetteville just listening to that stereo.

Newman's tough side came out twice and reset John's course in ways he never forgot. While they were living in Stone Mountain and John was feeling sour and sorry for himself, he said something rude to his mother in the kitchen while Jim was there. John doesn't remember what words prompted the response, but Jim jumped up out of his chair and stood right in the boy's face, his eyes burning with rage only a couple of inches away.

"You never speak to your mother like that again," the ex-soldier ordered. "If you don't lose this attitude, I'm going to adjust it for ya, and you're not gonna like it."

Newman never laid a finger on him, but John saw in his stepfather's eyes that he wasn't kidding. The boy backed down, changed his attitude at that very moment, and gained a whole new respect for Jim Newman. Several years later, he saw that flash of temper again. John was in his early twenties and working with Newman to assemble a single-bay garage from a kit behind a used-car lot Newman owned at the time. It was hot, patience was thin, and the young man said something he can't remember but acknowledges was disrespectful.

"By then I was an adult and figured I could do what the hell I wanted to do, and I crossed him, and he got right pissed off," John said. "Tempers flared, and I smarted off, and he had a hammer in his hand. He was nailin' something, but when I saw that same look in his face that I had seen years earlier—and this time he had a hammer in his hand—coincidentally, I said to myself, 'Well, that's not a good combination,' so I took off. I ran and got in my car and left.

"The next day I saw him at work, everything was fine. I did apologize." Newman was a chain-smoker in those days and was puffing away without saying anything when John said he was sorry. "He accepted it, but Jim's not the type—he's just got a rough exterior—he's not the type to say, 'Okay that's fine, don't worry about it.' He just let me say my piece, and by his not saying anything, it's his acceptance. You have to assume that he's accepted your apology."

John and Jay referred to each other as brothers, and they were friendly, although their ten-year age difference meant they shared few of the same experiences, except the Friday night excursions with Jim to the local Baskin-Robbins for ice cream. Jay didn't know Jim had other sons of his own until one day, when he was about twelve, his mother broke the secret. In a fit of fury at her husband, Kim told Jay he wasn't Jim's only son. It was revenge for her husband's fling with yet another woman. There were many in those days. Jay thought his parents never should have gotten married since they fought so much. He couldn't remember them happy together. His mother, who had been raised in her native Korea but defied her family to marry an American soldier and go home with him, never gained her balance in the United States. Her own children, as they grew to adulthood, learned to recognize her emotionally precarious state and to keep their distance. Jay inherited his mother's dark hair. A hint of her Asian eyes in his barely discloses his ethnic heritage. He speaks like his father, though more correctly, and the lilt of his North Carolina accent is more gentle than Jimmy's rural Georgia vernacular.

Jay adored his father as long as he could remember, and as John said, his father spoiled him no end. Jay, of course, never knew the soldier Jim had been. The man he grew up with was funny, easy on him, always ready with a cool car to ride in and a joke for his son's playmates. He seemed to know everything about cars and kept a pocketful of cash in case he wanted to buy Jay and his friends a treat or a gadget. Jay didn't take to mechanical work as John had, but he loved the dirt bikes, motorcycles, and fast cars his father provided. He got toys and attention without limit, sometimes tested the patience of school authorities, and when he got in trouble, he knew his father had his back. Jim told a story about giving Jay a motorcycle well before the kid was old enough to ride it legally. Soon afterward, the father watched Jay race home, ditch the bike, and run to hide out back. The cops showed up, and Jim walked out to meet them, chatted for a few minutes to give his son time to get away, and never let on he knew the kid was hiding somewhere nearby. Jay apparently had been spotted driving recklessly or out of control but hadn't hit anything. When he was old enough, he got his license.

His father rarely, if ever, barked at the boy or got angry, at least as Jay remembers it. The boy grew up thinking of his dad's presence as his safe harbor from a mother who was frequently furious about something and often took it out on him. She was verbally abusive to Jay and got physical with Jim. Jay's parents lived under the same roof but went for long periods without speaking, and when they did talk, they often fought. Kim, in her uncontrolled rages, would attack Jim and throw things at him, from plates to books to lamps, whatever was at hand. Jay often sought refuge with his neighborhood buddies, who became lifelong friends.[89]

The boy learned his father had a girlfriend when he was about five years old. His mother found out about the affair and ranted at the little boy about his father's infidelity. It wasn't long after that Jim took Jay to meet the girlfriend. He met another one a couple of years later. Then, one evening on his way to take a bath when he was still a little boy, Jay heard his parents talking in the den and stopped outside the door to listen. His mother was crying, his father was apologizing, saying he was sorry about the other women. That night they agreed to reconcile, or at least stay together for Jay's good. And they did, although Jim often had another woman on the side.

Jay liked to think of himself as something of a troublemaker, encouraged and defended by his father. Before he was old enough to drive, he and some friends plotted an attack on a local mall. They rode their bikes into the shopping center, climbed onto the roof and shut down the power for the entire complex, making good their escape before the police could catch them. It may have been a foolish and costly prank, but nobody got hurt. Years later, Jim was unabashedly proud the boys had pulled off the caper. It was the kind of thing he might have done himself at that age. Jay also rode motorcycles and four-wheelers illegally on the streets of Fayetteville, and neighbors called the cops more than once. But Jay hardly could be described as a juvenile delinquent. He played hooky but kept his grades up in school because he knew his father expected him to.

Jay Newman

Although both his parents smoked cigarettes constantly throughout his youth, Jay couldn't stand the stinking blue cloud that hovered in his house and never tried a cigarette—or marijuana, either. Jim taught him to drive long before he was old enough to get a license and took him on the back roads, sometimes with a couple of Jay's buddies in the backseat. He showed them how to smoke the tires and leave dramatic skid marks, but he also taught Jay how to handle a fast car, like the souped-up Mustang GT 5-liter Jim gave him for his sixteenth birthday. Jim never raised his voice in his tutorials, but if Jay popped the clutch and caused the car to jerk forward, he'd hear Jim complain, "Goddamn! My neck's gonna hurt tomorrah."

Jim stayed in the home until Jay went off to college, then packed and left the house. Looking back on it years later, with a wife and children of his own, Jay wished his father hadn't stuck it out all those years for him. "I know I'm the reason that he stayed with her and they stayed together," he told me. "He sacrificed a lotta years for me that I wish he hadn't done. He was very unhappy. They lived under the same roof, but it was really a screwed-up situation for a kid to grow up in."

As for Jim's older sons, Roger and Ronald grew into adulthood without a father or his support. He simply cut them out of his life. Both struggled for years as a result.

Roger's earliest memories go back to his father's days as a gung-ho paratrooper. Jimmy had graduated from jump school at Fort Benning right after basic training and, following service with a tank battalion at Fort Bragg, he was assigned to the 187th Airborne Regimental Combat Team, the unit he expected to serve with in Korea before the armistice. The airborne demanded that its soldiers look sharp at all times, with uniforms pressed and boots shined to a mirror finish. Roger watched his father push his feet into fatigues so stiff with starch that the pant legs stuck to each other as if they were one. Paratroopers wore high, black leather jump boots polished endlessly with dabs of Kiwi wax dipped in water until they shined like patent leather. On weekends, Jimmy would ask his first-born son, then about three or four, "You ready to shine the boots?" He pulled out a footstool and propped his boots on it, then boosted the little boy above the boot tops and lowered the child's feet and legs into the boots. Roger put all his weight on one foot to hold a boot in place as his father spit-shined the leather until Roger could see his reflection in the toe. It was the little boy's proudest job, and he tried hard not to be knocked off the stool as his daddy whipped and popped the polishing cloth to buff the uppers.

Roger was four and Ronald was two when they and their mother accompanied Jimmy to West Germany for a three-year tour of duty with U.S. forces in Europe.

Ronald Newman, left, and his brother, Roger, in West Germany during their father's tour of duty with a U.S. Army mechanized cavalry unit.

Newman was a rising young noncommissioned officer with an American ground cavalry unit. An Army brat like the other kids on post, Roger thought of his father as a brave man in uniform, a disciplinarian who stood proudly in defense of his country. In the Army, when the bugle sounds retreat at the end of the day, soldiers on post stop their cars, and everyone gets out. If they can see the flag being lowered, they face it. If they can't see the flag, they turn toward the sound of the bugle. Soldiers in uniform salute, and children and other civilians stand straight and place their hands over their hearts. Roger respected the traditions—and admired his father for teaching them to him.Roger was twelve when his father left for Vietnam the first time. He proudly donned the Seiko watch Jimmy sent him as a gift. It ran until 1985, and when it wore out, long after his father had left home, Roger bought himself another one like it. Jimmy was his hero then.

The second time his father came home from the war Roger had just graduated from high school and had been accepted at the University of Georgia in Athens. He would be the first in his family to go to college. Then Jimmy ran off with Kim, and Roger felt he couldn't leave home. Without his father's financial support, he couldn't afford to go away to school. What's more, as the elder son, he didn't believe he should abandon his mother. He got a job driving a school bus. He was seventeen. He tried to join the Navy, but his mother told the recruiter her son had asthma as a child, and that ended that. The next year he went to work in the catalog department of Sears, then decided to take a marketing course at a technical school in Florida. He met a girl from West Virginia, married her, and moved to her hometown, which he hated. The marriage lasted a year, and he drifted back to Fayetteville without her. At Sears, he had made friends with a police officer who was moonlighting as a store security guard, and Roger thought being a policeman would be a good job. By the time he got home from West Virginia, he was almost twenty-one, old enough to join the force. He applied and was accepted to the police academy, graduated, and joined the police department in Fayetteville. He liked police work and fell in love again, this time with a young woman from Newnan, his parents' hometown in Georgia. They married, and his bride moved up to Fayetteville, but the sprawling military town proved too much for her, and she soon went home alone. Roger quit the police department and went to Newnan to try to put the marriage back together. He got a job in management in a fast-food chain. The second marriage collapsed in a year, and Roger worked his way back to North Carolina, where—like his father—he started selling insurance.

In 1986, fourteen years and two failed marriages since high school, Roger decided to get serious about an education and enrolled in the local community college. He earned highest honors in a two-year paralegal program while working nights running a Hampton Inn. One of his teachers, a local lawyer, suggested he consider law school. He transferred to a four-year state college, graduated magna cum laude in 1990 and was admitted to Campbell University School of Law, a small private college in Raleigh. By the time he passed the North Carolina bar in 1993, Roger Newman was thirty-eight years old and finally seemed to have found his way. Within two years, he had married a third time, to his high school sweetheart, who by then had two adolescent daughters, and started his own law practice in Fayetteville. But his life came undone abruptly again. Roger was disbarred for mishandling the firm's trust account, and he went back to work in the hotel business. The third marriage lasted ten years.

"I was hurt for a lot of years," Roger said of his father's leaving. "I grew out of being hurt, and I started being mad about it. And then I stopped being mad about it, and I got bitter, and I stayed bitter for a lot of years up until the time that I found out that he had cancer."[90]

It was shortly before their father's cancer diagnosis in early 1997 that Jim Newman's sons met for the first time. Jay's half brother, John Fogelquist, discovered through the neighborhood homeowners association that he and Roger, both of them married at the time and both members of the association, were living five houses apart in Fayetteville. John was stunned when he saw Roger because the eldest son looked so much like Jim Newman that John thought it was scary. The young men got to know each other as neighbors, and when Jay came home from college, he often stayed at John's and did his homework in the kitchen. John told him about Roger, and Jay wanted to meet him. Jay had never heard his father speak of the older sons, but he had heard Roger was an attorney, and he wanted to talk to him because he was thinking about going to law school. John had a cookout in his backyard and brought all of Newman's children and their spouses together. He has always thought Roger's talking to Jay that evening was a factor in Jay's decision to go to law school. Roger, meanwhile, harbored some resentment that Jay got to go to college and law school with financial support through their father's veterans benefits. Ron, the youngest, said the one man they all had in common was never mentioned.

After the cookout, Jay thought it would be a good idea to get Roger back in touch with their father. He brought it up with Jim, saying he knew it was an awkward subject but might be a good thing to do. Jim brushed it off. He had a way of saying no by not responding. Jay didn't push it. But Jay kept in touch with Roger for a while and told him about talking to "Dad" about a meeting.

"Y'know," Roger stopped him, "after all these years, I just can't call him 'Dad.'"[91] They saw each other only once after that while their father was still alive. Jay did wind up going to Campbell University School of Law. If he realized at the time it was the same institution where his half brother Roger had earned his law degree, he didn't remember it when asked years later.

It was not long after the cookout that Jim Newman was diagnosed with cancer. He had kept in touch with his first wife, Flora, stopping by to see her sometimes when the boys weren't around. He had mentioned to her the previous year that he had some rectal bleeding, and she urged him to see a doctor, even brought him some medical books from the doctor's office where she worked, but it took him many months to have it checked out. When the malignancy was identified, a large part of his colon was removed and he had his first encounter with chemotherapy. The doctors got rid of all the cancerous tissue that time, and Newman recovered well, though it left him connected to a colostomy bag. Jay was with him in his hospital room soon after the surgery when Roger walked in. The eldest son spoke to his father for the first time in more than two decades, saying something like, "Hi, you doin' okay?" Newman nodded, almost imperceptibly. Jay knew they recognized each other, even after so many years. And both he and Roger recognized the brush-off. Roger turned and left.[92] It was not for the last time.

Ron, two years younger than Roger, has few boyhood memories of his father other than getting spanked often because he was always testing the boundaries of good behavior. When his father returned from Vietnam the second time, Ron thought he was hard to talk to and seemed preoccupied by work or something and didn't show much interest in his boys or their activities. It was like one man walked out the door, and somebody else came back.[93]

When he was told his father was leaving home for good, he blamed himself, not an uncommon reaction among children of divorce. Ron thought maybe he could have been a better son somehow or done something differently. He had just turned sixteen. He was trying to be friendly and to stay in touch that day when he got in the car and drove to Kim's home, and his father closed the door in his face. Ron walked away furious and drove home. He doesn't remember if he was crying, but he remembers how the anger and bitterness of the momentary encounter welled up and stuck with him for years.

Nearly twenty years later, in 1990, when Ron was thirty-four years old, his first marriage had fallen apart, he was alone, without a friend, and he went to a Baptist church around the corner from his house in search of some direction, some human contact. He felt something was missing from his life, but he didn't know what it was. He had not gone to church since childhood, but he spoke to the pastor, who told him he could have a friend forever who stayed closer than a brother. The minister explained the plan of salvation as preached by the church. Ron learned a simple prayer asking for forgiveness of his sins and, in the eyes of the church, his soul was saved. He has been a devout believer ever since. He talks about that day as "when I got saved."

That experience "pretty much" gave him peace about his life and liberated him from the bitterness he had felt toward his father all those years. "There's things that I don't understand, that I never will understand this side of heaven," Ron said. "One day I hope to stand face-to-face with Jimmy and ask him, but it just gave me peace, and I was able to forgive him for anything that had happened in the past."

Seven or eight years later, when Ron had remarried and had two children, he took them to visit his mother in Fayetteville and discovered his father was staying in a separate bedroom in the house after his cancer surgery. They had nothing to say to each other.

When his father died, Ron at first chose not to go to Arlington for the funeral. But his brother Roger and others in the family, including his mother and his fifteen-year-old son Matthew, who knew nothing about his grandfather, could not understand why Ron would stay home. "I said, 'Son, there's things in life you're not going to understand.' But then I decided that if I didn't go, later in life, if I wished I had, that's something I can't change. So out of respect for my mom, I went. And I'm glad I did. I learned a lot about him from talking to the other gentlemen that were with him, that served with him in the Condors." Whether because of his father or in spite of him, Ron chose to center his life around his own children. He eventually had four and has coached all of them in sports, follows what they do in school, and is determined that they will all go on to college one way or another. Ron himself didn't go to college. He went to work for a grocery company when he was sixteen, kept at it after high school, and has worked his way into senior management in the food business.

THE FIRST CONDOR

The first Condor was a career military officer named Bill Zierdt. Zierdt was a West Pointer (class of 1959) and the son of a professional soldier who had commanded a tank-destroyer company in World War II. His was a military family. An uncle and two cousins had gone to the U.S. Military Academy, too, and Bill thought of himself as someone going into the family business. He had been captivated since boyhood by cavalry doctrine that called for a small force traveling fast and light to find the enemy, engage him, and call in reinforcements to pile on. As a cadet, Zierdt developed a conviction, not widely shared at the time by Army generals, that helicopters were the horses of the future, and he wanted to fly them into battle. The superintendent of West Point had him summoned to the office and told him that becoming an aviator would be a career-wrecking mistake. Zierdt was stubborn, though, and after graduating from the academy, he went on to flight school to fly small, fixed-wing airplanes, a mandatory step in those days before he could qualify in rotary-wing aircraft. Aviation was not yet a branch of the Army like the combat arms such as infantry, artillery, and armor. Zierdt was commissioned as an armor officer, a descendant of the cavalry but with heavy tanks and armored personnel carriers instead of horses. His first command was as a platoon leader in an armored cavalry unit in West Germany before he got his wish to fly helicopters. After Zierdt graduated from helicopter flight school, the Army sent him to Vietnam in 1965 in the early months of President Lyndon Johnson's escalation of the U.S. war effort. As a young captain, Zierdt was among the first air cavalry troop commanders to go into combat. He arrived only a few months before Newman and finished his tour shortly before Newman was wounded and evacuated. Although they didn't meet for nearly forty years, both men were early and eager helicopter warriors helping invent the tactics for a new kind of warfare. Both would later command C Troop, 2/17 Air Cavalry, with the personal call sign Condor Six.

After his first year in Vietnam, Zierdt returned to Fort Rucker to teach aviators the practical, combat-tested tactics he had learned in air assault operations. As it became evident that helicopters could be used not just for reconnaissance and carrying troops and supplies but also to train firepower on the enemy from above, he helped set up and run a helicopter gunnery school and became a test pilot to try out the Army's prototype Cobra gunships.

Two years after his first Vietnam tour, he was sent to Fort Hood, Texas, to assume command of an experimental air cavalry troop, one of three that would be attached to the 101st Airborne Division, the proud Screaming Eagles of World War II fame. The division of more than fifteen thousand paratroopers, already in Vietnam, was being converted into the Army's second fully airmobile division, following the model of the 1st Air Cavalry Division. On August 7, 1968, Zierdt filed the mandatory Morning Report that every unit uses to inform superiors up the line of its strength and readiness. "G Packet," as the unit being assembled was then called, had a personnel strength of one: Major William H. Zierdt III. He had six months to build the new troop, drawing fresh pilots and flight crews coming out of schools that trained them for helicopter combat. He topped out at 338 men, including forty-four pilots, when he was ordered to take his troop to war. The unit was renamed C Troop, 2nd Squadron, 17th Cavalry, 101st Airborne Division, usually abbreviated as C/2/17. By that time, troop ships had been succeeded by airplanes and most of Zierdt's men flew to Vietnam on a chartered World Airways stretch DC-8 commercial airliner. The aircrews and specialists who were needed to load and unload their practically new helicopters accompanied the equipment across the Pacific on an aging World War II aircraft carrier converted for aircraft transfer duty.

When they got to Danang, the largest city in the northern sector of South Vietnam and a major port, they stripped the protective plastic from their Hueys, loaches, and Cobras, mounted the rotor blades, added some fuel, and flew the birds off the ship. Flying north along the coast of the South China Sea, they settled at Landing Zone Sally, a flat, fenced-in fortress in the comparatively secure coastal plain near the old imperial capital of Hue. Sally was the headquarters of the Screaming Eagles' 2nd Brigade, a unit made up mostly of infantry grunts who were about to get a lot more choppers to help them find and chase down the enemy. The land around Sally was checkered with bright-green paddies, where families planted rice, their staple crop, flooded the young shoots in fields surrounded by hand-dug earthen dikes, and stooped in the mud to tend their plants to maturity as the thunder of war echoed in the mountains to their west. Out there, in the forbidding, fog-shrouded jungled hillsides, the North Vietnamese Army fought like tigers to protect their supply lines into the populated lowlands. To get at them, the Americans had to hunt them down in the dangerous, tunnel-infested world where fast jets, big bombs, and undisputed control of the air were pitted against the primitive tactics of a seasoned, utterly determined, and disciplined ground force. It was March 1969, and U.S. combat deaths were running more than five hundred a month. Vietnamese casualties, both northern and southern, were far higher.

Not long after C Troop arrived, the first sergeant relayed a message from squadron headquarters one morning telling the commanding officer to come up with a radio call sign beginning with the letter "C." He had until noon. Zierdt thought of Cyclops, the big eye in the sky, and Condor, which he figured was the biggest bird that flies and will eat anything.[94]

He tried them out on two of his subordinates who couldn't do any better, and they picked Condor because they agreed the hard "c" would be heard more clearly on the radio when the flight crews talked to each other and to headquarters. C Troop became the Condors. Not long after that, Zierdt was flying his command-and-control ship over the A Shau Valley, which was becoming the troop's primary area of operations. The impatient commander was hammering his scout pilots for quicker reports on any signs of enemy activity on the valley floor. During what he would later acknowledge were unmerciful, unreasonable demands for more information, he heard a click in his helmet earpiece as an anonymous flier keyed his microphone and pleaded, "Patience, patience."

"Patience my ass," the commander shouted into his mouthpiece. "I want to kill something!" That line became the unit's motto. An image of a redheaded California condor perched on a dead tree branch under a full moon was embroidered into a circular patch worn by C Troopers on their flight jackets, over the right breast pocket on their fatigues, or just about anywhere they thought it would attract attention. Many years later, Frank Sama, who had been a Cobra pilot in

Zierdt's troop, confessed it was he who had anonymously urged the commander to practice patience during the mission.[95]

The men had barely settled in when the Condors got their first mission: to open a new fire support base overlooking the northern A Shau Valley from which a couple of batteries with 105 mm howitzers could fire at North Vietnamese strongholds below. It was to be called Fire Support Base Airborne and, at more than five thousand feet, would be nearly a mile above sea level, the highest artillery base in the country. The plan was to use it to support a major offensive to drive the North Vietnamese out of the valley. To operate at that altitude, fully loaded helicopters had to fly early in the morning when the cool air was denser and provided more lift for the ships' rotors. To lighten the load, they carried only half their usual fuel, which slashed the time available for delays, trouble, or unforeseen events. The military's announcement that U.S. troops were coming shook the ground for miles, shredded huge trees into toothpicks, and spread choking smoke and fire through the jungled mountains. The Air Force used the Arc Light mission as "ground preparation" to kill or drive underground any enemy troops in the area before the Americans landed by helicopter. A half-dozen giant B-52 bombers, invisible at thirty thousand feet, dumped up to seventy thousand pounds of bombs from each plane to devastate the ground below, thin the jungle forest, and, it was hoped, provide easy entry for the assaulting infantry. F-4 Phantom fighter-bombers roared in low for more pinpoint bombing, while from firebases miles away, eight-inch guns and 155 mm howitzers pounded the area with high-explosive projectiles. Rocket-firing helicopters from the 101st's aerial rocket artillery battalion and the cavalry's own Cobras hit targets picked for them by the scouts. Fire and smoke erupted with the impact of every bomb and shell. The rumbling thunder echoed down the valley for miles. It was always a wonder that anything survived those softening-up attacks, but tenacious North Vietnamese soldiers knew how to hide in bunkers and spider holes to get through the shelling and come out shooting.

Charlie Troop's lead Huey carried two combat engineers, one with a chainsaw and one with a coil of detonation cord to cut down or blow down a tall tree in the center of the chosen landing zone. Riflemen from the Blues Platoon and soldiers borrowed from other troops were aboard the first ship. It circled in to land beside the tree and came to a hover sixty feet off the ground. Zierdt, watching from his command-and-control ship about two hundred feet behind and to the left, saw a rope drop from each side door of the chopper, and the first man stepped off and started to rappel down the rope toward the ground. A small, black-clad figure stood up from hiding in the rocks and bushes and pointed his AK-47 at the chopper above him. Zierdt was close enough to see the brass shell casings popping out of the AK's receiver as the shots aimed at the lead Huey rat-tat-tatted from the barrel. The gunman emptied all fifty-one rounds in his fully loaded banana clip, and Zierdt saw a puff of white spray escape from the left side of the engine cowling of the lead helicopter.

The seasoned aviator instantly realized the white puff meant the gunman had hit the Huey's high-pressure fuel line, a breach that would quickly doom the bird if it didn't get on the ground. The options, none of them good, zipped through Major Zierdt's mind: Crash in place; just put it down where it was. Drift to the left, where the trees were lower, and autorotate in. Drop down the side of the mountain to more open space in the valley below and land there.

Zierdt squeezed the mic button under his finger and barked, "You're on fire! Head for the valley floor."

He got no reply and never knew if the pilot heard him. The aircraft nosed over and started down the mountain, following a streambed that dropped over a waterfall into the valley. Perhaps the pilot did hear the command, or maybe he realized he was losing power and turned downward on his own. He was barely off the ground but still flying. About halfway down, as the pristine mountain stream plunged over the waterfall, the wounded Huey's stubby nose flared sharply upward, and the tail boom dropped toward the ground. It was a desperate maneuver pilots were trained to use if they were about to crash. The pilot may have attempted to use the tail as a shock absorber to ease the impact when the fuselage hit. Instead, the tail hit a rock at the crest of the waterfall and smacked the nose down like a hammerhead, breaking the aircraft in two as it burst into a ball of flame.

Zierdt still had five Hueys with the rest of the Blues platoon circling to land and burning through their limited fuel supply. He switched tactics immediately from a combat assault to a recovery operation and ordered the scouts to find a landing zone downhill, where the Blues could unload. A scout pilot quickly located a knoll covered in high grass near the bottom of the waterfall. It was still early morning, and there was time to scramble up the mountain. Zierdt radioed squadron headquarters that he needed an infantry company to help his severely diminished platoon secure the mountainside and recover the bodies high above. The 101st stood up a company it had on standby at Camp Eagle and flew a couple hundred men to the A Shau in less than a half hour. The grunts were still making their way up the mountain when a scout pilot reported seeing movement near the burning aircraft. It wasn't clear at first whether he had seen friendly or enemy activity. The troops and choppers had been taking random fire all morning from bunkers in the area. A Cobra gunship covered the scout from behind as it buzzed the site, getting in so close the crew could make out the two downed pilots, both still strapped into their armored seats that had been thrown at least twenty feet in front of their chopper when it slammed into the earth. The crew could tell they were still breathing. It had been five hours since the shootdown.

With hope of a rescue instead of recovering remains, the infantrymen scrambled the rest of the way up the hill and moved in around the wreck as a medevac ship nosed into the open and slowed to a hover above the downed pilots. Zierdt thought the medevac pilot was the gutsiest aviator he had ever seen as the flying ambulance hovered above the wreckage, holding steady despite constant rifle fire from enemy soldiers below. The crew lowered a cable with a medic and a bright-yellow jungle penetrator rescue device toward the wounded men below. One crewman was conscious, the other alive but unconscious as the medic rigged lifting straps around them, hooked them to the penetrator and signaled the crew chief above to haul them into the air with him and pull them aboard.[96] Both men survived the trip out, but one, the aircraft commander, died aboard a U.S. Navy hospital ship offshore; the other was evacuated to the States where, like many of the wounded, he disappeared into the Army's stateside hospital system. A report years later said the survivor was paralyzed from the neck down.[97] He had been a Condor for less than three weeks, assigned to the unit after its arrival in Vietnam. Zierdt remembered him as an excellent pilot but couldn't recall his name and never knew what had become of him.

Zierdt, following cavalry doctrine, asked the division to send in a battalion to sweep the mountain, secure the landing zone, and root out the North Vietnamese defenders, who were later determined to be a skeleton crew of maintenance people looking after the bunker network. But the top brass of the 101st didn't think that way. By 5:00 p.m., Zierdt's troop and the infantry company that had come to its aid were ordered off the mountain, and they went back to Sally to lick their wounds. The Condors' commander had lost thirteen men of his own or other units in the crash and during the daylong struggle up the mountain. He knew he'd got his ass kicked in what he regarded for the rest of his career and many years beyond as "the god-awful day."[98]

During the next three weeks, C Troop scouts reported heavy infiltration of the A Shau by North Vietnamese regulars from Base Area 611, the enemy supply and staging base on the Laotian side of the border. By the time the leaders of the 101st were ready to try again, the enemy was waiting for the Screaming Eagles.

The Condors were in the lead again when they put down on the side of Dong Ap Bia, seven miles to the west across the valley from Firebase Airborne. Known to soldiers at the time as Hill 937 for the height of its summit in meters on military maps, the mountain was the scene of one of the most memorable set-to battles of the war. Before it was over, the bloody, costly, and controversial operation to seize the summit was notoriously dubbed the Battle of Hamburger Hill, a name more or less invented by a reporter for United Press International to the consternation of military top brass.[99] For ten days, the Americans fought for every inch of the mountain until they conquered it. After losing fifty-six men killed and some four hundred wounded, they abandoned Hamburger Hill to the enemy. U.S. commanders insisted they had won the day because they had killed an estimated six hundred North Vietnamese troops. The body count was in America's favor. Their point, however, was lost on American public opinion, which had turned against the war. Just as President Richard M. Nixon was beginning the American withdrawal from Vietnam, the desperate fighting and mounting casualties half a world away seemed more and more pointless to Americans watching the war on television and reading about it in newspapers.

After the battle, the Condors continued to fly the A Shau, planting sensors to track North Vietnamese troops and supplies moving back into the valley. On June 10, barely three weeks after the withdrawal from Dong Ap Bia, a Cobra gunship from A Troop, 2/17, crashed on the side of the mountain. Charlie Troop's Blues were sent in to rescue the two-man crew and put down in the same small landing zone on the mountain that had been used to begin the attack.[100] The platoon leader jumped out one side of the aircraft, and Specialist 4 Robert L. Howard, the unit's twenty-four-year-old "point man," jumped out the other. As the two moved off to get beyond the whirling blades of their Huey, an enemy soldier popped up from a spider hole only a few yards away and fired point-blank at Howard, hitting him in the chest. The American soldier died on the mountain. So did the man who shot him, quickly gunned down by others in Howard's platoon. When Zierdt got back to LZ Sally that night, the troop's first sergeant was waiting for him to tell him the only record the division had for Howard's next of kin was the name and address of a four-year-old boy. Not Howard's wife, from whom he was divorced, or a guardian of the boy, just an address in Connecticut. Zierdt asked division headquarters for guidance, knowing he was supposed to send his "regret to inform" letter out as quickly as possible. The Army didn't wait for the mail to tell families of tragedy. The policy when a soldier was killed was to dispatch casualty notification personnel, usually an officer and a chaplain, to inform the next of kin in person. The dead soldier's commanding officer would follow up with a form letter over his name, giving the family a written record that named the dead and bore the signature of the commander. Major Zierdt, thirty-one, sat down at the desk on the office side of his hooch and wrote a special letter to Robert L. Howard II, not the standard regret-to-inform missive dictated by Army regulation.

> Dear Robert:
>
> This letter is written to you for some day in the future when you will ask of and understand your father's death. I am writing as both a personal friend of your father's and as his troop commander, because I want you to know what a very special kind of man your father was, and how great was his loss to me and to his many friends.

Although your father only recently joined us, he was already a friend whom we admired and respected. He was a hard working and conscientious young man and an outstanding soldier whose personal devotion won him the esteem of all the officers and men of C Troop.

Your father was with his platoon attempting to rescue the crew of a crashed helicopter when death came to him. After landing by helicopter, your father and other men from the platoon established positions surrounding the landing zone to secure it for additional troops. As your father advanced, he was mortally wounded in the chest by enemy small arms fire. Death was instantaneous and he did not suffer any pain.

Our Squadron Chaplain has conducted memorial services in remembrance of your father.

I know that the sense of loss over your father's death is very great to you, but it is also shared by each member of our troop who will always remember him as a happy and wonderful man. I hope that is the way you will remember him also.

Sincerely yours,
[signed]
William H. Zierdt III
MAJ, Armor
Commanding[101]

That letter would come back to bite its author—hard—many years later.

Like most career officers picked to lead troops in battle in Vietnam, Zierdt's one-year tour was split between time in the field and a staff post at headquarters. The Army policy was intended to protect leaders from burnout—and give as many officers as possible a chance at combat command, regarded as a plum in the ticket-punching culture of career officers. In Zierdt's case, as in Newman's, leading C Troop in war was the best command he ever got. After seven months in-country, and consistent with the reconnaissance role of the cavalry, he went on to serve as military intelligence officer at the 101st's division headquarters at Camp Eagle, up the road from the Condors at LZ Sally. Sometime during his last five months in Vietnam, he began to revisit his role in the crash of the Huey on that mountainside in the A Shau. Seeing that puff of white smoke, reviewing his options and watching the pilot try but fail to save his ship became a daily ritual in Zierdt's life. Sometimes it would take a couple of hours, going over the details time and again, but the result was always the same. He never thought of himself as disabled by those repetitious thoughts. He just carried on.

Zierdt's career took an academic turn after Vietnam. He picked up two master's degrees, one in engineering systems management and another in sociology; taught behavioral science and leadership at West Point; and ran a sort of skunk works for the Army's chief of staff to figure out how to handle the critical social issues of the time. The military, like civilian society, was struggling with racial integration, spousal abuse, drug and alcohol problems, and the changing role of women. Even in the '70s, Zierdt's group was trying to figure out what to do about homosexuals in uniform, although the military didn't officially alter its ban on gays for twenty more years. Zierdt retired as a lieutenant colonel in 1979 and went into consulting and teaching.

He was working at a small college in Fond du Lac, Wisconsin, in 2002 when he received an email through the West Point alumni forwarding service asking if he could help direct the son of a soldier in the 101st Airborne to the site where the father had been killed during the war. The only thing the son knew about his father's death was contained in a letter written to him by a commanding officer named William H. Zierdt III. The writer of the email message was helping a group plan a trip to Vietnam, and the son hoped to visit the place where his father died. The writer was seeking help to determine where that was. Zierdt fired off what he later called a snarky reply telling the writer he didn't remember but if he saw the letter he had written it might help jog his memory.

When a copy of the letter he had sent to a four-year-old boy about the combat death of Robert L. Howard arrived in his email inbox as an attachment, Zierdt sent it to the printer, picked up the paper copy—and froze.

Seeing his own signature on the letter he had written thirty-two years earlier triggered a paralyzing mental firestorm. In his own words, he just absolutely lost it. The former commander, long retired from the Army and steeped in the academic world of a college professor, sat at his desk, unable to move. It wasn't the shooting of the point man, which he had not witnessed, that boiled to the surface; it was the Huey crash that had preceded it. It was that god-awful day. Zierdt stuck to his chair, reliving every second of that twenty-hour day, dredging up details, remembering his order: "You're on fire! Head for the valley floor." Was he right? Hell, he didn't know. All these years later he was still struggling with that question. It was the most critical order he gave in twenty years of military service, and he didn't even know if the pilot heard him.

As he had day after day for years, he relived the moments and their aftermath. The Hueys made a circular approach to avoid giving away their destination or being targeted too early. The scout dropped a purple smoke grenade exactly where Zierdt wanted him to in the center of the chosen landing zone. Then the lead ship came in flat, just as planned. But he saw the NVA soldier stand and start firing up at the chopper, the white puff, the pilot's desperate attempt to save his ship. The young aviator did everything he'd been trained to do. He kept the aircraft up until the power bled off and the bird wouldn't fly anymore. Then he pulled back on the cyclic to drop the tail boom and slow his forward speed in a maneuver known as a flare. If executed correctly at the right moment, the flare cushions the helicopter's fall while bringing its forward motion to a stop, minimizing the impact and skid when the craft touches the ground. The pilot did as he had been trained, but the tail hit something, and the ship exploded.

Racing through the madness of that day, Zierdt reviewed the aftermath again and again: putting his troops on the ground, watching them struggle up the mountain meeting resistance at every turn, learning hours later that the two pilots appeared to be alive, still strapped in their seats. Zierdt even remembered a humorous, if sobering, aside. A few hours after the crash, the commander landed at Firebase Birmingham to refuel. He had to pee but didn't want to unplug his helmet from the radios to walk a reasonable distance from the aircraft, so he climbed out onto a skid with the helmet's cable still attached. As he was standing there relieving himself, the door gunner tapped him on the back, and when Zierdt turned around, he saw the ashen-faced soldier with a horrified look on his face pointing toward the tail boom of their aircraft. Five bullet holes from ground fire had pierced the ship's skin, probably about the time the lead Huey was shot down. No one had noticed until the refueling stop. Zierdt unplugged his helmet, walked to the rear of the craft, and opened an access panel to see if anything vital had been damaged. He saw that the structural part of the tail was intact, closed the panel, gave the gunner a comforting pat on the shoulder, and climbed back into his seat to return to the mile-high mountain.

Still in his seat at the college, the memories kept erupting. Zierdt finally dragged himself to the office of the college president, Dr. Richard Ridenour, a psychiatrist, retired rear admiral, and former chief of Bethesda Naval Hospital outside Washington.

"Dick, I have a problem" was as much as Zierdt could manage to get out. Ridenour put him in touch with a psychiatric social worker, who calmly helped him describe what was going on in his mind. By the next morning, he could put a few words together but wasn't making much sense. It was the first time he had ever described his war experiences to anyone. Not even his wife and children knew about the most dramatic and demanding times in his life. They knew—or thought they knew—not to ask.

For Zierdt, seeing his signature on the long-ago letter was the beginning of what many experts now recognize as a second wave of post-traumatic stress disorder. The acute onset of this PTSD strikes veterans late in life, often when they retire or begin thinking more about the past, or, in some cases, go to reunions of their old war buddies.

Zierdt marked that day in 2002 that he started to tell his story to the psychiatric social worker, thirty-two years after he left Vietnam for the last time, as the beginning of his recovery.

ANOTHER GENERATION

In the summer of 1969, when the soldiers came to the house in Norwich, Connecticut, to inform Robert Howard's family that he had been killed in Vietnam, four-year-old Robert Louis Howard II stood at the door with his mother and listened to them talk about his father. He didn't understand what it meant, but he remembered the visit and, sometime later, the funeral and burial in Norwich. Although his parents were divorced, which is why the boy was listed as next of kin, his mother made sure that young Robert grew up as part of his father's family as well as hers. And she told him what a good man his father had been. He spent lots of time with his uncles and aunts and grew up hearing stories about his father's athletic prowess and battlefield courage.

Like two of his brothers before him, Robert L. Howard Sr. was a star athlete at Norwich Free Academy, long known for producing some of the state's premier athletes. Robert, who was known as Bobby on the field, was a football standout who also lettered in basketball and track. He was named the school's best athlete of 1964. In a town that celebrated its sports teams, people remembered the great running back with the distinctive stutter and friendly manner that befitted a local hero.

His son didn't like hearing it. Young Robert grew increasingly bitter that everybody else in town seemed to know his dad but that he didn't. Norwich is a small city, and the Howard brothers were big names, especially in football and basketball. Bobby Howard and two of his older brothers took top honors in sports at the academy three years in a row. Well-meaning people were always telling young Robert stories they remembered about his father, and young Robert didn't have any of his own. He hardly even knew his father.

"What I had was a funeral and a memory that my father was killed in action," he said. "I don't have any memory of him holding me, me sitting on his lap, you know, playing with a basketball."

Young Robert said Howie Dickenman, another standout at Norwich Free Academy and later a Hall of Fame basketball coach for Central Connecticut State University, told him that his father "used to bring me to practice and I'd be running around the gym in a diaper" while his father worked out with the team.[102]

Even years later, when young Robert was playing football for St. Bernard School in Norwich, he heard announcers on the radio talking about Bobby Howard's son playing football that day. The boy dedicated himself to doing better on the football field than his father had. He watched tapes of his father and tried to mimic his running style. And in 1982, the fall of his senior year, he fully intended to break his father's record for yards gained rushing. It was his one goal, and he committed everything to it. He was on that path when, in the fifth game of the season, he got hit hard and suffered a separated collarbone that would put him out for the rest of the season. At first, he refused to leave the field, despite the pain. The coaches ordered him out. He was shattered. Weeks later, while still recovering, the youth begged them to put him back in for the last game. They let him dress, but not start. They had played football with his father and cherished his memory. They knew the boy's obsession. Finally, they relented and let young Robert go in. He played only a couple of downs before he was hit again and reinjured his collarbone. That sent him into a downward spiral.

He graduated in the spring and entered Howard University in Washington, D.C., the following fall, but he failed to make the football team and lost direction. He got into drugs and, by his account, lost any fear of death. He was so engrossed in his father's dying young that he thought he'd be better off if he joined his father. Robert dropped out of college, went home, and worked as a laborer to feed his habit. The drugs got harder, and the crowd he hung with tougher. By his own reckoning, he was working but not making anything of himself. He was back in Norwich when, on June 8, 1989—two days before the twentieth anniversary of his father's death—he had a drug-induced seizure that nearly killed him. His mother went crazy at the hospital and lit into him. The doctors brought him around, and his mother took him out of the hospital in time to get him to a ceremony at which his father was inducted into the Norwich Sports Hall of Fame, still a hero a quarter century after he left the field. The son wept as he accepted the citation on his father's behalf.

"I don't have as many memories as everybody else who knew him," the son told the audience. "I know in my heart my father gave his best, regardless of whether it was football, basketball or track, and to his family and his country.

"I'm proud of you, Dad. I miss you, and I love you."[103]

But young Robert still had a chip on his shoulder and felt sorry for himself when someone told him, in the early 1990s, about Sons and

Daughters In Touch, an organization set up to bring together the children of American troops killed in Vietnam. Robert was drawn to it because his godson, a cousin, was having problems getting along with his own father, and Robert went in search of advice about the importance of reestablishing the relationship. Members of the group gather in Washington on Father's Day to celebrate and pay tribute to their own fathers by visiting the Vietnam Veterans Memorial, where the names of 58,300 servicemen and women are carved into the famous, reflective black rock panels on the sunken surface known as the Wall. For Robert, the group sessions that were part of the trip gave him, for the first time, a sense that he was not alone in his loss. Others his age stood up and spoke, and Robert, then in his midtwenties, began to cry. He cried a lot on that trip and opened up some to the others. There were thousands of children who lost their fathers in the war, and he found comfort in discovering he was one of many. Robert marked that trip as the beginning of a long period of recovery. He got a real job and worked his way up to manager in a local cell phone company. He married and raised three children. Although the marriage didn't last, he proudly shared the responsibilities of parenthood and named his youngest son Robert Louis Howard III. Photos of the boy as a teenager look remarkably like those of his grandfather at the same age.

Robert remained active in the support group and in 2003 traveled to Vietnam with other Sons and Daughters In Touch to see where their fathers died. In his case, he had only a few clues about where his father had died. After he was killed, Robert L. Howard Sr. was promoted to sergeant and awarded the Bronze Star with "V" device for valor and the Purple Heart. The citation for the Bronze Star medal identified his unit as the rifle platoon of Troop C, 2nd Squadron, 17th Cavalry, 101st Airborne Division and said he was "on a helicopter recovery mission in the A Shau Valley, Republic of Vietnam. He was the first man into the hostile landing zone, and he immediately began drawing fire from the enemy positions on top of the hill. He got into a position to return fire and was able to keep the enemy force from firing at the other helicopters as they landed. With complete disregard for his own safety, Specialist Howard subjected himself to intense enemy fire, thereby saving the lives of many of his fellow men. Trying to move closer to the insurgents, he was fatally wounded by enemy small arms fire."[104]

Robert also had Major Zierdt's letter to him dated July 8, 1969, less than three weeks after his father was killed in action. It didn't give much detail about the place, but it did have the commanding officer's name. One of the people helping organize the trip recognized the name from his own childhood, knew Zierdt had gone to West Point, and wrote him the email that the military academy's alumni association forwarded to Zierdt.

Robert said he was told first that Zierdt refused to speak to him. He had no idea that seeing the letter again had triggered a crippling attack of post-traumatic stress in the retired officer. Some days later, the intermediary told Robert that Zierdt had agreed to talk. The first time they spoke, by phone, Robert couldn't say a word. He just listened as the man he came to know as Bill described the flight into the A Shau, his father jumping off the chopper first, and getting shot. He also told the son where the incident occurred, giving Robert the destination he had requested. One other person on the trip, the son of an Air Force pilot, lost a father in the A Shau, and the group went to that site first. Representatives of the long-ago enemy, now part of the Vietnamese government, accompanied the group and conducted a traditional ceremony for the dead in the valley with offerings of food and burning of incense in an age-old ritual and gesture of respect.

Robert, who had wondered if he would hate the Vietnamese for killing his father, was touched by their show of concern and welcomed the tribute. The party was unable to reach the actual landing zone where the fighting took place because of concern about unexploded ordnance in the area, but when Robert got as close as he could, he removed a gold medallion he had worn since he had his father's image etched into it in 1993. Taking the chain off his neck felt like lifting a thousand pounds from his back. He finally felt, more than three decades since his father's death, that he was able to lay him to rest and focus on his own life, his own children. Looking out across the dense green foliage on the mountains on either side of the valley, Robert saw two white birds in a tree off in the distance. He couldn't see them well enough to identify them, but he interpreted their presence as a sign just for him. Robert pocketed the medallion and chain and carried them home, where they still hang over the mantel, in a place where he and his three children can see them. Robert's life became simpler, and he has never worn the medallion again. Robert L. Howard Sr. is buried in Maplewood Cemetery in Norwich, and his son, who now lives in Hartford, Connecticut, returns to the grave site every year, sometimes on June 10, sometimes on another day when he feels like it. He used to get fidgety and anxious around the time of the anniversary but is more comfortable with it now. When he visits, he gives his father an update, tells him what's going on in his life, how the kids are doing, and just has what he calls a little alone time with his father.

After the Vietnam trip, Robert kept in touch with Bill Zierdt by phone, and Zierdt invited him to a C Troop reunion in San Antonio, where the two men met face-to-face for the first time. Zierdt, who had cut off his military contacts when he retired from the Army, said he probably would not have gone to the reunion if Robert hadn't accepted his invitation. He described it as "a very difficult meeting for both of us" but one that turned out quite well.

Robert was nervous at first, the only child there of a Condor lost in the war. He spent most of the time with Bill, whom he described as a real catalyst in his life, and he was thrilled when the Condors welcomed him into their alumni association as an honorary member. He was surprised they seemed as happy to see him as he was to meet all of them. He felt as if he were being welcomed into their family, one that included his father.

Reflecting on the experience later, Zierdt said, "Had it not been for Robert Howard, I'm not sure I ever would have sought help and come out of this. I don't know how far out I am; I'm never going to be cured."

That May, a former soldier from a different unit of the 101st left a note on one of several websites devoted to the Vietnam Veterans Memorial. He said his unit, B Company, 2nd of the 502nd, was sent in on June 10, 1969, to bail out the Condors, who had rescued the downed Cobra crew on Hamburger Hill but were in trouble themselves trying to get off the mountain. "As it turned out, my squad took the hill top and pulled the Cav out of a jam," wrote Randy Page of San Antonio. "When we reached the top, the first thing we saw was Robert's body. I did not know, until recently, that it was Robert who died on Hamburger Hill that day. Just a note to honor his sacrifice and memory. RIP Brother."[105]

On another site, one maintained by the Vietnam Veterans Memorial Fund, which built the Wall, a note on Sergeant Howard's page was addressed to him:

> Dearest Robert,
>
> Your Son has visited you in Vietnam, he has walked in your footsteps and felt your presence around him. Robert has experienced a peace which will allow him to live his life with no regrets. You would be so very proud of him; we could not have asked for any more in a Son. He is a Husband and a Father and now as he places you within that special place in his heart, he will soon experience the joy of a new life in his

> Family. Be at peace, know that we love you and you are ever present in our lives and our hearts.
>
> Posted by: Roberta J Vincent
> Relationship: He is my husband
> Wednesday, March 19, 2003[106]

Two years later, when he was forty and the father of three, young Robert visited the same website and added his own note to the father he never knew:

> Thanks for everything. I've learned a lot about you in the past couple of years and it has made me a better father and a stronger person. Love you always
>
> your Son

On May 26, 2014, Robert Howard II visited the White House with members of Sons and Daughters In Touch and other family members of Americans killed in war and was welcomed by President Barack Obama. Obama had just returned from a secret overnight flight to Afghanistan to pay tribute to more than thirty-two thousand American troops, nearly all of whom were to be withdrawn from that embattled land by the end of the year. Howard went from the White House to the Vietnam Veterans Memorial, where he showed me his father's name engraved high overhead on the mirrorlike black wall.

Every five years, a delegation of the sons and daughters group visits Washington to wash the memorial wall that bears their fathers' names. In 2014, Howard joined representatives of American Gold Star Mothers and other organizations to present wreaths at the wall during the annual Memorial Day ceremony. When it was over, a speaker thanked all those who had lost husbands, sons, and loved ones in Vietnam. There was no mention of their children.

Robert Howard II points to his father's name high overhead on The Wall.

"They still don't get it," Howard said in a muffled and now-rare flash of anger. "They don't even know we're here." Robert Howard's experience with Bill Zierdt, his father's commanding officer, helped him find the way past his fury and self-destruction and toward building a better life for himself and his family. For Zierdt, the encounter served as a catalyst that forced his own emotional struggle into the open, where he learned to face it—and fight it. But Zierdt knew he would never be free of his memories. He was visiting his ninety-one-year-old father one morning in 2005, when the old man, whose health had been slipping for three years, laid his head back on his pillow for the last time, looked up at his son, and said, "I dreamt of Kasserine last night."

The son knew he meant February 1943, when German Field Marshal Erwin Rommel drew the U.S. First Armored Division into a deadly trap at the Kasserine Pass in the mountains of Tunisia. German guns destroyed nearly all the American tanks in that first large-scale battle between German and American forces in World War II. Zierdt's father had three half-tracks shot out from under him that week, and his best friend's body, missing its head, fell on him.

"PTSD is forever," Zierdt wrote me some years later. "I had never realized he had the same issues as I."[107]

HARD ROAD BACK

RICHARD FRAZEE, THE CREW CHIEF WHO JUMPED out of his chopper in the Laotian wilderness to search for Jim Kane and Jim Casher after their Cobra was shot down, went home from the war and tried to figure out what he wanted to do with the rest of his life. Like most of the enlisted men he knew in Vietnam and many of the officers, he smoked a lot of pot, both in-country and back in the States afterward. A thoughtful, introspective person, he sought comfort in the company of other Vietnam vets who shared the language and experience of war.

The Army was shedding people, and Frazee got an "early out" to go home to Kansas and join an Army Reserve aviation unit. There he found a couple of vets like himself who had manned a lonely radio listening post in a tiny hut on the edge of the A Shau. Frazee remembered seeing the place from the air and wondering who the poor bastards were who were stuck out there. In Olathe, Kansas, the three became friends, dependent on each other because their common experience gave them reference points they didn't have to explain or apologize for. They rented an apartment together, did a lot of dope, and tried to put the war behind them. The drugs helped take the edge off, but they didn't make the future any clearer.

Frazee got out of the reserves as soon as he could and went back to school. He had started college at Kansas State before the Army, but dropped out after a semester. He decided to get his degree in natural resource management, thinking he could find another career in public service and maybe rekindle the esprit de corps he had treasured in C Troop. Frazee realized that the adrenaline rush of combat, terrifying as the experience had been day after day, became an addiction of sorts. The ear-shattering dashes in and out of hot landing zones, his blasting away with his M-60 machine gun at the muzzle flashes from enemy rifles, even the shells piercing his helicopter generated an excitement he could never find anywhere else. Nor did he want to. Drugs kept him loose, but he struggled to understand what the war had done to him.

He managed pretty well for a while: finished college, got a job with the Kansas City park system, worked his way up to park manager, and became superintendent of parks for his home county south of Kansas City. It wasn't as neat as it might have looked on his résumé, however. Frazee married a woman who shared his fondness for a variety of drugs, as well as alcohol, and their lives descended into dependency. Frazee graduated to cocaine, a popular but expensive escalation of his drug habit. Nearly a decade after he got home from the war, he realized he had never gotten over Vietnam.

He didn't identify it as post-traumatic stress—and still doesn't in any official sense. He thought maybe he was living too much in the past, so he gathered the souvenirs and memorabilia he had brought home from the war and burned them. Photos of friends and choppers and landscapes. Machine-gun rounds taken from his helicopter, enemy bullets and shot-up pieces of aircraft, shrapnel he picked up off the ground at Khe Sanh—all went into the fire. What didn't burn up he disposed of. But not his "Cav hat," the black Stetson he eventually wore to Major Newman's funeral, nor the floppy cotton "boonie hat" that jungle warriors treasured. The ceremonial fire helped, but not enough.

His marriage dissolved, mostly a result of substance abuse, and he decided to get away. A couple, who had been good friends in college, had moved to the Northwest and told him it was a great place. There was a recession at the time, and not many jobs were available, but Frazee moved to Seattle and found work as a gardener, partly just to make a break with his past. As he put it, he had been living his life "leaning forward, trying to just keep going."[108]

He also tackled what he had come to realize was a problem with drugs. It had taken years, but he "connected the dots" and told himself he had acquired the habit in Vietnam as medication to get through those terrifying days, and he just didn't need that anymore. He went from being high a lot of the time to occasional recreational use to none. It took a year or so to give up drugs completely, but he did it on his own.

Seattle, he decided, wasn't away enough. He needed time to think, to reflect on what had happened to him, to remove the mask, and deal with his feelings about the war without thinking so much about career goals and measures of his achievement. Frazee found a small hut in the foothills of the Cascade Mountains east of Seattle and settled into the woods to read, relax, and be quiet. His new home had no heat, no electricity, no running water, but he found he could read there, and think. He wasn't a hermit; he took a part-time job as a cook at the Silver Spoon, a restaurant in the nearby town of Duvall, and met a lot of people in town. He lived that way for almost two years before he decided to embark again on a different career and a more normal lifestyle.

Although Frazee gave up his longtime desire to work for the government as a way of doing public service, he still wanted to do something he considered meaningful. The first job he landed was as a clerk in a small private company that did consulting on occupational health and safety. He must have been good at it, because he rose to general manager within a couple of years, and about two years after that, he left to start his own environmental consulting and training firm. Frazee is president of Argus Pacific, which boasts a number of well-known clients in the Northwest, including Boeing, Microsoft, Safeway, and the city of Seattle.

The one Condor he kept in close touch with for years was Gary Schuler, the door gunner who jumped out of the helicopter into Laos with him. Schuler, who once welcomed the military draft as a way out of a dreary, noisy, assembly-line job in a General Motors plant in Michigan, eventually went to work for the Veterans Administration and helped many friends and other former soldiers apply for benefits they had coming as a result of their service. He learned, long after the war, that a lot of veterans who seemed to be leading successful lives were still struggling with their war experiences.

"I see it all the time," he said. "It's good that people could carry out their lives and be successful. It's very good, but there's a lot of us Vietnam vets out there that really still have our issues big-time, even though people look at us as being successful. We continue to be successful, but those issues will never go away, and it has its impact on us."[109] Schuler himself sought treatment and got better, but in recent years, his fears, his nightmares, and trouble sleeping have returned.

After he got out of the Army, he went home to Michigan and went back to work in an auto plant, but a year or so later decided he hated his job and ought to try college. He was drinking a lot, spending most of his nights in bars, and he got nowhere in school. He eventually followed a friend to Lincoln, Nebraska, to restart his life, as he put it. Schuler made another run at a college career, got married, graduated from the University of Nebraska at Lincoln in 1984 and—seventeen years after Vietnam—earned a master's degree in public administration from the University of Nebraska Omaha in 1988. The marriage lasted ten years but ended in divorce. During that time, he reconnected with Frazee, who had been one of the closest friends he ever had.

At some point, after Schuler had learned the ropes at the Veterans Administration and reestablished his friendship with his old crew chief, he suggested Frazee was struggling with post-traumatic stress disorder. His friend didn't want to hear it. But now and then, when Frazee talked about his life since the war, Schuler would tell him, "That's the PTSD talkin'." Frazee refused to listen.

Schuler himself learned to avoid watching things on television he found "too dramatic" because they brought back memories of the friends he lost and his own worst day, the day he and Frazee jumped into the elephant grass in Laos and couldn't figure out where they were or how to get back. There were other bad times, like the day his friend Greg Crandall and two others were shot down and killed in Laos and Schuler saw the charred bodies in the wreckage but couldn't get to them. It was, nevertheless, the desperate attempt to find Kane and Casher in enemy-held territory that kept coming back to rekindle his personal terror.

Schuler went to one of the first Condor reunions in about 2001, primarily to see his old friends, and he went back several times to encourage those with problems to seek help from the VA. He had become a specialist in reviewing case files for final approval of disability benefits, and he thought he could help former buddies who didn't realize they suffered from PTSD or that they were entitled to treatment and benefits. There were physical illnesses as well, such as Type 2 diabetes, many cancers, and hearing loss, that were presumptively traced to Vietnam, exposure to Agent Orange, or other environmental factors related to service during the war. He told people the process could take a long time and that many people got frustrated by it—one claim took him five years before it won final approval—but Schuler told his friends they were likely to receive benefits in the end and that made it worth the investment in time. That was years before the delays in the VA system's treatment of vets and administrators' attempts to cover them up exploded into scandal in 2014.

Like many of those who have attended the reunions, Schuler found the experience both rewarding and deeply troubling. Reconnecting with old friends who shared the most exciting, yet terrifying, time in his life was a joy, but reliving those events while listening to his comrades share their war stories and memories brought back the fear, the shock, and the agony of it all. The PTSD he had learned to control got its grip on him again.

In Vietnam, he always slept with his .45-caliber automatic pistol close at hand "so I could grab it if I needed it." He felt more comfortable with it at his side. When he came home, he thought it was over and never had a desire to own a weapon, but in recent years he has felt the need. He lives in a small, quiet town north of Denver and knows his family is secure, but after the economic collapse in 2008, he sensed that someone might steal something "or come in and harm us."

He started keeping weapons at home because they make him feel better knowing he has them around, although they're not loaded for fear his ten-year-old granddaughter might find one and hurt herself. He thought his fear of being stalked or attacked had gone away, too. He has gone deer hunting in Michigan but recently began to feel "there was somebody out there," and he couldn't relax in the woods.

Someone tried to steal the wheels off his twelve-year-old Bonneville, so he started parking it on a pad out back, where it was less visible from the street. That was before he retired, and he had to leave for work when it was still dark.

"I was scared to death to go out and get in my car," Schuler said. "I thought the enemy was in my backyard. It scares the shit out of me to get in my car. It still does. I can't go in the backyard at night hardly at all unless the lights are on. And I like my backyard."

Schuler said he told that to a counselor at the VA clinic where he goes for periodic talks about his PTSD, but other vets who don't have his experience watching for the symptoms of post-traumatic stress don't associate their problems with Vietnam and don't know to seek help for them.

Schuler suffered for years from frequent and severe headaches and took aspirin to dull the pain. In 2012, he was hospitalized with bleeding ulcers and was given seven units of blood, but doctors weren't able to locate the source of the problem without exploratory surgery, which Schuler declined. Two years later, he had a recurrence and was back in the hospital, where he passed out and fell, pulling an IV rack down on his face. The good news, he said, was that he fought off the aspirin habit, and his headaches receded.

Years after he came home from Vietnam, Schuler's crewmate, Frazee, wrote a description of a mental snapshot he had kept in his head since Khe Sanh but never mentioned to anyone. It was late in the Laos operation, and he was in his usual place as crew chief aboard Huey 736. He couldn't remember any details of the mission, what day it was, or who was with him. Those were blotted out, leaving only the image of the incident itself. Sometime in the 1980s, probably thirteen to fifteen years after it happened, he thought it would help to put it into words:

It was a really early morning of thick, deep, impenetrable fog. The morning had a cold and damp feel but mostly it was surreal, yet incredibly tranquil and quiet—total silence except the swoosh of the rotor blades. It would soon become eerie and stunningly sad.

We sat in line on the runway at idle RPM for a long time. Just quietly sitting there in the fog and the damp, misty cold. Facing me as I sat there was a wide strip of grass between the runway and the revetments beyond. At first I couldn't see ten feet, but as the minutes passed, I began to make out the grassy strip and what appeared to be a small building or bunker barely visible.

Sleepy-eyed and already saddened by recent events, I seemed to be in a quiet, melancholy state, just staring into the fog—a dead stare—watching the little bunker become more and more visible.

The long line of helicopters ahead began to creep forward, but I just kept looking into the fog that enveloped us and across the grassy strip. Finally, my ship began to increase RPM and slowly lift a few inches off the ground. I hardly noticed. I was entranced in the eerie calmness of the morning and the fog-shrouded and misty apparition.

As the helicopter moved forward ever so slowly, I could see more of the bunker. It had corrugated sheeting on the sides. Now we were nearly parallel to it. Then I saw.

I could barely make it out. I squinted my eyes as a figure took shape. I thought, "Is that a person? Yes, a person." The twilight was still dim, and the fog was still too thick to see clearly, but now I could tell there was a young soldier sitting on the ground with his back against the corrugated sheeting. Fog was swirling now from the rotor wash, and then I saw something more, the shape of a weapon.

But the rifle was in his mouth with the butt between his knees. I wasn't sure anymore if any of it was real. It was still foggy, still surreal, still not quite visible and still strangely tranquil. I said nothing. I just kept watching the fog slowly thin out and swirl like cotton candy in the rotor wash.

And then I saw the blood. It was all over the side of the bunker behind his head.

For a moment, my mind sprang to life, and my heart seized. My instant impulse was to grab the trigger grip of my M-60, key my mic with my thumb and shout what I had seen. But then I relaxed my thumb, and I said nothing. I suppose I didn't want to disturb him in his desperate escape. I quietly sympathized with his lonely act and with my own lonely sadness and depression of spirit. Then I thought about all that he and I had experienced in this place. Had he gotten a "Dear John letter," as I would three months later? Or maybe he'd failed to save his best friend in a firefight, killed too many, or lied to a dying trooper, "You're gonna make it." I'd never know. I still don't. But I dream about knowing, seeing, and my wet streaks of quiet tears.

The aircraft continued to taxi down the runway. I slowly rotated my head with silently fixed eyes as we moved past the bunker and I stared quietly at the kid in the grassy strip who had just ended it once and for all. I kept looking back at him as the image quietly faded from sight. I said nothing and hoped that I, too, was not disappearing from sight; fading away.[110]

Sometimes, when Frazee refused another prod to go in for an evaluation, Schuler would get angry at him for his obstinacy. Frazee wanted to work it out on his own. He remembered years after one such conversation that Schuler had told him: "Give me a break, Frazee. You got a Bronze Star with V device, an air medal with V device. You got eleven air medals, had alcohol problems, drug problems and two failed marriages. What do you think this adds up to?"[111]

Frazee understood, but he was determined not to let the war get the better of his life. "Vietnam didn't kill me," he said, "and I am not going to let it ruin me." There were times, however, when he lost his iron self-control. One was while watching the movie *Saving Private Ryan*, the 1998 World War II epic about the loss of an American patrol sent to find and bring to safety the sole survivor of four brothers sent off to war. Captain Miller, the commander of the band of eight soldiers, played by actor Tom Hanks, is mortally wounded and tells Private Ryan with his dying breath to earn the price his fellow soldiers paid to get him home safely. In the closing scene, Ryan, who was a paratrooper in the 101st Airborne Division, visits the American cemetery at Normandy decades after the war and crouches before the simple white stone cross engraved with Captain Miller's name. In the casual dress of a retired traveler with a tiny Screaming Eagle embroidered on the breast of his jacket, Ryan tells his dead captain, "Every day I think of what you said to me that day on the bridge. I've tried to live my life the best I could. I hope that it was enough. I hope that at least in your eyes, I've earned what all of you have done for me."

As his wife walks over to join him at the grave site, he turns to her and says, implores, "Tell me I have led a good life... Tell me I'm a good man."

Watching that famous ending, Frazee broke down, crying hysterically, something that rarely happened, even on the day he had to clean the pieces of Sergeant Keith's leg out of his helicopter. Frazee saw himself in Ryan, who had thought of the captain's words every day since the war.

"If I admit that I am damaged somehow by Vietnam, can I keep hold of that self-image I have?" Frazee asked. "That's the nut I can't seem to crack.

"And I don't feel bad about it."

WAR WITHOUT END

Nobody told the men coming back that they would have trouble adjusting to "the World," as they called anyplace but Vietnam. They were glad to be alive, glad to be going home, and although the military knew from long experience that returnees sometimes bore psychological scars from war, there was no system to identify who would suffer—or what, exactly, caused their pain. The systems developed since, based on painful experience, are woefully inadequate at determining who will or will not prove resilient enough to put the war in perspective and carry on a happy, well-adjusted life.

Even less understood was that the onset of symptoms could begin immediately, frequently as excessive drinking or drug use to dull the senses and memories, or might not break into the open for many years, as in the case of Bill Zierdt, the first Condor, and Chuck Vehlow, whose PTSD was diagnosed while he was being treated for prostate cancer, some three decades after the war.

The officers and crews of Charlie Troop, highly trained volunteers for the most part and led into battle by an acclaimed commander, were presumed less likely than others to be upended by combat. They were the gung-ho ones, the true believers. War fighters, they called themselves, and they were proud. They were also immune to the life of the infantry grunt who humped seventy-five pounds on his back, dug a hole to sleep in at night, and never knew what awaited him in the jungle ahead. Yet the intensity of enemy fire during the Laos operation and the crews' exposure to danger, often several times a day for more than six weeks, tested the limits of endurance and, sometimes, sanity.

When the war ended with the collapse of South Vietnam on April 30, 1975—well after all American combat troops had left the country—psychiatric doctrine in the United States did not yet recognize post-traumatic stress disorder.

The American Psychiatric Association's *Diagnostic and Statistical Manual of Mental Disorders,* then in its second edition, had actually dropped a diagnosis of "Gross Stress Reaction," the closest the manual came to identifying battle fatigue, and substituted something it called "Adjustment Reaction to Adult Life" in a category of transient disturbances that were expected to go away by themselves. The manual, frequently referred to as psychiatry's "bible," was revised again in 1980, and by that time, the profession had encountered numerous cases of returning servicemen whose war-related problems did not abate after their return from the combat zone. That edition of the manual, the third, identified a condition it called Post-Traumatic Stress Disorder and acknowledged it could come on soon after the traumatic event that caused it and might last for months or could show up as a delayed reaction many months or years after the trauma occurred.

The mental health professions, the military, and the Veterans Administration (which was elevated to cabinet status and renamed the Department of Veterans Affairs in 1989) have focused on the problem with increasing concern in the years since and have come to acknowledge that PTSD is far more common and more difficult to identify and treat than anyone knew before or during Vietnam.[112]

Chuck Vehlow, Newman's trusted gun pilot and later the troop's operations officer, thought he had put Vietnam behind him and didn't think much about PTSD. He built a professional career on his military experience and is recognized for helping design and develop the modern successors to the Cobra he flew in C Troop.

Vehlow led what many considered a storybook life. A school and college football star, he married his high school sweetheart in a traditional academy wedding ten days after graduating from West Point. When he came home from the war, Chuck and Kate raised their children in comfort as he rose through military and civilian careers that led to top executive posts in the defense industry. Vehlow didn't look back to reexamine what he had done or how he had survived in Vietnam, believing that he and his comrades had performed their duties well. He was busy managing his career, going from one challenging job to another, and looking out for his family, not reliving the past. "I really didn't think much about what we had gone through," he told me years later. "I felt we did what was expected of us as aviators."

Statistics change with each new study, but there is general agreement that healthy people put grief and fright behind them, letting their memories fade with time and thinking about the present more than the past.

"Forgetting can be healthy," one noted specialist in post-traumatic stress told me. He explained that many soldiers deal successfully with their combat experiences, not necessarily by forgetting entirely but by letting their memories of past events recede, a process familiar to people who endure grief after the loss of family or friends.

Dr. Stephen Cozza, like Vehlow a West Point graduate, spent his military career as a psychiatrist studying and treating PTSD. After he retired from the Army, he stayed on at the Uniformed Services University of the Health Sciences, a federally funded medical and nursing school for military and Public Health Service officers located in a suburb of Washington, D.C. As associate director of the university's Center for the Study of Traumatic Stress, Cozza is among the country's most respected PTSD specialists.

Cozza is skeptical of the concept of late-onset PTSD, that people suddenly develop the disorder many years after a traumatic event. But he said, "Everybody comes back different, and so it's really hard to determine whether your experience is going to be a problem or not." It is more likely, he said, that people with underlying PTSD successfully repress their memories and symptoms for a long time until some event triggers a reexposure and the PTSD "suddenly resurfaces."[113]

Vehlow thought he had tucked his memories safely away. His training, from his undergraduate days studying engineering at the academy, taught him to be a problem solver, and he prided himself on his ability to tackle complex challenges. After training to be an Army Ranger and qualifying to jump out of airplanes, he was sent to Fort Belvoir for basic combat engineer training, then to Fort Carson, Colorado, to practice building and repairing roads, bridges, and airstrips as he might be called upon to do in combat zones. It was there he saw helicopters and got excited about flying. The Army's sudden appetite for chopper pilots to go to Vietnam gave him his shot at flight school and the chance to pilot Cobras, but after his wartime tour, he was expected to resume the more conventional life of an Army engineer.

Picked for a coveted job as a general's aide at the Defense Systems Management College just outside Washington, Vehlow discovered the Army was struggling to keep pace in an increasingly complex and expensive new world. The revolution in technology was spreading to weapons systems, and most military officers weren't ready or eager to change as fast as the industry that was building and promoting futuristic war machines. The Cold War was raging, and political pressure helped drive a U.S.-Soviet arms race that spurred the military-industrial complex to develop ever newer, more deadly weapons, even in peacetime. Vehlow wanted out of the bridge-building business to get back to flying machines. To earn another shot at air cavalry, he switched to the Army's armor branch, which was in charge of all cavalry, whether tanks on the ground or helicopters in the air. He spent a year studying strategy and tactics, then commanded a ground cavalry troop driving Sheridan tanks across dirt practice fields and through forests at Fort Knox. The Army sent him to MIT for a master's degree in aeronautical engineering, then to the Naval War College in Newport, Rhode Island, for strategic studies intended to groom promising senior officers for promotion.

A year in South Korea with an air cavalry squadron was followed by three years teaching helicopter design and engineering at West Point. That was a great job, and he got to keep flying, but afterward, when he asked for assignment to the Pentagon to develop the next generation of helicopters, the Army tried instead to send him back to the ground cavalry, to West Germany, where U.S. forces trained for conventional tank warfare. Still a major, Vehlow resigned his commission and gave up a shot at making general someday to put his experience and training to work for defense contractors designing and building military helicopters. He arrived late to the development team at McDonnell Douglas that was promoting its version of the ill-fated Comanche helicopter as the successor to the loach and venerable Huey. The Comanche contract went instead to Boeing and Sikorsky, but that may have been Vehlow's good fortune. Fed up after two decades of frustrating technical setbacks and seemingly endless cost overruns, the Army finally scrapped the Comanche program without ever adopting the aircraft for military deployment. Boeing bought McDonnell Douglas, and Vehlow wound up as vice president of the merged company's helicopter division. It was his office that developed and produced the AH-64D Apache Longbow, successor to the AH-1 Cobra gunship that Vehlow had flown in Vietnam.

When he left active duty, Vehlow took a commission in the Army Reserve and spent his required summer service at the Pentagon working on defense equipment budgets for fourteen years. He retired as a full colonel.

In 2000, Vehlow traveled to the first of the Condors reunions. He wanted to see the guys again, and when they got together, of course, they began telling war stories, recalling details of the events they had shared. Exchanging those stories brought back memories Vehlow had put away many years before. He began to reflect on some of the worst parts, especially the day Mickey McLeod and Clyde Wilkinson crashed and burned before his eyes in Laos. Afterward, he started having flashbacks and would wake up in a cold sweat thinking of Mickey, one of his closest friends at the time. Some of the roughest parts of the war, moments that barely got a mention in the tiny spaces in his pocket diary, came back, again, then again.

In 2004, Vehlow was diagnosed with an aggressive form of prostate cancer, and—characteristically—he attacked the disease as a complex problem to be solved, seeking medical advice from top specialists around the country and also consulting the Disabled American Veterans about the disease's possible link to his service in Vietnam. He learned the VA had recently put prostate cancer on its list of service-related disabilities, making sufferers eligible for treatment and benefits. There was no doubt he was entitled to a benefit check. Practically all Vietnam veterans are presumed to have been exposed to Agent Orange, the herbicide widely used by American forces to strip the jungles and mangrove swamps of their green growth and expose enemy positions. Widespread spraying of the chemical from the air was later implicated in a panoply of cancers, heart problems, neurological disorders, even spina bifida in veterans' children. Any Vietnam vet who develops prostate cancer is automatically eligible for benefits because the disease may have been caused by the since-banned chemical agent.

In Vehlow's case, it wasn't just about Agent Orange. By the time he was evaluated at the VA, standard medical history questionnaires included queries designed to identify symptoms of mental, as well as physical, illness. Vehlow's responses led doctors to think he might be experiencing PTSD in addition to his cancer. He was asked if he got depressed, ever had suicidal feelings, lost his temper, or had flashbacks. He answered yes to some of the questions and was advised to go in for further evaluation. A follow-up exam led to a positive diagnosis, and Vehlow agreed to begin therapy for post-traumatic stress.

Chuck Vehlow isn't the type of person to sit around a circle and talk about his personal problems. It's not that he didn't want help—it's that he believed Kate and the family suffered more than he when he snapped at them or lost his temper, and he wanted to fix that. He signed up for group counseling and started going to the VA for meetings with other victims of PTSD. He also saw an individual counselor, but he wasn't comfortable with the treatment. He talked some at the meetings and tried to help others in the group, but he'd never had much patience with what he called "the soft and squishy stuff." He resisted talking about his own feelings or "opening the back reaches of my mind," as he put it.[114] But he stuck with it for a couple of years, then decided to deal with the problems on his own.

Vehlow thinks of himself as an engineer, a problem solver, and decided his PTSD was a problem he could figure out on his own. One of the things he learned in combat, largely from Newman, was to control his fear, not let the situation shake him up but to ratchet down, stay calm, and think about what he needed to do, what the next step should be. He doesn't get nervous in a crisis. Just as he managed weapons systems development projects, he spent lots of time studying his options in fighting cancer, as well as managing PTSD, and he lived with both for years.

Once thought to affect perhaps one in twenty soldiers and regarded by military brass as a sign of cowardice or weak character, PTSD is now considered far more common, especially among troops subjected to prolonged and furious combat. Both the intensity of fighting, sometimes measured by the number of casualties suffered, and the amount of time troops are exposed to fire without respite are key indicators of who is most likely to crack. That much has been known at least since World War II.

The military's focus, however, was to deal with the tactical problem of fighters who quit, collapsed, or ran away. It was only after Vietnam that psychiatrists and psychologists recognized that the emotional effects of combat often show up long after the fight—and may last a lifetime.

Dr. Cozza, the PTSD specialist, though he did not treat Zierdt or Vehlow, would be inclined to say PTSD like theirs was probably present all along but just went undiagnosed until triggered by an event, such as Vehlow's participation in the reunions or Bill Zierdt's being given a copy of the letter he had written to a little boy about the death of the boy's father. Zierdt would certainly agree. He didn't recognize he was suffering from a mental health disorder, but he spent at least some part of every day—and sometimes hours—remembering and rethinking his order to a doomed pilot: "You're on fire! Head for the valley floor."

So far as is known, Jim Newman never considered himself a victim of PTSD or sought treatment for it, but the stunning, self-destructive reversals in his behavior after returning from the war are practically impossible to square with his remarkable leadership and heroic conduct as commander of C Troop. I never found a plausible explanation for the changes in him.

Gary Schuler, the door gunner who witnessed the crash of scout pilot Greg Crandall and his two crewmen, can't think of seeing their bodies in the wreckage in Laos without triggering his PTSD. His voice still cracks when he imagines Crandall's parents suffering all those years without knowing for sure what he knew at the time. He and Zierdt believe that practically everyone in C Troop developed PTSD at some point, at least all those who experienced combat. Schuler doesn't remember a day in his yearlong tour that someone in the unit didn't get shot at or shot down. After twelve years working with veterans at the VA and trying to help them, especially his friends, he claims he can spot signs of their suffering when he looks at them or listens to them talk.

Schuler walks into a room at a reunion or gathering of veterans and glances around to see how former war fighters carry themselves, how they face each other and position themselves in the room. Nobody stands with his back to anyone else or to a door or open space. They are still protecting themselves, watching their backs, looking furtively around the room with what experts in the field call hypervigilance.[115] The irony of PTSD is that its symptoms are not an accident of war or even an unintended byproduct. They are the skills, often drummed into troops by military training, that are critical to success and survival in combat. It is no wonder that hypervigilance, hair-trigger reactions to potentially threatening movements, lack of sleep, sudden increase in heart rate and breathing, impatience, high anxiety, and closing down emotional responses are keys to survival under fire. Back at home, however, they can wreck family relationships, interfere with work, and lead to dangerous instability. Depression, panic attacks, alcohol and drug abuse, divorce, child abuse, job loss, even suicide may stem from a soldier's inability to make the transition from necessary conduct under fire to a healthy, happy home life.

Dr. Charles W. Hoge, a retired Army psychiatrist who has written extensively on PTSD for leading medical journals, told veterans in his recent book on the subject: "Virtually every reaction that mental health professionals label a 'symptom,' and which indeed can cause havoc in your life after returning home from combat, is an essential survival skill in the war zone."[116]

Unfortunately, Hoge has found, no one knows which returning troops will adjust successfully on their own and which will be unable to adapt and suffer the consequences. Even more discouraging is that treatment of those who are diagnosed with PTSD fails as often as it succeeds in helping veterans recover.[117]

Treating PTSD can take several forms and frequently begins with helping a returned warrior tell his or her own story. That by itself often proves difficult. Few veterans talk openly about their combat experiences after they return, either because they can't or because they think no one would understand. Bottling up their memories, feelings of survivor's guilt, and brooding about what cannot be changed often lead to crashes like the one Bill Zierdt experienced. Careful exposure of the veteran to the places or events where the trauma originated can be an effective element of treatment—but also can be dangerous. In February 2013, a celebrated former sniper for a Navy SEAL team was murdered with a friend by an Iraq War veteran when the sniper took him to a firing range in Texas to help him deal with his PTSD.

Psychotropic drugs are frequently prescribed to help treat PTSD victims, often in combination with psychotherapy. The same drugs used to treat depression, anxiety, and chronic insomnia are frequently prescribed for the symptoms PTSD shares with other mental health disorders.

A less conventional but VA-recognized therapy called eye-movement desensitization and reprocessing, or EMDR, attempts to alter the effects of remembering traumatic, stressful events by changing the brain's association of events to neutral or positive sensations. In a limited number of sessions with a specially trained therapist, PTSD sufferers are retrained to think briefly about some traumatic event they have experienced while moving their eyes, tapping their hands, or listening with headphones to sounds that alternate from one ear to another. The therapy is thought to break the link between the memory and the terror, anxiety, and stress associated with that memory.

Hoge, who began his medical career as an infectious disease specialist, argues that PTSD "is not an 'emotional' or 'psychological' disorder, but a physiological condition that affects the entire body, including cardiovascular functioning, hormone system balance, and immune functioning. PTSD can result in physical, cognitive, psychological, emotional, and behavioral reactions that all have a physiological basis. The body's limbic system that triggers the fight-or-flight response causes the release of stress hormones, dulls pain, quickens blood flow, and unleashes rage as well as fear. The physical responses so critical to survival in war may return just as involuntarily in peacetime as the unwelcome symptoms of PTSD."[118]

In recent years, experts studying the long-term effects of war on the warriors have developed a concept that has come to be called "moral injury." Moral injury is not recognized by the Defense Department or Department of Veterans Affairs as a disabling condition. However, it is gaining acceptance among psychiatrists and religious and military scholars seeking to explain soldiers' lifelong struggles with feelings of shame, guilt, and sorrow traced to their wartime experiences. Some symptoms, such as substance abuse, anger, and depression, overlap with those associated with PTSD, but as war correspondent David Wood wrote in a series for the *Huffington Post*, PTSD stems from a reaction to fear, while moral injury grows from a conflict between the ethical values people learn growing up and the ugly, morally ambiguous situations they encounter in combat.[119]

* * *

A rubbing from The Wall showing Paul Johnson's name.

On August 4, 2005, Ricky Miller sat up all night writing a long email to the officers who had led him in Vietnam.

"Thirty-five years ago today I flew into a place called Three Rivers," he began. He was the crew chief aboard Gunky, the battered Huey he regarded as his personal pet. He described a mission to extract a reconnaissance team from the Blues platoon that was surrounded by the NVA in the notoriously hostile jungle valley called the A Shau. The troops, three of them already severely wounded, were under attack from all sides. The first two Hueys got in and out without serious damage, but the third took several hits from small arms and .51-caliber machines guns. Gunky was No. 4, the last ship in. Enemy soldiers were climbing the sloping hillside toward the small clearing where Gunky was trying to land. Its machine guns rattled off streams of fire to buy the Blues precious moments.[120]

Miller saw that one of the three Americans shooting back at the North Vietnamese was only a few feet from the aircraft but was blinded by blood covering his face and couldn't see to aim his rifle.

The crew chief abandoned his machine gun, grabbed a pistol, and jumped off his lift ship to help pull people aboard. He recognized the closest of the wounded as Private First Class Ed Long, who had been hit back and front by mortar shells and was crawling toward the ship, feeling for the skids with outstretched arms. Miller scooped him up with one arm and boosted him onto the floor of the chopper. He turned and saw another familiar soldier from the Blues platoon and ran toward him, zigzagging to dodge enemy fire. It was a short, stocky blond corporal named Larry Banton. Miller dragged him toward Gunky and hoisted him aboard. Banton landed on top of Long, who told Miller years later he thought it was a dead body that fell on him.

At the edge of the landing zone, perhaps thirty yards away, Miller saw the unit's radioman struggling to pick up another fallen soldier. He ran through the incoming fire to help and glanced over his shoulder to see enemy soldiers firing their AK-47 assault rifles in his direction. When he reached the wounded soldier, he looked down and recognized twenty-two-year-old Paul A. Johnson, the acting platoon sergeant and Miller's best friend.

"He had been hit directly in his back, and there was a hole so big that you could see all of his insides—his lungs, everything," Miller wrote. He shouted at the radioman to run for the chopper, saying he would carry Johnson. "From then on my world went quiet. . . . I got down on my knees, held Paul up. He opened his eyes but didn't say anything but gave me a big grin. . . . I tried to keep the tears down as much as I could as I didn't want Paul to think he was that badly wounded. It was hard though. . . . I told him I was going to carry him back and for him to just try and relax so the bleeding would slow down. Paul was a pale white . . . I stumbled one foot in front of the other trying to keep my wobbly knees locked in place so as not to fall down with Paul on my back. All I could think of was, 'Why, God? Why my friend? Why did you get me to come here today?'" He remembered being knocked down by the concussion of a mortar round exploding nearby, getting up, and going on, then being knocked down again. As he approached the helicopter, he could see the peter pilot, Warrant Officer Mark "Mighty Mouth" Minear, watching him from the cockpit. He stumbled and went down again, exhausted. He thought he would die there with his friend and started to signal Minear to take off without them. Then he heard Sergeant Johnson speak, just enough to tell him to save himself and leave Johnson behind.

"My back was killing me, and I could feel my heart beating so hard that I could feel my heart hitting my chicken plate," Miller's email recounted. "I remember back in high school when I ran the five-mile, I think it was, the taste I would get in my mouth about three-fourths of the way through the run. I had that taste in my mouth now, and I knew then I was pushing myself to my fullest."

Eventually, they reached the slick, boosted Johnson's limp body aboard, and Miller told the aircraft commander—too soon—to take off. The ship shot upward, and Miller just managed to grab the skid with one arm to keep from being left behind. With the aircraft rising out of the trees, he swung his body over the skid, reached for the barrel of the mounted machine gun, and grabbed a solid metal canister on the Huey's floor. It held two thousand rounds of ammunition for the M-60 and wasn't going anywhere. Miller pulled himself on board as Gunky headed for Phu Bai and the 85th Evacuation Hospital.

He opened the craft's first-aid kit, took out a couple rolls of gauze, and stuck them in Johnson's gaping wound without bothering to unwrap them first. The sergeant opened his eyes, motioned for Miller to bend toward him, "and he told me to make sure that his mom and dad and brother and sister knew that he loved them all and he had thought of them in his last moments. I told him to shut up. You're not going to die on me."

Gunky was flying so fast the whole aircraft began to shake as the crew raced its cargo of wounded to the hospital.

"Paul again woke up and pulled my head down again. 'Promise me, Rick, that you will tell my family I loved them and I thought of them...' I told him I would but that he could tell them himself because he wasn't going to die now. . . ." Tears swelled in the crew chief's eyes, and he pulled the dark sun visor on his flight helmet down to hide his face.

"I stroked his hair, tried to clean up his face somewhat," and in minutes the helicopter landed at 85th Evac. Johnson clutched Miller's hand as the orderlies loaded him onto a gurney, and as Miller freed his grip, the sergeant told him, "Bye, my friend. We were the best, weren't we?"

The crew chief's Army green flight suit was so soaked in blood that medics tried to put him on a gurney, too, but he pulled away and sent them after the other wounded. Johnson died a couple of hours later on the operating table.

Minear told Miller afterward that he would put the crew chief in for a Medal of Honor for the heroics he had shown during the rescue mission, but the paperwork never got completed. Twenty-five days later, on August 29, Minear, who had been promoted to aircraft commander in the interim, was flying a mission to insert a team of five Rangers into the jungle not far from where the earlier incident had occurred. The North Vietnamese were waiting for them, and as the Huey set down, a blast of fire from a .51-caliber machine gun ripped through the cockpit and killed both pilots, Minear and his copilot, First Lieutenant John Frederick Shiefer, and two of the Rangers. Only three Rangers and two crewmen survived.

Just two days later, Mac Jones, still reeling from the loss of Minear and Shiefer, was leading two other slicks to a pickup point where a B Troop loach had been shot down trying to insert a handful of Rangers for a reconnaissance mission. Thirteen or fourteen men, including the loach crew, were pinned down in a bomb crater under heavy enemy fire. The Hueys each had twenty-five-foot, roll-up aluminum ladders they could drop into the trees to pick up the marooned soldiers without touching down.

The intensity of the battle drove the helicopters away repeatedly before one managed to get in close enough to pick up seven men and Jones dropped down to get the rest. The Rangers' leader, Staff Sergeant Perry R. Tipton, was carrying his unit's radio and made sure everyone else got onto the ladder ahead of him. He grabbed the bottom of the ladder with one hand and pressed the transmit button on his handset with the other to tell the pilot, "Take off! Take off!"

Jones pulled pitch to get going and lift the troops on the ladder out of the trees. Then he heard the voice on the radio say, "I'm still here." The sergeant was so exhausted he couldn't hold on to the ladder and was left behind. The helicopter crews overhead heard Tipton's voice come back on the air: "Oh my God, I'm the only one left." And after a momentary pause, the pilots aloft heard him add, "I'm the coolest motherfucker in the jungle."

With six men already clinging to the twenty-five-foot ladder hanging from his slick, Jones couldn't go back. But Chief Warrant Officer 2 Harvey Rients, the twenty-one-year-old pilot of the third Huey, which had left to refuel and was just arriving back on station, announced over the radio, "This is Four-two. I'm back. I'm inbound and will go get him." He slipped into the clearing, and the crew dangled the ladder for the last Ranger. Loaded down with his rucksack, M-16 rifle, and the team's PRC-25 field radio, which weighed nearly twenty-five pounds, Tipton grabbed hold of the ladder a few rungs up from the bottom and hung on that time. As the Huey lifted him out of the jungle, its machine guns firing back at the enemy, crew chief Michael Horsch watched as the man on the ladder grimaced and loosened his heavy gear. He let the radio drop, then his rifle, and finally the rucksack before he slipped and just caught himself upside down, clinging to the ladder with his knees over one rung.

Horsch had rigged the ladders to insert and extract grunts, but he had never been on one. He stripped off his flight helmet, chicken plate, and pistol belt with his .45-caliber pistol, grabbed the ladder and went out the open doorway. As he let himself down past the skid, he thought, "Damn, this is a windy ride." He kept climbing down from rung to rung until he could reach down, grab Tipton, and pin his legs around a ladder rung to keep the Ranger from falling off. As he wrote Jones in an email several years later, "At that point I had to trust the people in the aircraft to do the right thing because the wind was going by so hard that it was watering my eyes and was difficult to breathe."

Rients spotted a dirt road that cut a wide enough swath in the foliage to let him land, and he descended toward it, slowing his aircraft as it approached the ground. A few feet before the ladder touched down, Tipton and Horsch fell off, and Rients landed about thirty feet away. Horsch got up, grabbed Tipton, who was dazed, exhausted, and in shock but not bleeding, and guided him toward the helicopter. Both men survived the war, but Tipton struggled with PTSD for decades.[121]

Ricky Miller kept Gunky flying for another year, extending his Vietnam tour to twenty-two months, most of that time with C Troop. The Army eventually awarded him a Bronze Star with V for his actions in rescuing the Blues riflemen that day. He tried several times to get it upgraded, if not to the Medal of Honor, at least to a Distinguished Flying Cross that would recognize his service in aviation. In the fall of 1971, he went home to Texas and was stationed at Fort Hood, but he couldn't find the excitement and pride he had felt during the war. He talked to some shadowy recruiters about flying black operations in Central America, but nothing came of it, and he decided to leave the Army. After his discharge, Miller "just sort of disappeared," as he put it. He left friends and family behind, ignoring attempts to contact him and hung around an abandoned airfield outside the West Texas town of Big Spring, where he took up dirt-track car racing to get his adrenaline pumping. He said he was trying to emulate the exhilaration he got from combat. He also drank a lot.

Miller eventually settled down and took a job with a large discount jewelry chain. But guilt dogged him because he couldn't bring himself to keep his promise to tell Sergeant Johnson's family about his friend's final thoughts of home. After the company he worked for was sold, he traveled through the South doing consulting work for smaller jewelers. At Christmastime, about twenty years after Johnson was killed, Miller found himself in Nashville, Tennessee, and realized he was less than two hundred miles south of Johnson's family home near the village of New Haven, Kentucky. On Christmas Day, he drove north to find the Johnsons at last and fulfill his obligation. On his first attempt, he pulled into the wrong driveway and was greeted by a bunch of bootleggers, who came toward his car carrying rifles and shotguns. He explained who he was looking for, and they sent him off with better directions. When he arrived, three generations of Johnsons were gathered for the holiday and welcomed him in to talk about Paul. They had never known what happened, only that Paul was killed in action.

Miller showed them pictures of the platoon sergeant in uniform from a Condors photo book he had with him and gave them the printed sheet he carried from a memorial service that the troop held for Johnson at its headquarters in Phu Bai the week he was killed. Then he asked Paul's sister if his mother was around. No, he was told, she had died the year before.

He felt awful that she never heard the story of her son's last hours and his final thoughts of love for his parents and siblings. But Miller simply hadn't been able to summon the strength earlier. On his way to the house, he tried to find his friend's gravestone, but without a map or identifier, he didn't know where to look. He stopped at one small cemetery he came to on the road and saw a Vietnam veteran's grave marker with a similar name, but the date of death on the stone was August 13, 1970, and Miller concluded it had to be someone else. Indeed, it was. On the Vietnam Veterans Memorial in Washington, the name of another Sergeant Johnson from the same tiny town in Kentucky is carved into the polished black stone panel where Paul Johnson's name appears. He was Staff Sergeant Nicholas G. Johnson, killed in the Mekong Delta far to the south just nine days after Paul Johnson was mortally wounded up north in the A Shau. The men even shared a birthday, October 1.

Paul Johnson's family gave Miller directions to the correct burial site, and on his way out, he pulled off the road at that cemetery and stopped. He sat in the car for quite a while but didn't get out. He never did visit Johnson's grave.

Early in 2013, a dozen years after the visit to New Haven, Miller received a tip that someone had posted a note on the Virtual Wall, an enhanced, Internet version of the memorial in Washington, asking for information about Paul Johnson from anyone who knew him in Vietnam. It was from Trina Judson, who identified herself as Johnson's niece.

"I am looking for any servicemen that had served with Paul," the posting said. "Myself and his family would be forever grateful if someone could reach me that knew of Paul. Please contact me anytime via email. Also, just want to say thank you so much to Ed Long whom posted such a beautiful piece about Paul. Unfortunately, there was no contact information so I could reach him. Please Please contact me if you have any information at all regarding Paul. Again, I would be forever grateful. Bless to all that had served."

She knew about Long, who was severely wounded in the firefight in which Johnson was killed, because eleven years earlier, he had added his own post to the web page for Johnson on the same site.[122] In a remembrance entitled "my sgt.," Long said, "I just wanted to give a long overdue salute of respect to my sgt. paul Johnson. He was only 22 and I was 19. I often think of him and of that fateful day as I was injured and sent to a hospital in Japan. Fortunately for me I survived but the memories continue to be difficult. I was there that day. If any family member wishes to contact me I would be honored to speak with you and perhaps answer some questions that have remained unanswered for so many years. Rest assured he was indeed a hero in every description of the word and for that you can be proud. Respectfully, edward long."

When Miller saw Trina Judson's appeal, he contacted her to tell her about her uncle's death and pass along contact information for Ed Long, whom he hadn't seen since he tossed the wounded rifleman onto his Huey under fire. Long was living in Maryland, only about an hour's drive from Washington, and Judson was in Virginia. She hastily arranged to meet Long at the Wall on Memorial Day the following week, and they persuaded Miller to fly up from Texas to join them. They met at the Metro subway station on the National Mall, Miller wearing his beloved Cav hat and Long a floppy "boonie hat," favored by Blues Platoon grunts, and an old Army field jacket. Long's gray hair and nearly white mustache made him instantly recognizable as a vet from the Vietnam era. As they walked the well-trodden dirt paths to the Wall, nearly everyone they passed expressed the now-standard gratitude they always felt was denied them when they came home: "Thank you for your service."

They stopped to be interviewed by a local television station, and Judson presented each of them with a flag, flowers, and an angel statuette she said would look over them. Both men told her they still felt terrible guilt that her uncle had died and they had survived.

Long also told Miller, his long-ago buddy, "I want to say thank you for my life." He had been quietly grateful for forty-two years.

The three then approached the Wall to find Paul Johnson's name on Panel 8W, Line 82. They brushed their fingers over the polished black stone and felt the depression of the capital letters etched deeply into the slab. A volunteer helped them make rubbings of the name to take home.

Miller recounted for Trina Judson his attempt to save and comfort her uncle.

"'I know I'm gonna die, Rick,'" the platoon sergeant told his friend. "I said, 'No, you're not. Be quiet. Think about Kentucky. Think about something nice at home.' He said something, and I couldn't hear him. He grabbed hold of my shirt, and he said, 'I want you to do something for me.' I said, 'Sure, buddy. What?' He said, 'When you go home, if you make it back, I want you to go by my parents' house in New Haven and tell them I love them.'"

Miller's voice broke, and the big West Texas cowboy began to cry, but he forced himself to finish his confession: "I told him I would. I got back. They asked me if I would escort Paul back, and I said, 'I don't think I can.' I felt like I let Paul down. He died. It was my fault, I thought. I couldn't do it. Twenty years later I did make it up there. His mother was already passed away. That's it."

Ricky Miller, left, Trina Judson, and Ed Long met at The Wall on Memorial Day 2013, the first time the men had seen each other since Vietnam.

Trina Judson tried to comfort him. "I beg each of you to let any guilt you feel go," she told both men. "There was nothing you could have done. . . . You are truly heroes in our eyes. You have our undying gratitude, and you'll always be the heroes in our lives. And there's no way we can repay you for not only going beyond the call of duty, but also, spending the last few moments of Paul's life and making sure that he was comfortable and that he knew that he had friends around and someone there with him. That means more to us than anything. And we can never repay you guys for everything."

"He was wounded pretty bad, and I don't think he was in pain," Miller offered. "We gave him morphine."

"I know he wasn't in pain when he died," Long added. "When he was taking his last breath and just letting it out, he was not in any pain.

He seemed to be at peace. And the nurses and the doctor that was on the floor with him worked, I mean, like, you know, banshees to try to save Paul. And, when he passed away, it was no pain, no crying or yelling out. It was just peace, like he went to sleep."

ONE MORE RESCUE MISSION

Hunched over the computer in his bedroom, Jim Newman pecked at the keys with his stubby fingers, punching in names from the past. He was feeling a bit stronger, but the radiation and chemo had wrecked his body. He'd lost thirty pounds and could hardly lift his bad leg.

J-A-M-E-S . . . He had tried this name before but not for quite a while. C-A-S-H-E-R. His searches had never produced a meaningful result, but he kept trying when he thought about it. Newman had been reflecting a lot lately, gathering and uploading old photos to the Vietnam Helicopter Pilots Association website, exchanging email with fellow Condors, hunting for those he had never been able to find. This time: BINGO.

James Casher was Jim Kane's frontseater who had been pulled from the grove of trees that day in Laos. He recovered from his wounds, finished his tour, and went home—everyone thought—to fulfill a dream of going to medical school and becoming a doctor.

Somehow (Newman couldn't remember later where the search engines had taken him), Condor Six found Jim Casher's name coupled with an address in Winlock, Washington, and an age of 58, which he calculated would be about right for a man who had been a young helicopter pilot in Vietnam in 1971.

Thirty-five years later, Newman was spurred to action again. He fired off email messages to a couple of aging Condors who he knew lived somewhere in the Pacific Northwest.

Richard Frazee was the first to react. A long-ago Charlie Troop crew chief whom Mac Jones had put on the ground in Laos that day to look for Casher and Kane, Frazee was living in Seattle, about two hours from Winlock. He got the message while traveling in California and five days later stopped on his way home to try to find Casher.

"I spent about an hour talking in person to James Casher this morning," he reported to his old commander by email. He had found the former Cobra gunship pilot living in a dilapidated one-room shack in the woods off a backcountry road. Once one of the most clean-cut of Condors, Casher was dressed in rags, his hair long and straggly. Most of his teeth were rotted or missing. Casher shared his tiny quarters with a pack of dogs, at least seven or eight of them. There was no electricity or running water. Frazee couldn't get much out of him but said, "When I shook his hand and said good-bye, he seemed not to want to let go. I think that he felt like a meaningful connection had returned in his life."

Newman stood up the troops, such as they were. Chuck Vehlow, Casher's one-time gun platoon commander, who was living in Arizona, flew thousands of miles to see Casher and offer him help. Others consulted specialists at the VA on what could be done. Gary Swift, the scout pilot whom Kane and Casher's Cobra had been guarding that day in Laos, made several trips to Winlock.

They tried to tread lightly for fear of making a bad situation worse, but everyone wanted to save Jim Casher—again. They understood Six never left anyone behind.

The day Newman cut down those trees with his rotor blade and plucked Casher and Kane from imminent capture or death was Condor lore.

Now, with his own body giving out on him, the Old Man figured he had one more rescue operation in him. He concocted a plan to bring Casher back out of the woods.

* * *

What Newman never knew was that Casher had slipped into a distant, uncommunicative state after Vietnam and had been living alone in those woods—with his dogs—for twenty years.

Jim Casher got a tough start. The son of a black American soldier and a Japanese war bride, he had a light complexion and showed few signs of his Asian heritage, but as a child, he was branded as black. Other children in the mostly white neighborhood where he lived in Tacoma, Washington, hated the African American they saw in him.

His father, a career enlisted man in the Army, was stationed nearby at Fort Lewis. His mother worked in a clothing factory. Jim, the eldest of six siblings, was largely in charge at home after school.

"We were just niggers at that time," his younger sister Josephine Robinson remembered many years later. She was six or seven, her brother seven years older, and she vividly recalled being chased by neighborhood children who hated the only black kids in the neighborhood. She looked at Jim as a father figure and the family protector. There were times when he gathered his brothers and sisters to lie down in the living room while he stood guard with one of his father's rifles cradled in his arm. James Vernon Casher Sr. had taken him hunting, and young Jim knew how to use a gun, but he never shot at anyone—until Vietnam. Jim had a difficult relationship with his drill-sergeant-type father, who beat his wife when his temper flared and whipped his children with his uniform belt when they misbehaved. But Jim loved the military. He helped his siblings dig trenches in the yard and divided the kids into sides to play endless games of war. He watched every available episode of the World War II series *Combat* on TV and dreamed of being a pilot. With money from his paper route, he bought model airplanes and joined the Civil Air Patrol to feed his appetite for flying.

Then, when Jim was in high school, his father retired from the Army, and the family moved to St. Albans, a predominantly black neighborhood in Queens, New York, where, as Josephine put it, "we were no longer niggers; we were chinks. . . . A lot of black kids wanted to fight us because we were different." Jim hated it. He never liked being tagged as black, preferring his mother's Japanese heritage. He quickly came to despise New York. As soon as he graduated from high school, Jim returned to the Pacific Northwest, where he enrolled in Washington State University and joined ROTC. He lasted two years. In the fall of 1968—after dropping out of college and losing his draft deferment at the height of the Vietnam War—he chose to enlist. The Army promised to teach him to fly if he passed the tests, and he agreed to extend his years of active duty to make it worth the Army's investment to put him through flight school. A year later, Casher graduated eleventh of seventy-one in his class at helicopter flight school at Fort Rucker and was promoted out of the enlisted ranks to warrant officer (WO1). Like practically all Rucker graduates, he was shipped off to Vietnam.

The men of Charlie Troop accepted the new pilot and remembered him kindly. He was quiet, though. Jim Kane, his aircraft commander in their Cobra, called him cerebral, "a guy who was really at peace."

Others marveled at how he always seemed to remain cool under fire. Cobra crews took a lot of ground fire, but it didn't seem to faze Casher, even after the shootdown, when he might have been expected to get skittish. Gary Swift, the loach pilot Kane and Casher were guarding that day, remembered, "There were guys over there you could trust. I could always trust Jim Casher. He knew what was going on every minute." After the Laos operation, C Troop returned to patrolling the A Shau Valley, and Casher, by then promoted to aircraft commander, knocked out three .51-caliber machine guns, making him a hero to his fellow aviators who regarded the .51 as their most frequent and deadly threat. Casher was awarded a Silver Star for that feat and Air Medals for other exploits.[123]

When Casher's tour was up seven months after he and Kane were shot down and rescued by Newman, Casher was ordered to Fort Hood, Texas, where the Army was developing new tactics and strategies for airmobile warfare and wanted experienced combat pilots to help.

Josephine remembered her brother coming to New York to visit and expressing his disappointment when he learned she had gotten pregnant at fifteen and dropped out of school to get married. She loved her older brother but had chosen a different escape route from the home both of them fled. He wanted her to go back to school. She promised she would, but it took her years to make good on it. She almost completed a degree in accounting before she dropped out again to start a company with her husband. She became a successful businesswoman and restaurateur in Queens.

After almost two years at Fort Hood, Jim Casher completed his military obligation and was discharged from active duty. When he returned to New York to visit his family, Josephine thought he acted weird, that he had become a totally different person. They had dinner at their parents' house, and Jim hardly spoke at all. If asked a question, he might just look up and say, "Oh," and let out a little giggle.

The gunship pilot who had flown the fastest helicopter in the Army drove a car in New York at a snail's pace. He wouldn't exceed twenty miles per hour anywhere and got stopped by a police officer one day for holding up traffic while driving with his brother. George Casher was shocked when Jim quietly slipped a pistol onto the seat beside him as the officer approached. Fortunately, the policeman didn't see it and was satisfied when Jim showed him his identification and something indicating he was or had been in the military. The officer told him not to drive that way in New York and let him go. George was grateful his brother hadn't gone for the gun.

During that time, Jim called his parents more than once to say people were after him, the first sign of the paranoia that stuck with him the rest of his life. He moved back to Tacoma and rented an apartment for himself and a small dog, one of many Jim treated as his best friends. At some point, he told his mother and sister that a person in Tacoma was trying to have him committed to a mental institution. Whatever prompted it, he begged them not to let him be taken involuntarily. Josephine Robinson fell out of touch with her brother for a few years but went to see him during a trip across the country that she, her husband, and oldest daughter took in 1978. He was living in South Tacoma in a small house that she said was fairly clean and had running water, but her brother didn't seem normal to her. He was so gentle that he wouldn't hurt a fly, but he didn't engage in conversation or respond to questions about himself. Jim had been a good musician when he was a boy, loved classical music, and could play a couple of instruments. During Josephine's visit, he took out a violin and started to play for them. Josephine thought the music sounded gruesome, like something out of a scary movie. It was scratchy and made her daughter feel uncomfortable. They left the next day.

Jim's mother kept in touch with him for several years. She stopped to see him three or four times on her way to or from visits with relatives in Japan. Jim had always been closer to his mother than his father and wrote her letters from Washington, but his writing wasn't always legible. The family would puzzle over what he had written.

It's not clear whether he held a job after the Army, but he got money from somewhere that enabled him to pursue his love of flying and a passion for cars. A fixed-wing logbook shows he started taking lessons in 1979, got his private pilot's license, and kept flying for about eight years.

Josephine thought he was receiving some sort of government assistance, probably from the VA. It was, more likely, a monthly check for Supplemental Security Income, a federal program for the aged, blind, and disabled. She lost track of him again, but after their mother died in 2000, four of the siblings went out to Washington to deliver a knapsack and some papers and things his mother had been keeping for him.

By that time Jim was living in the woods outside Winlock, a farming community of about four hundred homes in southwestern Washington. He had let his black hair grow in thick mats that hung below his shoulders, and a scruffy beard darkened his once clean-shaven face. Casher had bought ten acres of undeveloped land in 1990 and lived on it. He cleared a place in the woods for his vehicles. His first dwelling was the cab of an old Dodge Power Wagon pickup truck. He had no electricity or source of water on the place but managed to get by somehow with a permanent entourage of small dogs that lived with him in whatever enclosure he had. The Krenelka family, three generations from a North Dakota farm community, bought the land around Casher's shortly after he did, built their own modest homes, and settled in.

Jim Casher in Vietnam, left, and with his dogs in Winlock, Washington, in the 1990s.

His neighbors understood he was a shell-shocked veteran and pretty much left him alone but helped out when he'd let them. Dan Krenelka, the family patriarch and Casher's closest neighbor, gave Jim permission to draw water from his well, and Jim would stop by regularly to fill a five-gallon jug half full and carry it back to his own land. The Krenelkas noticed he would never take water from a hose and preferred the outdoor spigot closest to the well, even if another faucet seemed more convenient. Not long after he moved down from Tacoma onto his land, Casher went back north to bring more of his possessions to the site. Two standouts were flashy MGB sports cars, the last of a classic line of British imports from the 1960s and 1970s that were the envy of millions of young men Casher's age. They were in great condition, like new, when he parked the pair, one red, one green, in the clearing off the road that ran past his property. Over the years, nearly a dozen more vehicles would join them as they sat there, neglected. All of the machines rotted away, some for twenty years. Big, old Cadillacs were favorites, too. He tried to keep one of them running for driving into town and such and sometimes made meticulous notes on needed repairs.

"Things I must fix on the cadillac," he wrote in 2004.

"1. Right front Hood Hinge.

"2. Right rear Trunk Hinge.

"3. Differential or rather Universal . . ."

That car needed major work: muffler, brakes and master cylinder, power steering unit, interior. It's doubtful he ever got to his thirteen-point list. Eventually, just about every vehicle was sold for junk after he was gone.

Another of Jim Casher's passions was books. He collected them incessantly and read almost anything: Greek classics, poetry, pattern making, geology, history from the ancients to modern politics. He seemed not to discriminate, but also couldn't take care of the hundreds of books he collected. They piled up around him, got stuffed in an old orange van, and swelled with mold and moisture when the van leaked. One of several that were still sealed in their original plastic wrappings was a book called *The Clinton Tapes,* an historian's memoir of his secret White House conversations with then-President Bill Clinton. Ruined volumes of several encyclopedias were scattered about.

Early on, while Casher was living in the cab of his pickup, a neighbor gave him an old camper that fit in the truck bed to give him a larger living space. The ex-pilot lived in it until it rusted and fell apart, and other well-meaning neighbors gave him another that sat on the ground, resting more or less on the level. There weren't many people around, but those who knew about the shy man living alone in the woods liked him or, at least, tried to help him.

Casher established a rapport with Dan Krenelka, although he hardly spoke. One bitterly cold winter night he knocked on the door of the

Krenelkas' house nearly freezing to death. They propped him up by the wood-burning stove, where he sat for a couple of hours while they fed him hot soup and coffee and got him over his uncontrollable shivering.

It was after that incident that one of the boys who lived in a nearby house collected some money and material from local merchants and got his high school shop class to build Casher a primitive, one-room cabin about twelve feet by twelve feet. It wasn't much, but it had a wood stove for heat.

At some point, he apparently spent enough time with a VA doctor to be diagnosed as schizophrenic and was classified as having a service-connected disability, which entitled him to monthly benefit payments. Neighbors noticed he sometimes seemed to be talking to invisible companions or thought he heard voices. He would duck his head in the middle of a conversation and whisper "Not now" into his shoulder as if speaking insistently into a microphone to silence an interrupting speaker.

One of his sisters sent him money from time to time, but VA records indicated the benefit checks he received for a period in the early '80s were cut off in 1983 or 1984 because he failed to return a required form saying he was still disabled. After the Army, Casher developed an abiding distrust of institutions, which may be why he neglected to file the necessary report.

Not long after Casher and the Krenelka family moved to the land along Antrim Road, Dan Krenelka's ten-year-old grandson Daniel wrote a story about Mr. Casher, his unusual neighbor, and the neighbor's cats, chickens, dogs, cows, and pigs.

"The problem begins where the fence begins," wrote the home-schooled youngster, "because, you see, Mr. Casher doesn't have any fences. His method for keeping his animals on his farm is to give them a firm talking to. However, they must not have listened, because one day they showed up in Grandma's garden."

The story recounts the family's protracted efforts to keep Casher's pigs out of the garden by scaring them away with sticks, revving up a motorcycle engine to frighten them and talk, at least, of shooting the beasts. "We didn't really shoot them, but we wanted to," young Daniel wrote. "What could we do? Just hope I guess. Mr. Casher had spoken of building a large sailboat (A fifty-four footer!). Maybe he and his crew would be going to sea and that would solve our problem." Casher never built that boat, but the Krenelkas eventually got a dog that kept the pigs at bay.[124]

As the years went by, Casher's living area off the lonely county road filled up with his castoffs: rusted hulks of old pickups and cars, piles of plastic jugs, old tires, metal parts of all kinds, rubber boots, and heaps of rocks that Jim had delivered to the site saying he was going to build himself a stone house. He managed two six-foot-high, V-shaped, rock walls at the entrance to his land, but he never got a start on the house. By the time Condor Six discovered where he was, in August 2006, Jim Casher's condition had deteriorated. Richard Frazee, who had jumped off his helicopter into high grass in Laos in a vain attempt to find Casher and Kane after they were shot down, told Newman it took some sleuthing to get to him this time.

He went to a local cafe and asked the regulars if they knew Jim Casher, but they were instantly protective and unhelpful. He finally found someone who acknowledged knowing the man and pointed Frazee in the right direction.

"He said he had just gotten a letter from you," Frazee reported. Indeed, Newman had mailed a letter to the address he found on the Internet the same day he made his discovery, and Frazee arrived at Casher's shack five days later, not far behind the letter.

"Needless to say, he was a bit shocked when I came strolling up," Frazee wrote. "He is living in a one-room shack way out in the countryside about ten miles out of town. I think he is basically living in poverty and is barely getting by but is well liked by the people in town and his neighbors. He was dressed in rags basically and his hair was long and uncut and most of his teeth are gone. He's gotten a little bald but then so have I and he's gained a little weight since those days. He remembers everyone by name and all the details of the day he was shot down."

Newman may have invited Casher to an upcoming Condors reunion because Frazee said, "I doubt that he could manage to make it to a reunion without financial assistance. Even then he might not go—he seems self-conscious and a little embarrassed about his condition. If you remember he was really soft-spoken and a little shy back then and is even more so now." Newman remembered him as polite, quiet, and bashful.

Told that Casher had no phone or power at the shack, Newman decided to send him a "throw-away" cell phone by UPS courier, track the package, and call the phone number after it was delivered and, he hoped, switched on.

Jim Kane, Casher's aircraft commander the day of the shootdown, had settled into what looked like a picture-book life after the war, living in the comfort of a solid marriage, suburban home, growing kids, and a secure career as a bond salesman in Richmond, Virginia. When he learned about his crewmate from Newman and Frazee, he proposed getting Casher an advocate in Veterans Affairs who could guide him to benefits and treatment. "I'd like to figure out the steps to take to help him," Kane told Newman, "but I want it to be good help," not just a Band-Aid like getting a few Condors to send him some cash.

Major Newman told the Condor Alumni Association, made up mostly of Charlie troopers from the Vietnam days, that he had located Casher at last and that Frazee had been to see him, but he cautioned the leadership of the organization not to bandy about details of Casher's condition, only that he might need some help from the membership.

"Sounds like PTSD big-time," messaged John Barron, who flew with Casher in the gun platoon and fought his own demons for years after the war. He also wanted to get the VA involved if Casher would agree and told Newman: "Standing by for your instructions, sir."

Gary Swift was the next to pay a visit to Winlock. A businessman in Seattle, Swift remembered Casher well, although they had not been particularly close friends in the troop. He drove south about seventy-five miles and located the place without trouble, but when he got there, he found no sign of Casher and left a note in the mailbox, which he signed Condor One-Zero, his old call sign. When Swift drove down again the next week, he had to park out on the road because Casher's car occupied the only space big enough to pull into. Swift, who knew the forestry and lumber business, sized up the shack, noticing its siding was made of a cheap plywood material known in the trade as T1-11. It is notoriously subject to rot and mold when used in wet environments like those in Washington State. He spotted a metal smokestack punching through the roof and saw a pile of firewood outside that had been collected for the oncoming winter. He also counted eight scruffy-looking mutts. Casher walked out to greet him and recognized him immediately. They stood in the road and talked, but it was a mostly one-sided conversation. Casher was quiet and hard to talk to. Swift shot the breeze for a while, told him what the Condors Alumni Association was up to and how glad he was they had finally found him again. He offered the ex-pilot any help he might need, said he could work with the VA or whatever, but Casher didn't nibble. Casher told Swift he was fine, that relatives back east would be sending him some money, and that he was going to fix up the place. It was the first of several visits.

Swift returned later that fall and took Casher to a sandwich place in town for lunch. Another time, they went to a hardware store, where Casher picked out some plywood, nails, and other things for fixing the shack. Swift paid, telling Casher it was a present from the Condors. Casher smiled and accepted, but he had been willing to pay for the supplies himself and pulled out a Visa card from somewhere, indicating he had at least some connection with a bank and perhaps some means of support. Swift noticed that Casher was quite self-conscious about his teeth and tended to cover his mouth with his hand when he spoke. When Gary Schuler, the ex-door gunner who had jumped out of the slick to look for Kane and Casher on the ground and who was working for the VA all those years later, learned what had happened to Casher, he encouraged his fellow Condors to help the aging snake pilot get his benefits reinstated. Apparently, nothing ever came of it, because Casher wouldn't—or couldn't—ask for assistance.

Kane wanted to help, but he worried that "charging in on Jim to attack his problems as we see them may make us feel better about ourselves, but may do irreparable damage to Jim." That slowed Newman down some. He still wanted to try the cell-phone gambit but held off while Vehlow made his own reconnaissance trip from his home in Phoenix, 1,500 miles to the south. Chuck Vehlow had been Casher's platoon commander and Newman's most trusted officer in Vietnam. He remained Six's devoted friend.

"Casher is not in good shape," Vehlow confided. He had found the same sorry sight at the shack but was more insistent in trying to get the man to talk. The former platoon leader wanted to know how Casher cared for himself, how he got food, whether he had a job, saw other people. The answers were vague, and Vehlow didn't believe them. He asked if Casher could use help from Veterans Affairs or the Disabled American Veterans, a group Vehlow had talked to for guidance before making his trip. Casher said he didn't need any help and wouldn't bite when Vehlow offered. "He did say he was interested in getting vocational assistance and using his veterans benefits to start flying again," Vehlow told Six. Vehlow thought the idea preposterous but didn't say so.

Newman, never shy about his ability to motivate people, considered going out to Winlock himself. He was still enduring his cancer treatments and was hardly up to flying across the country, but he hated thinking Casher was out there in need of another rescue. Then, in January, Jim Newman suffered a severe stroke, ending his efforts to save Casher again. Newman was partially paralyzed for a time and never completely recovered his ability to speak.

Casher went on living in the shack for a couple more years, odd possessions and trash piling up around him.

Jim Casher's one-room shack on land outside Winlock was so crammed with objects that there was no apparent place for him to lie down to sleep.

A grandfather clock stood against one wall; a huge, stringless bass fiddle was crammed between the wall and a stovepipe. Lighting a fire in the stove would have burned the place down. Loren Krenelka, the late Dan Krenelka's son, who built his own tidy home and office nearby, found so much junk piled inside that the door would open only a few inches. He speculated Casher was sleeping in a near-standing position, leaning against the piles. Until one day in the spring of 2011.

Loren Krenelka had noticed Jim seemed to have got rid of his dogs but had no other clue that anything was seriously wrong. One night, with no one around to notice, Casher climbed into his last running Cadillac and drove himself to Providence Centralia Hospital, fifteen miles up the interstate. He left his car in the hospital parking lot and went inside. Former Chief Warrant Officer 2 James Vernon Casher Jr. died of liver failure two days later, apparently a result of chronic dehydration. He was sixty-three years old.

Loren Krenelka, who learned of Casher's death from the local sheriff, went by the place at the sheriff's request to secure the door. Looking through the jumbles of Casher's belongings crammed into vehicles and piled nearly six feet high in the shack, he found the moldy remains of a soldier's dress uniform. He could make out three rows of ribbons above the left breast pocket, an aviator's wings pinned above them, a black-on-silver chief warrant officer's insignia on the epaulets, and the name tag, CASHER, still pinned in place on the flap over the right pocket. A Vietnam veteran himself, Krenelka recognized the ribbons on the top row representing the Distinguished Flying Cross and an Air Medal with devices attached indicating its recipient had earned more than one with valor. At the center of the second row was a Purple Heart ribbon signifying Casher had been wounded in action.

At the top left of the three rows, in the place where the wearer's highest award should be, was a bare bar for another decoration. As he sorted through the detritus in a rotted-out camper, Loren Krenelka discovered a small cardboard box, and inside it a pristine ribbon with the blue, white, and red stripes that signify the Silver Star, the nation's third highest award for valor in the face of the enemy. He suddenly realized that his troubled friend of twenty years had once been a recognized war hero several times over.

Ex-Chief Warrant Officer 2 James Casher's gravestone,
Tahoma National Cemetery, Kent, Washington

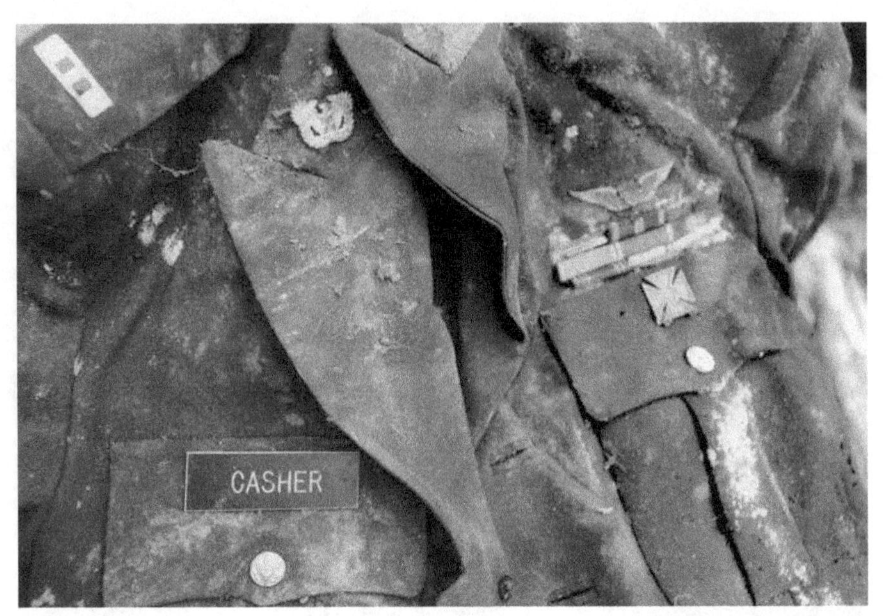

Jim Casher's Uniform

EPILOGUE

MAJOR NEWMAN

Jim Newman was sixty years old when he was diagnosed with colon cancer. He telephoned his son Jay at college sometime after he learned of it in 1995 and said there were some procedures he had to go through but that everything was going to be fine. It started with chemotherapy, then a very long day of surgery to remove a section of his colon, then more chemo. His kidneys failed, and he lost so much weight that a photo taken to renew his driver's license shows him looking like a skeleton. After he got better, he laughed about that picture and showed it to friends, but Jay said he looked scared in that photo.

Remarkably, he made a full recovery, and that cancer never came back, but his health spiraled downward from there. In 2002, the former chain smoker went for his annual scan to check for a recurrence of the colon cancer, and doctors spotted a tiny dot on his lung that turned out to be malignant. They considered it fortunate that they caught it so early, and he underwent another operation to remove one of the five lobes of his lungs. He thought that would take care of it, but the chemo afterward nearly killed him. He developed sepsis, an infection that attacks the blood and spreads through the body, frequently causing multiple organ failure. His kidneys stopped working again.

Newman was taken to Womack Army Hospital near his home, where powerful antibiotics failed to halt his deterioration. He began hallucinating, and Jay thought he was dying. Jay wanted to transfer him to the University of North Carolina Medical Center at Chapel Hill, where he had undergone the lung surgery, but he resisted at first, and the Army hospital refused to move him against his will. In desperation, his last wife, Cheryl, who had met him in a hospital during an earlier illness, helped him out of bed and into a car and drove him seventy-five miles to the hospital in Chapel Hill. He was critically ill when they got there, and the treatment took weeks, but the medical team saved him.

The nursing staff and orderlies remembered him as an impossibly difficult patient. He treated them like dirt, swore at them, complained constantly, and ordered them around. When a nurse came on duty, she knew that if Jim Newman was on her rotation she was in for a bad day.[125] Newman was an officer but never a gentleman, and although he lavished praise on those he found worthy, as he got older, he grew more demanding, and was especially hard on waiters, store clerks, and those he regarded as service people. He could be that way with wives and girlfriends and, some thought, women in general. When he was in the hospital, female nurses and hospital aides seemed to get the worst of his bad temper.

Pain may have been a factor. Even during his many months of hospitalization and repeated surgeries on his wounded leg, Newman stubbornly refused to take pain medications, not even over-the-counter Tylenol. Flora said he was in so much pain sometimes that it was pitiful, but he just suffered and toughed it out. He ran a high fever with the sepsis after lung surgery, and doctors wanted to give him Tylenol to lower his temperature, but he refused.[126] He would just sit or lie in bed and suffer. He rarely watched television or read and wasn't able to manage email or web surfing, to which he had become addicted. It took weeks before he was well enough to leave the hospital.

After the lung cancer crisis, he sold all his used car lots and gave up his last job as general manager of a Chrysler dealership in Fayetteville. He didn't need the money. He was drawing maximum veterans benefits as 100 percent disabled by service-related injuries, received free medical care, a Social Security pension, and his Army retirement pay. By the time of his death, his various annuities amounted to about $8,000 a month.

Former Condor Rick "The Mayor" Daly, who was flying a Cobra in the A Shau on July 4, 1971—the day Charlie Troop lost three aircraft to enemy fire all at once—still regarded Jim Newman as an underappreciated hero. Daly set out to get him a Medal of Honor for his rescue of the other Cobra crew from the jungle floor that day. He gathered a sheaf of official records and testimonials from witnesses and persuaded his congressman, Texas Republican Sam Johnson, to press the Pentagon to consider the case. As it turned out, Newman had been approved for a Distinguished Flying Cross with V for that mission about the time he rotated back to the States in 1971, but the paperwork never caught up with him. A belated presentation by Newman's North Carolina congressman was set for November 21, 2005, in Fayetteville, and Cobra pilots Daly, Vehlow, and Mike Sherrer, one of the two crewmen Newman plucked from the jungle that day, flew in unannounced to surprise their one-time commander at the ceremony. I had corresponded with Newman and spoken to him from time to time but had not seen him since the war and decided to join the group for an impromptu reunion.

Comrades in arms (from left) Rick Daly, Newman, Vehlow, and Sherrer at belated award ceremony for Newman in 2005. His former gun pilots flew to North Carolina to surprise him.

The Old Man was rounder and balder than he had been when he was flying, but he appeared healthy and proud with his combat decorations pinned over his heart on his civilian suit jacket and his black Cav hat with insignia firmly in place. At a lunch afterward, however, he quietly told me his lung cancer was back and that he had been diagnosed with diabetes, which ran in his family, but is also presumptively caused by exposure to Agent Orange.

He endured more chemo and another long series of daily radiation treatments that sapped his stamina, but he refused to surrender. He was scheduled for a PET scan to see what the treatments accomplished, and the doctors told him if they found any remaining malignant tissue it would mean more radiation or a shorter life. "I voted for more radiation," Newman told me.[127]

I made plans to visit him in North Carolina, but he put me off, saying his life was consumed by lab tests, scans, and trips to various doctors. He found a hole in his schedule toward the end of January 2007, but just before I left to drive down, I got word he had suffered a stroke. He survived and, with intensive therapy, overcame partial paralysis, but he never fully recovered his speech. He understood what others said and tried to respond, but the words got jumbled.

Several months after the stroke, Newman telephoned me one day and just started talking.

"This is a strange guy that you're talking to, huh?" The voice was recognizable, but the wrong words came out often enough that he was difficult to understand. I mentioned that Cheryl had told me he needed to get a new copy of his driver's license.

"She shouldn't—" He paused. "The only thing I told her that she needs to know where it is, is that little—those things that cleared that—talk about the middle and talk about the people there I have to talk about the two senators and VA did one of them and up north where there was—there were both of them, she's only got one of them."

Yet there was no question he understood that his brain was sending signals his mouth didn't execute correctly. "I can see everything, but I cannot talk about everything," he said.

Cheryl decided to throw a surprise party for his seventy-second birthday and invited friends and neighbors from Fayetteville to their new suburban home. She passed the word a few days ahead of time to me and some of the Condors. I met Jim Kane in Richmond, and we drove several hours to see him. But he wasn't around, and the guests waited uncomfortably for hours, assured that he would have to come home at some point. When he finally showed up about 10:00 p.m., it turned out he and Jay had gone to Raleigh to buy a car, the last of his beloved Buicks.

He looked thinner than the year before, and his buckle was cinched to the last hole in his belt, but he was happy to see old friends—and furious at Cheryl for not alerting him or telling Jay to make sure he got home earlier. It was only a few months before the cancer laid him low again. By December, he had left Cheryl, and Jay moved him to a house in Raleigh and brought a family friend from Georgia to stay with him. His breathing was hampered by the spreading disease in his lungs, and he got around the house with an electric wheelchair, trailing an oxygen tube that snaked across the living room floor into a bedroom where its pump was running to push enriched air into his weakening lungs. On New Year's Eve, with his breathing increasingly difficult, he returned to the hospital at Chapel Hill. Jim Newman, Condor Six, died there on January 11, 2009. His son Jay and Jay's wife, Elizabeth, were the only ones with him.

Newman had signed a will two years earlier, notarized by his sister Elaine Bagby, that expressly disinherited his last wife, Cheryl, and his two eldest sons, Roger and Ronald Newman, leaving everything he owned to Jay. He never felt it necessary to explain why. Nor did he ever acknowledge that he had destroyed his own military career at its zenith.

"I don't know why I got out," he told me once. "It was a stupid decision, stupidest I ever made. General Berry told me I could get one star or two, said I was the most outstanding cavalry officer he'd ever seen."[128] "Vietnam changed him" was the only explanation Newman's first family could come up with. Never knowing more, they clung to it for years.

FLORA NEWMAN AND HER BOYS

Jim Newman's first wife, Flora, never remarried and, her sons said, remained in love with the memory of the husband she knew before Vietnam.

She left the family home in Fayetteville after a health crisis during a Disney World vacation with her son Ronald's family several years ago and moved into a mobile home near Ronald's house in Mount Pleasant, North Carolina, to be closer to family. Mount Pleasant, about one hundred miles west of Fayetteville, is an old mill town near Charlotte, North Carolina's largest city. When Roger lost his job in Raleigh, he moved in with his mother during the depths of the financial collapse, and neither has found steady work since, due in part to serious health problems. At eighty, Flora fractured the large bone in her upper leg, which didn't heal properly, and Roger has struggled with complications from diabetes. Ronald has suffered severe hearing loss, partially corrected in one ear, but has kept his job as general manager of a regional wholesale food trading company.

CHUCK VEHLOW

Among the Condors who came to Arlington to say farewell to their former commander, Chuck Vehlow was the one pilot who participated in the three most dramatic rescues and the one who remained closest to Six and probably the most devoted to him. The West Pointer flew Cobra cover in the two daring pickups in Laos and was Newman's copilot going in to get Mike Sherrer and Ross Eliason out of the A Shau. He gave up his high-stress work as a defense industry executive to fight an aggressive prostate cancer that the VA presumes came from exposure to Agent Orange in Vietnam, although such cancers aren't traceable to any single cause or event. For five years after his initial prostate surgery, Vehlow was cancer-free, but in the course of treatment and follow-up in the VA health-care system, he was diagnosed with long-dormant post-traumatic stress syndrome traced to his wartime service. Then the malignancy returned.

Vehlow retired to Arizona to be with his family and spent summers at a lake house in Waukesha, Wisconsin, where he and his wife, Kate, had met in high school. He sought out top-tier oncologists around the country, participated in clinical trials, and endured seven rounds of increasingly difficult chemotherapy. Having kept himself in top physical condition all his life, playing competitive football in high school and college and tennis and golf in later years, the chemo in the summer of 2014 "really, really kicked his butt," Kate said. He lost his hair and his energy, and he felt awful a lot of the time. He developed numbness in his feet, known as peripheral neuropathy, and had to give up golf and tennis. In August 2014, the Vehlows reluctantly put their modest, century-old lake house on the market, sold it in two days, and made plans to return to Arizona, where Chuck could be closer to his doctors at the Mayo Clinic in Scottsdale.

MAC JONES

Mac Jones retired from the Army at forty-six after twenty years of service and moved to Florida to begin drawing his military pension and manage his investments and real estate. He compiled a book of the shared recollections of four Condors who found each other in the early days of email in the 1990s. Jones is the Condors Alumni Association's historian and has collected thousands of official and unofficial records of C Troop's Vietnam-era operations. He realized that after retirement he had drifted from drinking in moderation in the military to being drunk all day. At 3:00 p.m. on June 6, 2003, he decided to quit and hasn't had a drink since, although he confessed to taking a single sip of a companion's screwdriver a few years ago.

When he started working on the book of emails that he called *Four Condors,* Jones began having dreams about being back in the A Shau Valley with his colleagues from twenty years earlier. He had the dreams often enough that he called that period his "second Vietnam tour." The mountains looked more like the Rockies than the mountainous jungles of Vietnam, but the combat situations were realistic and scary, although nobody got killed. He never woke up screaming or thought of those dreams as symptoms of PTSD.

What stuck with him, however, was a hatred of telephones. When he came home from the war, he never wanted to hear a phone ring again. He refused for months to get a telephone at home, and four decades later still answers it with brusque annoyance.

When he was commander of the lift platoon and later the troop operations officer, he could not escape the reach of the telephone, and it never seemed to bring good news. At his desk were a field phone and a dial phone. There was a phone at the mess hall and one at the officers' club. Everywhere he went, when the phone rang, the room fell silent. He especially dreaded the one at the O Club because when it rang, it was usually dark outside, probably cloudy, and the tracer bullets were clearer when they slashed through the sky at night. Whoever answered the ring would announce, "Captain Jones," and everybody got really quiet, knowing that when he hung up, he would tell them how many aircraft he needed, how many people to fly them, and that those selected should head for the flight line. The ringing of the telephone became associated in Jones's mind with night flying, bad weather, dark mountains, and red, white, and green tracers. He never wanted to hear a phone ring again—and still doesn't pick it up if it rings at night.

Jones developed physical problems years after his flying days that doctors told him were directly traceable to his service as a pilot. He had noticed his first day in flight school that it hurt to lean back and look up, swiveling his head to check all the overhead circuit breakers in a Huey. Perhaps due to the genetic shape of his upper vertebrae, it always hurt when he turned his head or looked straight up. In 1987, after he retired, his left arm began to tingle, and he thought he was having a heart attack. When he went to the doctor, the physician told him, "Your heart's in great shape, but your neck is broken." The tingle was due to nerve damage in his neck. After a series of operations, Jones said, his neck is now "solid titanium" with five cervical disks screwed together. He almost certainly was eligible for service-connected disability payments, but he refused to apply, either for physical or psychological injury. "I don't feel disabled," he said. He can't play golf, tennis, or volleyball, as he used to, but he figures it's his duty to "tough it out."

"I don't have much faith in the VA anyway," he said.

One of quite a few Condors with strong, right-wing political views, Jones calls himself a "constitutional conservative" and is an unabashed fan of Glenn Beck and Fox News. Super patriots in the group frequently bandy about email chain letters and videos waving the flag, celebrating the military, and disparaging President Obama for perceived weakness. Many are still bitter about the ungrateful reception they received when they came home and still contend they could have won if the United States had devoted enough to the fight.

RICHARD FRAZEE

Richard Frazee, who founded an environmental consulting business in Seattle, built a website for the Condors and occasionally added thoughtful, sometimes haunting, stories of his Vietnam tour. Frazee battled for years to tame the aftereffects of Vietnam, but he refused to be tested or compensated for PTSD because he thought it would be an admission that he couldn't repair the emotional wounds of war on his own. In 2014, he was elected commanding officer of the Condors Alumni Association, whose membership consists largely of Vietnam veterans who served in C Troop, 2/17 Air Cavalry Squadron, 101st Airborne Division.

MIKE SHERRER

Mike Sherrer, the Cobra gunship commander rescued by Newman after he was shot down in the A Shau on July 4, 1971, returned to the United States and was discharged from the Army in 1976, but he quickly got a job as a civilian flight instructor at Fort Rucker teaching Huey pilots to fly by instruments. About the same time, he met Anita Griffis, who was on her way to becoming a marketing representative for IBM in Atlanta. They were married the next year, and Mike began dreaming of starting a store where they could work together selling aviation memorabilia to helicopter crews. Pappy Papin, who had been close friends with Sherrer since Sherrer's Cobra guarded Pappy's loach in the A Shau Valley, recalled that "Mikey" got into an altercation in a Florida bar that escalated into "overreaction" by both Sherrer and law enforcement officers. Sherrer wound up in the "drunk tank" of a local jail in what he insisted for years was a crass injustice that demonstrated the authorities' disdain for those who fought for their country in Vietnam. He left his job, and he, Anita, and an associate set up shop as Wings Aviation in Daleville, Alabama, just outside the gate at Fort Rucker. Despite being burned out by an arsonist, they built the business into an 11,000-square-foot store with thirty-five employees selling everything from shoulder patches and aviator sunglasses to survival gear and night vision goggles. After ten years and a bout Anita had with breast cancer, they sold the business in 1990 and went cruising in a thirty-nine-foot trawler just to "enjoy life."

Mike had another brush with the law soon afterward. They were at anchor in a quiet cove off the Intracoastal Waterway in South Florida and woke up to someone shouting and throwing sticks at their boat, ordering them to leave what he said was a private anchorage. It turned out the complainer was a deputy sheriff in Broward County, but Sherrer insisted he was within his rights in a public waterway, and he fought back, defending boaters' rights in interviews with several boating publications. The incident made him increasingly suspicious of authority. He was also struggling with a hangover from the war. He had always had trouble sleeping and drank to help with that, which was no solution. The shootdown and his survival haunted him. He remembered dreading getting shot down every time he went out on a mission. But when it happened, he was surprised that he wasn't afraid; he reacted admirably to save his copilot from the wreckage and get both of them rescued. But he looked back on it with bitterness because he had come to think of Vietnam as a political war in which he and his comrades were just pawns in a game. He tried to tell Anita about his wartime experience, but he couldn't finish the story. He started to tell a boyhood friend from his hometown of Picayune, Mississippi, too, but he couldn't get it out that time either. It was only years later, when he was seeing therapists and taking antidepressant drugs for PTSD that he could talk about what had happened.

In 1998, Sherrer was at an outdoor party listening to friends play music in Walton County, a rural area on the Gulf Coast, when two sheriff's deputies walked in without warning or warrant, unplugged the musicians' electrical equipment, and broke up the party. The manager of the place protested the aggressive disruption, but the deputies told him their badges entitled them to do as they pleased. Sherrer volunteered to be a witness for the manager and was promptly arrested on a misdemeanor charge that was later dropped. Outraged at what he considered a blatant violation of the Constitution he had fought to defend, Sherrer filed a civil suit against the Walton County authorities for false arrest. The impact of the incident, however, went much deeper, exacerbating Sherrer's post-traumatic stress disorder and dominating his thoughts. He became convinced he had been brainwashed into believing he had fought for justice in Vietnam when the authorities at home "trampled all over" his rights, showing no respect for the Silver Star and Purple Heart he had earned in combat.

"I lost my country," he told me some years later. "They took my freedom and still have it." The legal struggle went on for six years, but Sherrer lost his case at trial in the local courts and on appeal. He and Anita sought others who considered themselves victims of abuse of power by the Sheriff's Office, advertised in the local newspaper, and collected numerous case files, but they never got anywhere in court. Anita turned over all the materials she had gathered to the U.S. Justice Department and "let it go." Mike decided to leave the United States "to find the freedom that doesn't exist for me here."

He believed he found what he was searching for in the mountain village of Santa Fe, Panama, a would-be retirement haven about a five-hour drive from Panama City. He purchased a small, primitive house with several acres of land about five miles from town for $17,000 and hired two workers at five dollars a day each to help him gut the interior and make it suitable for a couple more accustomed to modern appliances, satellite television, and air conditioning. Anita went along with her husband's determined quest for a radically new life, although she kept a condo in Panama City, Panama, and returned to the States to check up on family, especially her aging mother in Panama City, Florida.

Mike struggled to learn Spanish, made friends easily, and embraced the villagers of Santa Fe, who reminded him of the innocent villagers in Vietnam whom he had watched suffer the agonies of war. Anita came to look on it as his "path of redemption . . . a peaceful place from which to begin the process of healing the many wounds caused by the fighting of battles here and abroad."

In July 2011, Sherrer was making coffee in his home at about 6:00 a.m. when he was bitten twice in the foot by a fer-de-lance pit viper, one of the deadliest snakes known. A friend drove him over the mountains to the nearest hospital, in Santiago, about an hour from his home. The venom had turned his foot blue and caused his leg to swell to twice its normal size. Doctors immediately administered an antitoxin to counter the venom, but that triggered a severe allergic reaction, and doctors had to switch from treating the wound to treating the reaction, then alternate treatments until the poison was under control.

When he was well enough, Sherrer returned to Santa Fe and resumed his life there, keeping in constant contact with Anita and Harvey Rients, a fellow pilot from the Condors who also moved to Panama and became one of Sherrer's closest friends. On December 12, 2013, while sitting at his computer tending to email, he passed out. Santa Fe's only doctor was away from town, and the closest hospital was in Santiago. His death was attributed to right ventricular fibrillation, a heart attack that causes loss of consciousness in seconds and death within minutes if not treated immediately.

More than two hundred people attended his funeral in the church at Santa Fe, and afterward, most of them walked through a misty rain to the local cemetery, where he was buried. Mike Sherrer was sixty-five years old.[129]

PAPPY PAPIN

Edward "Pappy" Papin flew scouts for three years in Vietnam, a rarely matched record in a danger-fraught occupation. "It was fun," he told me years later. "I was having a blast." He volunteered for a fourth tour but was called home when his unit, one of the last American combat units still in Vietnam, was ordered to return to the United States in 1972.

"Mikey was having fun, too," he said of Sherrer, whom he tagged as his best friend from July 4, 1971, the day his loach and Sherrer's gunship were shot down in the A Shau. Sherrer, he noted, flew low Cobra in a heavy pink team and was therefore "the guy who flung the first sets of rockets if I found something." He called his buddy the best rocket shooter in the world.

They met again by chance when assigned to pick up new helicopters in Saigon to fly back to C Troop and "got shit-faced together every night" at bars downtown. Getting drunk was what they did, and they kept it up after they returned to the States. Sherrer, Pappy said, developed severe PTSD, and Pappy might have as well, but he remained what he called a functional drunk for years, flying still-secret special ops missions, leading a SWAT team in Washington State after retirement from the military, and managing a radiation decontamination project in Chernobyl for American contractor Westinghouse. After he retired from Westinghouse and moved to Las Vegas in 1997, Pappy was diagnosed with PTSD and still goes to meetings to manage that disability. He quit smoking and drinking in 2003 and devoted his time to collecting and riding fast, custom-built motorcycles. Not long afterward, he rode his motorcycle to San Antonio, Texas, to a Condors reunion. He would not have gone, he said, because "I can't do those sort of things," but he figured it might be the last time he would see Newman or Sherrer. The next year, he developed a blood clot in his leg between two bullet wounds he had received in service, and he didn't feel it because that part of his leg was numb from the bullet holes. By the time he realized he had a problem, his leg had turned black with gangrene and had to be amputated.

Pappy's closest friend in Nevada is another Vietnam vet, a former medic, and they help each other deal with the emotional problems left over from their military days. "If we don't talk about it, we get it stored up, and something bad happens," Pappy said. "There's no gettin' around it. We have to. If we don't talk to one another about it, we can't function."[130]

STEVE KARSCHNER

Steve Karschner flew scouts in Vietnam for less than three weeks and in that brief time was shot down and wounded twice. He had graduated from Army Aviation School and qualified to fly scouts, but he had not flown enough in combat to command his own aircraft in C Troop's scout platoon. He was still flying as an observer for veteran pilot Pappy Papin when he was shot down the second time and wounded so severely that he was evacuated from Vietnam and sent home to Pennsylvania. He never got over the guilt of not finishing his tour.

After more than a year in military hospitals and multiple surgeries to repair his wounds, he was, as he put it, "forced into retirement" at twenty-one, told that he was too disabled to fly again and no longer useful to the Army. He got drunk and stayed that way for quite a while.

Karschner had a fling with one of his nurses at the hospital in Valley Forge, Pennsylvania, and after his release and discharge from the Army, he moved in with her for a while, but the relationship didn't last. Then he heard about a private flight school in Gettysburg, about ninety miles from his hometown of Lewistown, Pennsylvania, that could qualify him to fly helicopters in civilian life. The Veterans Administration paid his tuition under the GI Bill, and Karschner went back to flying.

He had a succession of jobs after that, mostly flying crop dusters in rural Maine, Florida, Wisconsin, and—for a year in the mid-1970s—Central America. He did some spraying in Honduras, El Salvador, and Nicaragua, although he is vague about the contract work there, saying only that he wasn't involved in the drug trade that was rampant in the region at that time, as was civil strife.

He learned that drinking was the only way he could sleep at night, and he leaped at the toughest flying assignments, fighting forest fires or spraying timber at treetop level, because it kept his adrenaline pumping. He craved excitement and the rush he got from the most hazardous jobs. He was told he seemed driven to self-destruction, and he doesn't dispute that. It caught up with him.

The first time he got seriously hurt after the Army was on the ground. He had gotten married in 1979 and planned to get out of flying and take a job working in the woods in Utah come spring, but he needed winter work until then and got a job cutting timber in Pennsylvania. A coworker felled a tree that struck Karschner in the head as it crashed to the ground. The other woodsman, afraid he had killed a man, fled the forest. When Karschner regained consciousness, he was alone in the woods, his scalp hanging over his ear, and he was bleeding profusely. He staggered to his truck and drove thirty miles to a hospital, where it took fifty stitches to close the wound in his scalp. He recovered and went back to flying, but after a succession of bad jobs and bad bosses, he decided he wasn't cut out to work for others and started an aircraft company of his own. He flew helicopters for others or leased them to work jobs that he found himself. He built the business until he was operating nine helicopters at a time, but his marriage fell apart, and he shut down the company.

On June 4, 1994, while spraying timber for gypsy moths in a twenty-two-year-old helicopter, Karschner's aircraft lost power and crashed into a mountainside. The impact broke all the bones in his chest, crushed a vertebra in his lower back, compressed his spine, and knocked him unconscious for an undetermined time. He was in intensive care for days, then in a full body brace for nine months. His doctor told him his flying days were done. A number of tiny bone fragments remained in his spinal canal that could paralyze him if he were to have another accident, he was told, and with a history of concussions, he probably couldn't renew his commercial flying license in any case. The former combat helicopter pilot was forty-three years old.

Left with few means after his divorce and helping raise a son, Karschner took any job he could find. He was a shoe salesman for a while, selling sneakers to high school teams, then did overnight radio in

DuBois, Pennsylvania, where he has lived for many years, about one hundred miles west of his birthplace.

The Veterans Administration, which judged him 40 percent disabled when he left the Army, increased that classification over the course of several years as the VA acknowledged the broader long-term effects of combat. In 2003, Karschner was classified as fully disabled and essentially unable to work for a living.

He still picks up odd income as a "scrapper," walking the railroad tracks and picking up salable junk, such as old steel spikes and other scrap metal. He judges it better than sitting in a bar or watching endless TV. He got his drinking under control after many years and said he no longer takes any drugs that aren't prescribed by the VA. He still has what he calls "a real authority problem" and is happier if he doesn't have to answer to anyone. He counts Daly, Ricky Miller, and a few other Condors among his closest friends, although he knew them only briefly before he was shot down and evacuated. They rarely see each other but keep in touch, mainly by email.

ED KERSEY

Ed Kersey, the gung-ho West Pointer who took command of C Troop's "Blues" rifle platoon when it was on the verge of being overrun in the A Shau Valley, had what many soldiers would consider a long and nearly ideal military career. At Newman's urging after eight months as a platoon leader, Kersey was promoted from lieutenant to captain and a day later took command of Delta Troop, the only company-size infantry unit in the air cavalry squadron.

When he finished his Vietnam tour four months later, he was transferred directly to West Germany to command a mechanized infantry company. For an officer in the combat arms, command is both a coveted personal objective and a key to promotion, which makes it essential to most successful military careers.

Kersey's tour in Vietnam was notable because he not only held back-to-back commands, but also spent all his time in the most contested region in the country, followed Newman's example of "leading from the front," as the cavalry puts it, and during his tour lost only one soldier killed in action, a twenty-three-year-old radio-telephone operator in Delta Troop named Joe Cooper. Cooper was shot aboard a helicopter as it tried to land in a clearing where North Vietnamese soldiers were waiting in ambush.

Long after he retired, Kersey called Newman "the greatest leader I ever served with" and said he spent his career trying to emulate Newman's style, bravery, and relationship with his troops. Promoting Jim Newman out of the enlisted ranks and giving him command of troops and aircraft in combat were examples, Kersey said, of the Army "getting it right."

Kersey himself bounced from one sought-after assignment to another for years, but, to his great disappointment, never got another shot at command under fire. On August 1, 1990, he reported to the National War College, where the military sends its best midcareer candidates to study the "grand strategy" of foreign and defense policy that is the province of generals, admirals, and high-ranking diplomats. The next day, Iraq invaded Kuwait, triggering the first Gulf War with the United States leading a broad coalition of countries that went to the aid of oil-rich Kuwait and turned back the invasion. Kersey was trapped in school and couldn't persuade anyone at the Pentagon to give him a brigade to lead into battle. He sadly sat out the war in class while a fresh crop of younger officers logged the combat time they needed to get their own tickets punched. Kersey realized his real-war experience was too far in the past to compete and that he wasn't likely to have a star pinned on his shoulder. He turned his attention to rooting out waste, fraud, and abuse in the military and made enough enemies that, during his last tour, in Alabama, he felt so threatened by miscreants that he packed a concealed handgun wherever he went. He retired as a full colonel in 1997 after twenty-eight years in the Army. His seven best were as commanding officer of a company or battalion.

After he took off his uniform, Kersey went to work for a defense contractor helping develop simulation software to enable high-level combat teams to practice modern maneuvers against imaginary enemies. He also managed a piece of the since-canceled Future Combat Systems, a concept for fielding a high-tech, lightweight brigade that got more and more expensive and complicated as the generals came up with new things they would like it to do. Critics charged it was soaking up billions of dollars for dreamed-up technologies, while troops on the ground in Iraq were learning they were most vulnerable to cheap, simple, and deadly improvised explosive devices that the Future Combat Systems architecture was not designed to thwart.

Unlike many of his comrades in Charlie Troop, Kersey, who went to Vietnam a month after his brother was killed there and who saw his share of ground combat with his rifle platoon and later with Delta Troop, said he never had "one minute that I would identify as PTSD from all the shit that we got into over there with Newman." Like many senior officers, he remained skeptical of the diagnosis. As opposed to traumatic brain injury (TBI), which has received considerable attention since the war in Iraq and which Kersey regards as a complex, physical disorder, he labeled PTSD a crutch often used to excuse personal responsibility for bad behavior, alcoholism, or drug addiction.

"I think it probably does exist, that there are probably some people out there who have recurring nightmares," he told me. "But they are weak individuals who allow it to overtake and rule their life. I've been told from Day One, 'Suck it up, Ranger, and drive on.' Through the power of will, you overcome those things that are causing you problems and get on down the road and accomplish the mission. Suck it up, and drive on."[131]

GARY SWIFT AND JIM KANE

When Gary Swift, the former C Troop scout pilot, got laid off from his management job in the construction equipment industry after the 2008 financial crash, he went down to the unemployment office in Seattle to file for compensation and seek advice about how to get health insurance when his thirty days of emergency COBRA coverage ended. He learned—for the first time—that as a Vietnam veteran awarded a Purple Heart for wounds suffered in combat, he was entitled to free VA medical care for the rest of his life. He was advised to seek assistance from one of the veterans service organizations to file the necessary application and serve as his advocate in dealing with the VA's bureaucracy.

He also was told he was entitled to disability compensation for the ringing in his ears, if it was caused by his helicopter service, and the recurrent skin cancers that, in Vietnam vets, are presumed to result from exposure to the defoliant Agent Orange that was sprayed over much of the terrain where Swift flew.

In a later examination, while looking for the cause of hip pain that Swift described to him, his VA doctor spotted some irregularities on an X-ray, ordered more films, and asked if he also suffered from back pain. Swift told him his back had hurt for forty-one years, since the first of three crashes flying combat missions in his little bird.

It was August 21, 1970, and he was on a reconnaissance mission at treetop level over an enemy-infested area west of Hue that the Americans called the Tennessee Valley. He didn't hear the shot, but he felt the jolt when a large shell, probably from a .51-caliber machine gun, smashed into the underside of the aircraft. Swift immediately started looking for a place to put down to check the damage, spotted a small clearing in the forest, and headed for it. There wasn't room to make a measured approach. He just aimed for the clearing and when he reached it, flared to cut his forward speed to zero. The little bird hovered above the tall trees surrounding it as Swift tried to ease down into the clearing. Thirty or forty feet above the ground, the engine quit, and the helicopter fell out of the sky like a rock. It hit hard, collapsed the left skid, and rolled over on its side, its rotors smacking the ground. Swift and his crew escaped and were pulled aboard a chase ship just as a squad of North Vietnamese broke into the clearing and opened fire.

The doctor told Swift all those years later that the X-rays showed compression and bone spurs in several lumbar and sacral vertebrae that did not appear to be age-related like the pain in his hip. He may have been entitled to disability all that time but never realized it. The original injury was compounded a few months later when Swift's loach had a mechanical failure on a last-light mission near the base at Phu Bai, and he had to put it down in the trees. That broke his fall somewhat, but the aircraft again fell straight down from treetop height, cramming his spine into the armored seat beneath him.

Neither of those injuries got him the Purple Heart, though. That came from a low-altitude flight into Laos during the Lam Son operation. A North Vietnamese soldier stepped out from behind a bush in front of him with a rocket-propelled grenade launcher on his shoulder. He loosed the missile as Swift flew straight toward him. RPGs usually explode on impact, but, luckily for Swift, the projectile coming at his loach as he raced toward it inexplicably blew up before it got there. Shrapnel pierced the bubble-like windshield and peppered the cockpit, hitting Swift in the right knee and leg. He managed to fly back to Khe Sanh, got patched up by a doctor, and went back to work.

Many years later, when he was visiting VA hospitals and doctors after being laid off in the financial crisis, Swift was so impressed with the care he got in Washington State that he urged Jim Kane, his best friend since before Vietnam, to go to the VA in Virginia and get himself checked out. Kane, the Cobra gunship pilot shot down in Laos while flying gun cover for Swift's little bird, despised doctors and hospitals and had done his best to avoid them since his long convalescence at Walter Reed during the war.

But he listened to his friend, procrastinated for a while, and finally decided to go in for a checkup. Forty years after he was shot down in Laos and narrowly escaped from his burning gunship, Jim Kane told a VA hospital interviewer that he still dreamed of watching the flames walk up his legs and paint his hands with fire. He still couldn't go to backyard fireworks displays because he worried that an errant bottle rocket would go wild and hit him. He looked up at the young medical student as he described his recurring nightmare and realized she was in tears listening to him.

Kane had never thought of himself as someone with post-traumatic stress disorder. He was an ornery guy but a successful one. He'd done well as a bond broker, lived life as a Virginia gentleman with a nice home and enviable family. He and his wife, Maureen, raised three children and put them through college. He was charming and fun to drink with and always had a good story or fresh joke to put people at ease. What he didn't advertise was that he had gone from drinking with his pilot buddies to celebrate surviving another day in Vietnam to swigging mouthwash in the office to calm his nerves until he could leave work and get a real drink. After years of tolerating his increasing drinking, Maureen and the kids resorted to an intervention to compel him to enter a residential treatment center for alcoholism. He spent a month at Father Martin's Ashley in Maryland. Afterward, he fell off the wagon a couple of times before he got control of his habit.

Gary Swift had helped persuade him to seek more help when he relapsed, and after his experience with the VA, he urged Kane repeatedly to take advantage of the privilege he had earned to get attention for his mounting physical pain. The back pain Kane lived with ever since the crash was getting worse, one hip kept him tossing and awake nights for years, and he was having trouble with his left calf that he thought was related to the burns. The VA doctors diagnosed arthritis in his hip and pulmonary artery disease in his leg, neither of which was likely to have come from the war. The circulatory trouble probably came instead from a lifetime of heavy smoking, they told him.

But in the course of the examination, Kane realized that some of his problems, including the drinking and nightmares, had their roots in his head and went all the way back to Vietnam.

"It just went on and on and on," he said. "There was a lot of baggage that a lot of people had to tote around for a number of years. . . . It took an awfully long time."

His smoking was taking a toll, too. On a trip to Alaska with friends, he contracted pneumonia and had to drop off. That finally forced him to admit the smoking was killing him, and a few months later, he quit. It was 3:00 p.m. on November 13, 2012.

At sixty-six, he had chronic obstructive pulmonary disease, that trouble with his leg, and an arthritic hip. Walking any distance was painful. The VA increased the disability compensation that Kane had been awarded when he left the Army to acknowledge his post-traumatic stress and war-related injuries but not for the inevitable consequences of age and lifestyle.

DAVID FAUSNIGHT

People had known for a long time that former Cobra pilot David "Fuzzy" Fausnight drank a lot. Other pilots in Vietnam drank, too, but Fuzzy got worse after he went home. He is best remembered by his fellow Condors as the pilot who recorded their radio chatter during the Laos invasion.

A decade later, Fuzzy was convicted of drunken driving in Ohio in 1980 and again in 1987 but managed to hang on to his commercial flying license and hired out for many years as a civilian helicopter pilot around Canton, Ohio. On July 8, 1996, he picked up four passengers at the Salem, Ohio, Airpark for an aerial photographic mission to the nearby Little Beaver Creek. It was about 11:00 a.m. The sky was clear, and there was a light breeze—near perfect conditions for the Bell JetRanger, a civilian version of the OH-58 Kiowa used as a reconnaissance helicopter in Vietnam and still in service with various modifications four decades later. The JetRanger and its successors remain popular with television news, traffic, and weather reporters, and as an air ambulance and an executive shuttle. The aircraft Fuzzy was flying was twenty-two years old.

In addition to all five seats being filled, the chopper was carrying extra camera gear and equipment and was more than one hundred pounds above its allowable takeoff weight. About twenty minutes later, several witnesses saw and heard the aircraft flying noisily just over some tall trees near the creek. They watched it turn uncertainly and reverse course, then appear to hover perhaps one hundred feet off the ground. The fuselage began to rotate slowly under its prop, and the aircraft dropped out of the sky, crashing into an open field and killing Fausnight and all four passengers.

Ohio State Police reported the pilot's blood alcohol level was 0.158, nearly twice the legal limit for driving a car and four times what federal regulations permit for a pilot.[132]

C TROOP

Reorganized and reequipped with technologically advanced OH-58 Kiowa helicopters, C Troop went back to war in Iraq and Afghanistan, losing only one pilot, Chief Warrant Officer Michael Slebodnik, thirty-nine, who was fatally wounded by enemy ground fire in Afghanistan on September 11, 2008. Several Vietnam-era Condors got together with their modern counterparts at a 2014 ceremony at Fort Campbell, Kentucky, after C Troop returned from Afghanistan.

The Army announced that in late 2015, the 2nd Squadron, 17th Cavalry, will "case its colors," be deactivated, then be reactivated as an armed reconnaissance unit flying Apache helicopters that will serve as both scout and gunship. The Apache operates in a digitally enhanced environment that makes Cobras seem like classic sports cars. Thanks in part to C Troop's experience in Laos and the A Shau and Vehlow's decision to leave the Army to study aeronautical engineering and join the defense industry, Apaches now fly night and day in good weather and bad with GPS instead of maps and grease pencils to plot positions and targets. They identify enemy positions and weapons by sensor and fire computer-guided Hellfire missiles and a highly accurate autocannon that shoots bursts of high-explosive, 30 mm projectiles faster than five times a second. The frontseater can operate an accompanying drone while the aircraft commander flies the gunship.

* * *

Nearly all the old Condors interviewed for this book were drawing military disability checks for physical or emotional scars—and often for both. Cancers linked to the defoliant Agent Orange, a leg amputated due to long-ago war wounds, chronic pain, loss of eyesight, leftover shrapnel, drug and alcohol abuse, PTSD. One way or another, the war touched them all, and it didn't let go.

For a few, Charlie Troop was the launchpad for building a new Army and more effective weapons. For Pappy, it was the start of a life in black ops. Chuck Vehlow helped design and build the Apache gunship, successor to the Cobra he flew in Vietnam. Ed Kersey, who never lost a man on the ground leading his Blues platoon, helped invent a soldier of the future: a high-tech grunt tricked out with electronic gadgets and superweapons. The men of Charlie Troop never knew about Major Newman's about-face after he came home from the war. A few heard rumors of some domestic troubles, but those weren't so unusual and certainly didn't affect their lifelong admiration of the man they followed in Vietnam. What they had in common was their devotion to Condor Six, and thirty-five years after the war they were still trying to get him the Medal of Honor they thought he deserved for saving so many lives.

"PATIENCE MY ASS, I WANT TO KILL SOMETHING"

C TROOP, 2ND SQUADRON, 17TH CAVALRY

ACKNOWLEDGMENTS

SAYING THANK YOU is hardly just compensation for the incalculable help I received in reconstructing events of long ago and teasing the fine and fallible threads of memory through four decades of life after a war that brought the people in this story together and shaped them in so many unexpected ways.

I begin with Jim Newman, the military commander whose personal courage and leadership made an indelible impression on my own thinking. He helped me then, ignoring orders not to take journalists across the border, by flying me into a hostile part of Laos to see where colleagues of mine died in a helicopter shootdown he had witnessed. He helped again years later, but more guardedly, by telling me his own story—at least, the part he wanted to share. Newman's youngest son, Jay, gave me access to his father's personal records and described his own upbringing after the war. Newman's first wife, Flora, and her sons Roger and Ronald, born before the war, generously shared their own memories and family photos, home movies, and records that exposed a part of Newman's life he had protected from me. Other family members, especially Newman's sister, Elaine Bagby, late brother, Jack, and stepson, John Fogelquist, helped piece together a mystifying puzzle.

The soldiers who flew with Newman in his finest hour told me proudly how he led them and, when I finally thought to ask, shared accounts of their own painful struggles since the war. I am grateful to all the Condors, especially those named in the book, but a few deserve added thanks for help, insight, and for enduring my seemingly endless requests for details. Chuck Vehlow, while waging his own war on cancer, answered my questions with unstinting patience and care. Mac Jones, the Condors historian, dug through file cabinets of documents and a trove of memories to track down answers to questions, at least a few of which he had never been asked. Bill Zierdt, the first Condor, replied to my simple query about where the unit's nickname came from with an answer that exposed his late-life struggle with the ghosts of Vietnam and caused me to reconsider the premise of the book. Ed Kersey's keen eye for detail put color into the cold snow at Arlington Cemetery and the numbness of exhaustion on a foreboding mountainside above the A Shau. Ricky Miller's war stories flowed and flowed, and when he finally met Ed Long and Trina Judson at the Wall, so did his tears. Gary Swift not only provided a copy of old tapes of radio chatter but translated the jargon and made sense of segments rendered nearly indecipherable by noise and static. Richard Frazee took me to Jim Casher's shack and to the Krenelkas, whom I could not have found by myself. And without being asked, he snuffed out a soldier's misunderstanding that threatened my access to some of the Condors. Gary Schuler walked me through his own flashbacks and struggles with PTSD and his efforts to persuade others to seek help for theirs. Rick "The Mayor" Daly was a bridge and a cheerleader. Mike Sherrer generously gave his time to tell of his survival and later private battles. I am saddened he did not live to read the fruits of his efforts. Jim Kane drove with me for hours, telling story after story that helped me feel the fire and exposed the enduring scars. Steve Karschner's video-like recall of his first crash took me too close for comfort. Charles Davis trusted me with his photo album for years. Families, too, did their best to help, especially Robert L. Howard II and his mother, Roberta Vincent; Jim Casher's sister, Josephine Robinson; Joe Brown's brother, Larry, his sister, Sally Stone, and cousin, my old colleague, Skip Brown. Armond Simmons and Dustoff historian Phil Marshall steered me to Brown's surviving crew members, including Dr. Paul Simcoe and Dennis Fujii, who filled many gaps.

Anyone who writes about the past is dependent on documents, newspapers, books, recordings, and the institutions that preserve them. Many of those vital materials would never be unearthed were it not for the librarians, archivists, and researchers who guide writers through the immense stacks that they catalogue and store. The technical expertise of archivist Maarja Krusten resurrected parts of the diaries of H. R. Haldeman, President Richard Nixon's chief of staff, who had the foresight to have his daily records digitized—but in a format that died with an early Microsoft Windows operating system. Robert Reed of the National Archives borrowed time from his herculean effort to move the Nixon presidential papers across the country to help me find critical White House documents before they got packed and shipped west. Army Aviation historian Jim Williams steered me to videotaped interviews with key participants in the Laos operation, and Jill Redington, chief of the technical library at Fort Rucker, found a way to get them to me. Mike Sloniker, Vietnam Helicopter Pilots Association historian, has collected and disseminated more information about military helicopters in Vietnam and the people who flew them than any individual I know. Bill Geiger photographed Newman's funeral and sharpened a shoe box full of old snapshots to make them reproducible. Marc Cameron generously provided photos of the Laos operation taken by his late father, the noted photographer Denis Cameron. Theodore Keefer, former general editor of the official history Foreign Relations of the United States (FRUS), tipped me to fascinating material hiding in plain sight. Ernie Bruce loaned me his unpublished memoir that gave shape and color to Newman's first tour. John Prados, prolific author and forager in the National Security Archive, provided insight into why President Nixon decided to invade Laos when he did. Dr. Stephen Cozza helped trace the development of military and medical thinking about PTSD. Charles and Alex Karelis, founders of Writers Room DC, furnished my "cave," an invaluable hideout where I could write without the myriad distractions I encountered everywhere else. David Beaudreau transcribed hours of recordings, learning strange place names, military terms, acronyms, and aviators' lingo as he went. Marcia Kramer, AKA Three, edited the manuscript, catching countless problems large and small before a final reading by Mary Altbaum exposed even more. Any that got past their eagle eyes are attributable solely to me. Gwyn Kennedy Snider created the cover, made the map, and designed a book I could not envision without her. Jared Kuritz steered me through the new worlds of publishing and publicity.

Special thanks to friends and colleagues Heathcote Wales, Jim Dickinson, and Richard Pyle, who helped me think the story through, and Barbara Burkhardt, who listened over lunch for years, wondering, I'm sure, if it would ever end.

From the very beginning, my beloved Annie helped figure out what I had, sorted good from bad, read and improved many drafts, propped me up when I needed it, told me when I was wrong, and waited, and waited, and waited for me to finish. Now there will be time to go sailing.

PHOTO CREDITS

Where photographers could be identified, they have given permission for use of their photographs. In some cases, snapshots in possession of the subjects have been used with the subjects' permission if the photographer could not be identified.

Cover image........ Brandon Swanson for *The Chronicle of Lewis County*

Page No.

2, 3 Funeral caisson at Arlington......................... William K. Geiger

4 Wartime colleagues' farewell .... William K. Geiger

20 Huey extracting the Blues..Ed Kersey

26 Jimmy Newman's grandparents..... from family collection with permission, photographer unknown

31 PFC Newman, paratrooper ....official Army photograph

32 Jump wings pin, front and back........................ Michael Putzel

50 Captain Newman, fellow officer in Vietnam, 1966Ernest Bruce

57 Huey 091 .... Hugh Talman for Smithsonian Institution

78 Charles Davis, Newman's crew chief .... from Davis's collection photographer unknown

80 Newman and Vehlow.................from Jim Newman's collection photographer unknown

81 Scout pilot Pappy Papin, half-shaved ....Michael Sherrer

100 Reopened Khe Sanh combat base.......................Charles Davis

101 C Troop Hueys over Laos .... Michael Putzel

102 Major Newman at controls en route to Laos .... Michael Putzel

121 Jim Casher, rescued from Laos, lying wounded aboard Newman's command ship ....Ed Kersey

123 A rotor blade for an ax..Ed Kersey

NOTES

1. Author interview with Lonnie Turner, San Antonio, Texas, April 19, 2010.
2. Some weeks later, the Condors found a large telephone cable that snaked through the valley from Laos and perhaps from North Vietnam. With the help of military intelligence, they installed a tap on the line. Some days later, they got a message from Saigon chewing them out for burying the mortar tube. It was a violation of regulations that the American command learned of by listening in on phone conversations from North Vietnamese soldiers, who proudly reported to superiors they had found and dug up the weapon. Telephone conversation with Mac Jones, March 23, 2009.
3. Newnan Herald and Advertiser, April 4 and April 28, 1899, copyright 2007 Newnan Times-Herald Inc. (http://www.newnan.com:16080/samhose/). See also Edwin T. Arnold, What Virtue There Is in Fire: Cultural Memory and the Lynching of Sam Hose (Athens: University of Georgia Press, 2009).
4. Author conversation with Jay Newman, Alexandria, Virginia, April 25, 2013.
5. Obediah B. Stevens and Robert F. Wright, Georgia, Historical and Industrial (Atlanta: Franklin Printing and Publishing, 1901), 615–18.
6. Author interview with Jack Newman, May 19, 2009.
7. Author interview with Flora Newman, March 2, 2012.
8. Author interview with Elaine Bagby, February 6, 2009.
9. Author interview with Flora Newman, September 8, 2009.
10. The Delayed Certificate of Birth purportedly was signed January 4, 1944, by Coweta County Ordinary J. T. Pike based on the attending physician's affidavit and an affidavit signed by Jimmy's father, John Sam Newman. However, a certified copy of the document, dated January 10, 1952—eight years later and the month Jimmy enlisted, does not contain Sam Newman's actual signature and ignores the date of birth on the physician's affidavit. Pike's signature is on both documents, but the handwriting appears to be by different signers.
11. Author interview with Flora Newman, April 20, 2009; tank photo from Truman Library, Accession #73-4021.
12. Author interview with Jim Newman, near Raleigh-Durham Airport, North Carolina, January 18, 2006.

13. Ibid.
14. "Seven G.I.'s Slain in Vietcong Raid; 80 Are Wounded," New York Times, February 7, 1965: 1.
15. "History of the 52d Combat Aviation Battalion 1 January 1965 to 31 December 1965," Vietnam Center and Archive, Texas Tech University, Lubbock, Texas.
16. Victory in Vietnam: The Official History of the People's Army of Vietnam, 1954–1975, translated by Merle L. Pribbenow, Military Institute of Vietnam (Lawrence: University Press of Kansas, 2002), 142.
17. The Pentagon Papers, Gravel Edition, Volume 3, Chapter 4, "American Troops Enter the Ground War, March July 1965" (Boston: Beacon Press, 1971), 389–485.
18. James Williams, A History of Army Aviation: From Its Beginnings to the War on Terror (Lincoln: U.S. Army Aviation Museum Foundation, Inc., 2005), 99. Williams was the historian of the U.S. Army Aviation Center.
19. Unpublished memoir by retired Lieutenant Colonel Ernest E. Bruce Jr., associate professor of aviation (emeritus) at University of Louisiana, Monroe. Bruce served in the Robin Hoods with Newman.
20. Origin of the term "peter pilot" unknown.
21. Undated Reviewer's note appended to Newman's OER for the period June 11, 1966, to September 17, 1966, and dated October 27, 1966.
22. Author interview with Ed Walsh, March 9, 2010.
23. Letter to Newman dated April 8, 1970, signed by Lieutenant Colonel Douglas S. Smith, Commanding Officer, Headquarters, 1st Squadron, 17th Cavalry, Fort Bragg, North Carolina.
24. Malcolm Jones cassette tape recorded in 1970 and replayed by Jones for the author.
25. Author interview with Jim Newman, Chapel Hill, North Carolina, May 5, 2006.
26. Malcolm Jones cassette tape recorded in 1970 and replayed by Jones for the author.
27. Newman told this story to author in meeting near Raleigh-Durham Airport, January 18, 2006.
28. Author interview with Kate Vehlow, August 14, 2014.
29. Author interview with Jim Newman, May 5, 2006, Chapel Hill, North Carolina.
30. Ibid.

31. Colonel Richard Johnson, oral history interview by James Williams, PhD, Aviation Branch historian of the U.S. Army Aviation Center, September 21, 2000.
32. Colonel John M. Collins (retired), "Going to Tchepone: OPLAN El Paso," Joint Force Quarterly (Autumn/Winter 1997–98).
33. John Prados, The Hidden History of the Vietnam War (Chicago: Ivan R. Dee, 1995), 235–48.
34. Memorandum from K. Wayne Smith to Kissinger, National Archives, Nixon Presidential Materials, NSC Files NSC Institutional Files (H-Files), Box H-47, SRG Meeting, Cambodia.
35. H. R. Haldeman, The Haldeman Diaries: Inside the Nixon White House (New York: G. P. Putnam's Sons, 1994), 212.
36. Foreign Relations of the United States, 1964–1968, Vol. VII, Vietnam, September 1968–January 1969 (Washington: U.S. Government Printing Office, 2003), 200.
37. Galeazzo Ciano, Mussolini's son-in-law and foreign minister of Italy, executed for treason in 1944 after calling for Mussolini's ouster.
38. National Archives, Nixon Presidential Materials, NSC Files, Box 1012, Haig Special File, Haig Trip File—Vietnam, Phnom Penh, December 11–18, 1970. Top Secret; Sensitive; Eyes Only, Dec. 15, 1970, 1:40 a.m.
39. Willard J. Webb and Walter S. Poole, History of the Joint Chiefs of Staff; The Joint Chiefs of Staff and the War in Vietnam, 1971-1973 (U.S. Government Printing Office, 2007), 2.
40. Admiral Thomas H. Moorer diary, as related in ibid., 4 and footnote 7.
41. Ibid., 4–6 and footnote 12.
42. Transcript of telephone conversation, 9:15 a.m. January 29, 1971, National Security Archive, George Washington University Library.
43. Victory in Vietnam, 268–78.
44. Excerpts from Charles A. Vehlow's entry in personal diary, February 8, 1971.
45. Americans in Vietnam frequently referred to the enemy's 12.7 mm heavy machine guns as "51s" to differentiate them from the similar U.S. .50-caliber machine guns, whose cartridges were essentially the same diameter but shaped a bit differently. As the gun pilot did here, they also used the term "50" interchangeably to describe either the U.S. or Communist-bloc heavy weapon. Like other weapons and ammunition measured in calibers, the sizes are generally spoken as whole numbers without the decimal point, such as ".22," ".38," ".45," and ".50."

46. Author interview with Michael Horsch, March 6, 2009.

47. Author interviews with Larry Brown, Joe's brother, July 11, 2009; and Joe's cousin, Skip Brown, who was a distinguished CBS News cameraman in Vietnam, July 5, 2009.

48. Peter Dorland and James Nanney, Dust Off: Army Aeromedical Evacuation in Vietnam (Washington: U.S. Government Printing Office, 1982), 30.

49. Sally Stone, Joe Brown's sister, in email to author, July 12, 2009.

50. Simcoe email to author, July 9, 2009.

51. Newman interview, May 5, 2006.

52. Author interview with Vehlow, July 17, 2009.

53. Fuzzy Fausnight audiotape recording made from nearby Cobra gunship, February 18, 1971.

54. Author interview with George Schopfer, June 17, 2009.

55. Author interview with Dennis M. Fujii, July 22, 2009.

56. Boca Raton News, February 23, 1971.

57. Author interview with Dennis M. Fujii, July 23, 2009.

58. Videotape interview with Dennis M. Fujii by Tom Marshall, author of The Price of Exit: A True Story of Helicopter Pilots in Vietnam, February 8, 1971.

59. Joel Chandler Harris, Uncle Remus and His Legends of the Old Plantation (London: David Bogue, 1881), digitized by Google.

60. John A. G. Klose oral history interview with James Williams, PhD, Aviation Branch historian of the U.S. Army Aviation Center, Fort Rucker, Alabama, April 23, 2001; videotape on file, U.S. Army Aviation Technical Library, Fort Rucker.

61. Vietnam Helicopter Pilots Association, www.vhpa.org/KIA/incident/71021830KIA.HTM.

62. Author interview with Gary Schuler, San Antonio, Texas, February 12, 2013.

63. Richard A. Serrano, "Quest to Find MIAs Keeps Vietnam in U.S. Conscience," Los Angeles Times, October 31, 1993. Also, Arlington National Cemetery website (unofficial) at www.arlingtoncemetery.net/crandall.htm, and POW Network, www.pownetwork.org/bios/c/c433.htm.

64. Vehlow email to author, May 18, 2010.

65. Author interview with Don Wilson, June 29, 2014.

66. The informal practice of scout pilots training their crew chiefs to fly was not uncommon. The little OH-6 helicopters had dual controls but didn't normally have copilots. An eerily similar incident occurred less than six weeks earlier, on January 19, 1971, as C Troop was about to be dispatched to Khe Sanh. Captain Wilbur Dale Latimer, the troop's operations officer, wanted to fly scouts, but Newman hesitated to let him because he thought it was too dangerous. Latimer got his wish and was on an ordinarily routine pink team reconnaissance mission near Phu Bai when a single AK-47 rifle bullet hit him in the head and killed him outright. His crew chief took control of the aircraft and flew it back to base, where Captain Gary Swift and several other Condors ran down to the refueling area to watch the little bird land. It was a running landing, but the crew chief/observer got the aircraft on the ground. Chief Warrant Officer Jim Jones, who had arrived in Vietnam with Latimer, jumped into the left seat and flew the loach over to the 85th Evacuation Hospital on base, but Latimer was already dead.
67. "Wounded GI Tells of 13-Day Ordeal," Pacific Stars and Stripes, April 4, 1971: 6.
68. Some U.S. prisoners of war were held for more than eight years.
69. Author interview with Richard Frazee, Seattle, December 11, 2011.
70. Colonel Richard Johnson interview with James Williams, PhD, Aviation Branch historian of the U.S. Army Aviation Center, Fort Rucker, Alabama, September 21, 2000; videotape on file, U.S. Army Aviation Technical Library, Fort Rucker.
71. Unpublished paper of D. Vu Hieu, a former South Vietnamese officer, Dallas, Texas, July 25, 1995, posted on http://vnafmamn.com/.
72. Author interview with Stephen Karschner, April 25, 2006.
73. Author interview with Ricky Miller, February 4, 2011.
74. Text on back of Vietnam-era Emergency Signaling Mirror.
75. Based on author interviews with Newman, Vehlow, Karschner, Sherrer, Papin, Miller, Daly, Eliason; emails with Grubbs and others.
76. Michael Putzel, Associated Press staff writer, "Esprit de Corps Very Much Alive in One Outfit," as published in Fort Worth Star-Telegram, August 26, 1971.
77. Author interview with Jim Newman, January 18, 2006.
78. Author interview with Captain Richard Daly, April 18, 2010.
79. Newman interview with author, January 18, 2006.
80. "Conspiracy to Burn, Kill Is Charged to Army Major," Fayetteville Observer,

undated newspaper clipping.

81. Fayette County Superior Court records.
82. Fayette County Superior Court, April 12, 1972.
83. Cassette tape with Frank G. Budd's cover note in Newman's personal papers inherited by Jay Newman and made available to the author.
84. Email message from Donna Murphy, manager, Corporate Archives, Manulife Financial, April 5, 2012.
85. Author interview with Jack Newman, May 19, 2009.
86. Author interview with Jack Newman, May 5, 2009.
87. Author interview with Jay Newman, Raleigh, North Carolina, June 8, 2009.
88. Author interview with John K. Fogelquist, April 4, 2012; follow-up emails to author, April 11 and 17, 2012.
89. Author interview with Jay Newman, Raleigh, North Carolina, June 8, 2009.
90. Author interview with Roger Newman, Concord, North Carolina, April 20, 2009.
91. Author interview with Jay Newman, Raleigh, North Carolina, June 8, 2009.
92. Ibid.
93. Author interview with Ron Newman, Concord, North Carolina, April 20, 2009.
94. Email to author from Bill Zierdt, December 15, 2010.
95. Ibid.
96. Interviews and emails with Bill Zierdt; Tim Dyehouse, "'Condors' Fight Mile-High Battle," VFW, April 2008: 36–39; Samuel Zaffiri, Hamburger Hill: The Brutal Battle for Dong Ap Bia: May 11–20, 1969 (New York: Presidio Press, Ballantine Publishing Group, 1988), 151–76.
97. VHPA Vietnam Helicopter History CD-ROM, incident and accident reports, November 2007 edition.
98. Defense Department records are unclear on how many men from which units were killed or wounded in the daylong fight, but it is undisputed that the casualties aboard the Huey were the worst ever experienced in a single loss by C Troop, 2/17.
99. Richard Pyle and Horst Faas, Lost Over Laos: A True Story of Tragedy, Mystery and Friendship (Boston: Da Capo Press, 2003).
100. Bill Zierdt emails and interviews.

101. Copy of original provided to author by Roberta Delgado Howard Vincent, mother of Robert Howard II.

102. Author interview with Robert L. Howard II, August 14, 2012.

103. "Robert Howard, a Hero on the Fields of Play and War," article in The Day in New London, Connecticut, by columnist Steven Slosberg, undated clipping provided by Roberta Vincent.

104. Unidentified, undated newspaper clipping with a Norwich dateline describing a military awards ceremony honoring Howard in the State Armory, provided by Roberta Vincent.

105. http://thewall-usa.com/guest.asp?recid=24355

106. http://www.vvmf.org/thewall/Wall_Id_No=24333

107. Bill Zierdt email to author, April 24, 2012.

108. Frazee interview, December 11, 2011.

109. Schuler interview, April 16, 2010.

110. "Sadness in the Fog," entry submitted to Condors Alumni Association website by Richard Frazee, April 11, 2011, http://www.aircav-condors.org/node/42. Circumstances described by Frazee in discussion with author, December 11, 2011. Used with Frazee's permission granted July 28, 2014.

111. Author interview with Richard Frazee on drive from Winlock, Washington, to Seattle, December 11, 2011.

112. Nancy C. Andreasen, "Posttraumatic Stress Disorder: A History and a Critique," Annals of the New York Academy of Sciences 1208 (2010).

113. Author interview with Stephen J. Cozza, MD, Bethesda, Maryland, February 27, 2013.

114. Vehlow interview, March 3, 2012.

115. Schuler interview, February 12, 2013.

116. Charles W. Hoge, Once a Warrior Always a Warrior: Navigating the Transition from Combat to Home—Including Combat Stress, PTSD, and mTBI (Guilford: Lyons Press, 2010), xii, 15–47, 83–89.

117. Charles W. Hoge, "Interventions for War-Related Posttraumatic Stress Disorder: Meeting Veterans Where They Are," JAMA 306, no. 5 (2011): 549–51.

118. Hoge, Once a Warrior, Always a Warrior, 3.

119. David Wood, "A Warrior's Moral Dilemma," HuffingtonPost.com, March 18–20,

2014. See also Jonathan Shay, Achilles in Vietnam: Combat Trauma and the Undoing of Character (New York: Scribner, 1994), 74.

120. Former Specialist 5 Ricky Miller's email to Major General (Ret.) Benjamin L. Harrison, Major (Ret.) James T. Newman, Major (Ret.) Malcolm Jones, and former C Troop pilot Steve Karschner, August 4, 2005.

121. Author interviews with Malcolm Jones, Harvey Rients, Ricky Miller, Dennis Urick; unpublished book Four Condors compiled by Jones, 2000; television documentary, "A Soldier's Story," produced by LMNO Productions, 2002.

122. http://www.vvmf.org/Wall-of-Faces/26322/PAUL-A-JOHNSON

123. Putzel, "Esprit de Corps Very Much Alive in One Outfit."

124. Author interview with Linda and Loren Krenelka, Winlock, Washington, December 11, 2011.

125. Author interview with Jay Newman, Arlington, Virginia, April 25, 2013.

126. Author interview with Jay Newman, Raleigh, North Carolina, June 6, 2009.

127. Jim Newman email to author, July 17, 2006.

128. Author interview with Jim Newman, Raleigh-Durham Airport, January 18, 2006. Berry went on to be superintendent of West Point after the war and commanded the 5th U.S. Army Corps in Europe before he retired with three stars in 1980. When he was asked thirty years later, a year before he died at eighty-seven, if he remembered Newman, he said he could no longer trust his memory and preferred not to comment.

129. Author interview with Michael Sherrer, April 11, 2006; email correspondence with Anita Sherrer, 2014; email correspondence with Harvey Rients, December 12, 2013; April 22, 2014; August 1, 2014.

130. Author interview with Pappy Papin, January 5, 2015.

131. Author interview with Ed Kersey, May 30, 2013.

132. National Transportation Safety Board Report No. IAD96FA107 and Associated Press report from Youngstown, Ohio, July 12, 1996.